Critical Human Geography

'Critical Human Geography' is an international series which provides a critical examination and extension of the concepts and
consequences of work in human geography and the allied social
sciences and humanities. The volumes are written by scholars
currently engaged in substantive research, so that, wherever possible, the discussions are empirically grounded as well as theoretically informed. Existing studies and the traditions from which they
derive are carefully described and located in their historically
specific context, but the series at the same time introduces and
explores new ideas and insights from the human sciences as a
whole. The series is thus not intended as a collection of synthetic
reviews, but rather as a cluster of considered arguments which are
accessible enough to engage geographers at all levels in the development of geography. The series therefore reflects the continuing
methodological and philosophical diversity of the subject, and its
books are united only by their common commitment to the pros-
ecution of a genuinely human geography.

Department of Geography   MARK BILLINGE
University of Cambridge   DEREK GREGORY
England   RON MARTIN

Critical Human Geography

PUBLISHED

FORTHCOMING

Long Waves of Regional Development

Michael Marshall

MACMILLAN

First published 1987

Published by
MACMILLAN EDUCATION LTD
Houndmills, Basingstoke, Hampshire RG21 2XS
and London
Companies and representatives
throughout the world

Printed in Hong Kong

British Library Cataloguing in Publication Data

Marshall, Michael, *1957–*
Long waves of regional development.—
(Crucial human geography)
1. Long waves (Economics)
I. Title   II. Series
330.15'42   HB3729
ISBN 0–333–41983–9
ISBN 0–333–41984–7 Pbk

To my parents

To my parents

Contents

List of Figures

List of Tables

Preface

Comparisons between the contemporary economic slump and previous phases of prolonged depression in industrial capitalism's 200-year history have stimulated renewed interest in the theory of economic long waves. My own interest in the theory and its implications for our understanding of uneven regional development within the industrial capitalist economies stems from the winter of 1978–9. At that time I was reading Ernest Mandel's influential *Late Capitalism* while preparing a paper on regional planning in a period of economic decline as part of my undergraduate course in urban and regional planning at Oxford Polytechnic. One of the most novel features of Mandel's work was his reformulation of a long-wave perspective of capitalist development within the Marxist tradition. Mandel's thesis provided me with an intellectual rationalisation of what I already intuitively knew to be true. The deepening economic crises since the early 1970s, marked by widening interregional inequalities and accelerating inner urban decay, represented more than a temporary downturn in British capitalism's fluctuating fortunes. They reflected major structural shifts in the patterns of social, economic and spatial development. The collapse of the fragile 'Keynesian consensus' with the onset in 1979 of the deepest recession since the 1930s, accompanied by the return of mass unemployment and the election of a Conservative government committed to a monetarist deflationary programme, confirmed my fast-hardening views about the nature of these structural changes.

Much of mainstream regional analysis at that time remained preoccupied with theories of 'structural convergence' that were becoming decreasingly pertinent to contemporary spatial development. It was in this context that I became attracted to Marxist and other critical theories of spatial development which were the first to apprehend the changing nature of Britain's socio-economic geography. My undergraduate dissertation examined the changing nature of the 'regional problem' and regional policy responses since 1945, relating these changes to the underlying shifts in the direction of capitalist development with the evaporation of the post-war expansionary long wave. After graduating in 1980 I continued my research at Birmingham University's Centre for Urban and Regional Studies, intending to take a more comprehensive look at the process of regional development in Britain since the Industrial Revolution. The long-wave theory was to occupy a much more prominent place in this project, whose results are presented here.

During this time I was fortunate to experience life in a region where the changing patterns of industrial development were nowhere more dramatically evident. I was fortunate, which is more than can be said for the people of the West Midlands region where some 300 000 joined the dole queue in the four years it took to write this book. This real and immediate experience had a direct bearing on my academic research. I became increasingly dissatisfied, not only with the oft-repeated view of the Right that 'There Is No Alternative', but also with the interpretations of many Left theorists who reduced local patterns of economic change to the perverse and remorseless machinery of global capital accumulation. This approach excludes the possibility of any scope for self-determination by local communities in shaping the course of their own development. One central purpose of this book is to suggest that, both theoretically and historically, socio-economic forces based in particular localities can play and have played an important role in determining wider patterns of development. During the past eighteen months I have again been fortunate to work for the West Midlands County Council's Economic Development Unit which, along with many other like-minded local councils, is developing and implementing positive local alternatives to industrial slump, mounting unemployment and social debilitation.

The ideas in this book have, then, been subject to a variety of influences, academic, personal and political. I am particularly indebted to Mrs Barbara M. D. Smith at Birmingham University's Centre for Urban and Regional Studies, who supervised my research and suffered the unenviable task of reading and re-reading drafts. I would like to express my sincere gratitude to Barbara for her constant advice and encouragement throughout the preparation of this study. My thanks are also due to the staff and students of the Centre for incidental guidance and suggestions; to the Social Science Research Council, which funded this study; to Birmingham University Centre for Computing and Computer Studies for use of their facilities; to former colleagues at Oxford Polytechnic who inspired many of the initial ideas for this work; to my friends and colleagues at the West Midlands County Council's Economic Development Unit; and to Ron Martin, the series editor, for his encouragement and support. I have my best friend and brother Adrian to thank for sustaining my morale over the past four years. I am not married and I type my own work.

Birmingham   MICK MARSHALL

Acknowledgements

The author and publishers wish to thank the following who have kindly given permission for the use of copyright material:

Conference of Socialist Economists for diagram from *The Labour Process and Class Strategies*.

Van Gorcum & Comp BV for diagram from *The Long Wave in Economic Life* by J. J. van Duijn, Allen & Unwin Ltd (1983).

Francis Pinter (Publishers) Ltd for figure from *Long Waves of the World Economy* edited by Christopher Freeman (1984).

Every effort has been made to trace all the copyright-holders, but if any have been inadvertently overlooked the publishers will be pleased to make the necessary arrangement at the first opportunity.

Introduction

Regional Analysis and the Kondratieff Cycle: Methodological Problems and Perspectives

Capitalist Crisis and the Theory of Long Waves

Capitalism is in crisis. After a quarter-century of relative prosperity the Western capitalist bloc is once again in a state of deep depression. In Britain the 'hungry years' of the 1930s, supposedly banished for ever by the Keynesian saviour of economic planning and the welfare state, are back with a vengeance. The Two Nations society of mass unemployment, regional depression and inner-city decay penetrates every corner of British economic, social and political life.

Capitalism is in crisis – a banal and obvious statement. Yet this simple fact remains far from clear to many politicians, academics and other observers. Many commentators still see the economic difficulties of the recent past as just another short-term cyclical downturn in capitalist development rather than the product of more deep-seated structural problems. Others blame the West's current economic difficulties on 'external shocks' to the system, i.e. the oil price rises of the mid-1970s, rather than on structural processes inherent to the capitalist economic system itself. It is by no means universally accepted, then, that the current economic problems facing the Western countries constitute a crisis or that these problems can be traced to the internal contradictions of the capitalist mode of economic development.

In a preview of the Western economic summit at Williamsburg in June 1983 an article in *The Times* outlined three groups of opinion on the prevailing international recession.[1] The first group, led by the USA, sees the world crisis since 1979 as a temporary recession like any other which will soon give way to 'normality'.

The second group, represented by Japan and France, argues that the world economy has suffered a far-reaching structural shock which will not be fully resolved by any future cyclical upturn, but will necessitate a long phase of readjustment. The third group was not represented at the summit conference. It carries no weight in any national government or state department. Yet, as other theories have fallen by the wayside, victims of the recent history which they have so utterly failed to predict, the third approach has grown in popularity and influence among professional economists and others seeking an explanation for the current period of global capitalist decline. This is the theory of long waves or the 'Kondratieff cycle'.

The approach draws on the work of Nikolai Kondratieff in the 1920s who discovered long, fifty-year waves of economic expansion and contraction in capitalist development, reflected in the movements of commodity price data since the late eighteenth century. The first of these waves was represented by the Industrial Revolution in Britain during the first half of the nineteenth century; the second by the rapid rise of Continental industry from the 1850s followed by the Victorian depression of the 1880s; the third by the imperialist expansion led by Britain, Germany and the US in the late nineteenth century, reaching its climax in the First World War. Had Kondratieff lived to complete his work he might have correctly predicted the depression of the 1930s, the long post-war boom and the international recessions of the 1970s and 1980s.

Although Kondratieff himself attempted to explain the long waves through the uneven development of different economic sectors, the recent revival of interest in the theory owes much to the work of Joseph Schumpeter in the 1930s. Schumpeter explained the 'Kondratieff cycle' as the effect of periodic 'Technological Revolutions' which transformed the basis of capitalist production. He related the first 'Kondratieff' to innovations in iron-smelting and the mechanisation of the cotton industry; the second to steam power, the railways and Bessemer steel; the third to electric power, the chemicals and synthetic materials industries and the beginnings of the motor industry. Schumpeter's followers have subsequently related the fourth and most recent 'Kondratieff' to innovations in the electrical, petrochemicals and motor industries. They predict a future fifth 'Kondratieff' on the basis of the current technical advances in microelectronics and other areas.

For increasing numbers of such modern observers the severity and duration of the contemporary economic decline bears a striking similarity to its antecedents in the depressions of the interwar years and the mid-Victorian era. After over three decades of relative obscurity the 'Kondratieff cycle' is currently enjoying a phase – one might say a 'wave' – of unprecedented popularity. The theory of long waves is the subject of ongoing research projects at the Massachusetts Institute of Technology and at the University of Sussex Science Policy Research Unit.[2] It was the subject of conferences of the Organisation for Economic Co-operation and Development at Paris in 1977 and of the Long-Range Planning Society and the Institute of Measurement and Control at London in 1981.[3] No new book on technical change and employment is complete without reference to the theory.[4] The magazine *Futures* devoted a whole special issue to the theory in 1981.[5] One of Kondratieff's papers, first published in 1925, was reprinted in a 1978 issue of *Lloyds Bank Review*, a journal hardly noted for its services to the economic historian.[6] One stock-market analyst felt moved to publish a guide for investors on the subject.[7] Another has written a handbook on surviving the 'downwave', promising to reveal 'everything all the experts would tell you if only they dared'.[8] The same author has linked the long waves with trends in public morals and women's clothing fashions. Other researchers have related the long waves to trends in advertising strategies and even to tree growth in Arizona.[9] I mention these examples not to ridicule them, but to show just how pervasive the recent revival of interest in the long-wave thesis has been. During the space of a few months in 1982 the 'Kondratieff cycle' appeared in a three-page article in *Business Week*; a *Lloyds Bank Economic Bulletin* on house prices; a leading City stock-market consultant's mailing to investors; and a television interview with Clive Sinclair of home-computer fame.[10]

All this comes as no surprise to a handful of Marxist political economists who recognised the collapse of the post-war boom in the late 1960s and early 1970s long before their counterparts in mainstream economic thought.[11] Of these, Ernest Mandel's *Late Capitalism* is one of the most far-sighted analyses by a Marxist

thinker since the classical era and, at the time of its first publication in 1972, the only attempt to comprehensively and systematically analyse the economic formations of modern capitalism
through the principles of historical materialism bequeathed by
Marx and Engels.[12]

The most strikingly innovative feature of Mandel's approach was
his reconstruction of a theory of long waves in capitalist development within the Marxist tradition. Mandel did not explain the long
waves through superficial economic imbalances or the process of
technical change in the manner of Kondratieff and Schumpeter.
He related the long waves to the fundamental characteristics of
capital accumulation and the basic motor force of capitalist production in the movements of the rate of profit. Employing this
theoretical framework, Mandel was among the first to predict the
end of the expansionary post-war long wave and the arrival of a
new long wave of international capitalist stagnation.

Regional Analysis

That the crisis of the Western economies has been paralleled by a
crisis of economic theory is something of a conventional truism.[13]
The controversy that had been raging between Keynesians and
monetarists throughout the 1970s reached its inevitable conclusion
by the end of the decade. It was always a non-debate since events
in the economic and political worlds had long since pre-empted the
outcome of academic discussion. The Keynesian consensus, which
had been terminally ill for some considerable time, died a perhaps
surprisingly noisy death with the recession from 1979 accompanied, in Britain and elsewhere, by the election of national
governments committed to monetarist deflationary programmes.

If economic theory was slow in adjusting to the collapse of the
post-war economic order, however, writers in the field of regional
analysis did not even seem to recognise the need for adjustment.
The whole post-war ethos of regional development and planning
had been geared to Keynesian growth economics. The 'regional
problem' in Britain was seen as a historical legacy of nineteenth-
century industrialisation to be banished by redistributing growth
from the 'congested' or 'overheated' regions to the Assisted
Areas. When, quite simply, the growth ran out the objective basis

for regional planning evaporated with it.[14] Yet, until very recently indeed, the literature of regional analysis continued to celebrate the successes of the past rather than anticipate the problems of the future. The paralysis of regional policy in the late 1970s was commonly attributed, where it was considered at all, to the quirks of fickle government.[15]

It was against this background that a growing body of critical Marxist work on urban and regional analysis developed. This school was the first to appreciate the changing nature of contemporary spatial 'problems' and to apprehend the approaching symptoms of inner-city decay and regional depression which have since become such prominent features of Britain in the 1980s.

The initial development of this approach was characterised as much, if not more, by introspective theoretical debate as by its contributions to empirical knowledge. Indeed, the relationship betwen theory and concrete analysis was a source of great tension within the Marxist school. The early Marxist contributions were, for the most part, preoccupied with establishing a broad theoretical and methodological framework within which to 'locate' the process of regional development and which could form the analytical starting-point for subsequent empirical investigations. Elizabeth Lebas's comments on a sociological approach to regional analysis are illuminating:

> Quite soon it became apparent to us that a sociology of regional policy and planning entailed, almost by definition, a 'global approach', able to grasp in historical context some notion of the socio-economic and political whole. Also, it had to take into account the existence of power relations and socio-economic conflict, since planning and policy were in themselves ideological and political activities. Otherwise one could not even begin by posing such basic questions as the following. What really is regional policy and planning behind all the pronouncements and activities? Why are issues formulated or *not* formulated the way they are? What part does this form of state intervention play at a particular stage of capitalist society? After which, one could begin to ask about relationships between regional policy and planning and the management of the labour force in areas conveniently labelled 'disadvantaged', 'peripheral' or 'underdeveloped'.[16]

Not surprisingly, many Marxist theorists attempted in the first instance to 'borrow' theoretical frameworks constructed to tackle other fields of inquiry and apply them to the study of uneven regional development.[17] Perhaps the most influential of these was the 'internal colonialism' theory and related perspectives which likened the relationships between 'central' and 'peripheral' regions within the industrialised economies to relationships of imperialism or trading inequality between the advanced capitalist nations and the Third World.[18] This perspective was most widespread among Continental theorists attempting to analyse the spatial 'dualism' between the industrial heartlands and under-industrialised agricultural peripheries in countries like Italy and France.[19] In Britain the approach was applied to the study of uneven development between industrial regions as well as between the English heartland and the Scots and Welsh 'Celtic fringe'.[20]

Such early Marxist approaches were widely criticised from within the Marxist perspective for their high level of abstraction, their 'spatial fetishism', their 'functionalism' and their 'ahistoricism'.[21] They were seen as too abstract since they tended to superimpose a monolithic theoretical framework upon very disparate concrete phenomena. They tended to exclude the possibility, for example, that their might be very different relationships between industrial regions or between industrial and agricultural regions in different countries and at different times. The abstract perspectives were criticised for their spatial fetishism since they tended to interpret uneven regional development as arising from relationships between physical spaces rather than between social groups. They accepted too readily the conventional geographical definitions of 'regions' before having fully examined the ideological connotations underlying such concepts. The perspectives were seen as too functionalist since they assigned certain functional roles to different categories of region within the requirements set by the capitalist economic framework. Again, this tended to arbitrarily generalise very varied regional experiences into monolithic statements about the economic purpose (from capitalism's standpoint) of uneven development or spatial inequality as a necessary ingredient of the economic system. Finally, the abstract theories were criticised as ahistorical because they saw uneven regional development as a static phenomenon. They failed to examine how uneven development arose in the first place and how its form could change and evolve over time. Where the perspectives *did* introduce a historical dimension they again tended to do so in highly functionalist and mechanical ways. Alain Lipietz, for example, describes two mechanisms whereby central regions have exerted their dominance over the periphery during the successive historical periods of primitive commodity production and fully developed industrial capitalism.[22] But Lipietz assumes that a dominant region in the early historical phase will simply take on a different form of dominance over the periphery in the later period of its development. He neglects the possibility that a dominant region in one period may later itself become dominated during an ensuing period – precisely the phenomenon which I will argue has taken place across the historical long waves in Britain which has experienced a succession of different leading industrial regions.

Partly in response to these kind of criticisms, subsequent Marxist approaches in Britain at least tended to reject the notion of developing a specifically 'regional' theory of uneven development. Rather, they sought to situate the phenomenon of uneven regional development within a wider perspective of social, economic and political structures and processes governing the historical evolution of capitalist societies – an analysis which as Michael Dunford pointed out 'must be conducted in historical rather than functionalist terms'.[23] In addition to academic debates the new directon in Marxist regional theory was influenced by the deepening economic crisis affecting all industrialised countries since the international recession of 1974–5. In response to the new urban and regional crises Marxists were particularly concerned with posing alternatives to the dominant geographical explanation that blamed the cities and regions themselves for their degeneration due to their inflexible industrial structures or inadequate social fabric. The term 'regional' itself was extensively criticised as an imprecise or 'unscientific' label for phenomena which were deeply rooted in the capitalist economic fabric rather than governed by some spatially bounded dynamic.[24] As Enzo Mingione later put it:

There are no urban or regional questions as such: urban as opposed to rural or to regional is not a fundamental characteristic of social problems. It is only a feature of the general reproduction of current societies. So, although it is possible and reasonable to call a social problem urban or regional or rural, as the academic description of division of labour teaches us to do, this definition has no precise scientific meaning, apart from its obvious descriptive content.[25]

The term 'restructuring' became the new keyword for theorists concerned with examining industrial and social change in Britain's cities and regions. In practical terms this led to investigations which regarded the 'regional question' and 'capital restructuring and capitalist crisis' as synonymous fields of inquiry. Industrial decline and employment losses in the older urban areas were seen as symptomatic of the far-reaching restructuring of capitalist production brought on by the international recessions.[26] The forms of state intervention in this restructuring process commonly referred to as regional policies were not specifically 'regional' at all. They were 'but one dimen ion of a concerted political and economic attempt to invigorate industrial capital in Britain'[27] or 'a means by which accumulation by industrial capitalists is bolstered in a period of falling profitability' in which 'the "regional" element of the policy is completely subsidiary'.[28]

I do not deny the validity of these conclusions, but I dispute some of the thinking underlying them. The basic starting-point for this approach is that 'regional' problems, crises or whatever can be ultimately traced to wider national and international processes. Yet at the same time these wider processes take on particular forms in different regions. This hypothesis has been very clearly stated by Felix Damette and Edmond Poncet:

> Regional crises ultimately reflect the general crisis of the system. The initial force is provided by the general crisis.
> Regional crises are not the result of simple disaggregation of the overall crisis. There is a specifically regional dimension to the problem.[29]

This distinction between general crises or processes and regional processes seems to me to be a contradictory one. General processes are seen as global in scale and nature, distinct from any internally contained regional process. The logic of this approach is that it would be possible to take any region of any national territory and explain its character by reference to external processes, presumably located in other regions or nations. If the causal forces giving rise to a particular regional condition are not located internally to the region in question then they must be located elsewhere. Following this interpretation it makes little sense to attribute regional differentiation to 'general' processes because the activities taking place in the regions *are* the process, or at least a part of it. The approach leads to the disembodiment of regional processes, occurring everywhere and yet nowhere at the same time.

In response to this kind of problem some Marxist theorists adopted an alternative interpretation of the concept of 'general' processes. The latter were seen as abstract processes in the sense of historically invariant characteristics of the capitalist system, but with no particular association with spatial scale. The most influential of such approaches has been the 'labour process' perspective which sees the struggle between capital and labour over the technical organisation and social relationships of production as universal to capitalist economies, but goes on to analyse how this process has taken different forms in different places and at different times.[30] Other theorists rejected the idea of any general or universal capitalist process in the belief that since all regional situations are different it is impossible to subsume them all within any abstract, general framework.[31]

This book is partly a product of dissatisfaction with what I consider to be a false dichotomy between 'abstract' and 'concrete' analyses in Marxist and other critical theories of uneven regional development.[32] In my view general theories of the spatial dimension to capitalist development do not necessarily have to be monolithic or totalising. They do not have to rationalise different regional or, for that matter, national conditions within all-embracing concepts of abstract processes. What is needed is a general theory capable of bridging the gap between abstract and concrete modes of analysis; a theoretical framework which can systematically account for different concrete conditions within a general historical perspective of the development of the capitalist spatial and economic system. The theory of long waves provides the basis for such a framework. It is evidently a theory of the uneven development of different industrial sectors and of different regional and national territories. At the same time Mandel's influential reformulation of the theory has shown how the long waves can be traced back to the basic and general characteristics of the capitalist system; how the so-called 'laws of motion' of capital in fact produce a multiplicity of different concrete processes, varying both in time and in space.

Long Waves and Regional Analysis

Approaching the theory of long waves in this way, however, simultaneously revises our conception of the theory itself and its potential as a framework for regional analysis. It is not enough to simply take the long-wave theory and apply it to a fresh problematic. The long-wave approach cannot be merely employed as a descriptive framework within which to locate the evolution of different historical patterns of uneven regional development. Such an approach implicitly assumes a 'top-down' view of regional development as the outcome of general global tendencies. It presumes the notion that concrete regional experiences can be explained by abstract mechanisms as if regional conditions are somehow divorced from these general forces. What is needed is a perspective which identifies the role which uneven regional development plays in causing the long waves, rather than one which simply views regional differences as the outcome of pregiven global or abstract forces.

In this respect the theoretical stance of this book differs from those of others in the field who have also been attracted to the theory of long waves as a framework for regional analysis. One perspective uses the long-wave thesis simply as a descriptive background to recent changes in regional development.[33] This kind of approach makes no attempt to integrate the regional dimension within any causal explanation of the long waves. The ever-controversial Professor Peter Hall has proposed an undiluted Schumpeterian approach which sees technical change and entrepreneurship as the cause of the long waves.[34] In Hall's view the uneven spatial distribution of innovative activity is the ultimate reason for uneven regional economic development. Another interpretation views technical change and innovation as a key factor in the process of regional economic development, but not as the latter's ultimate cause. Roy Rothwell, for example, argues that while technical innovations may carry the long waves forward the initial stimulus must be provided by a confluence of other social and economic forces.[35] These factors may entail a particular regional dimension which determines why profoundly new industries based on technically new products and processes develop in some regions at particular times rather than in others. Along similar lines Herman Freudenberger and Gerhard Mensch have argued that the process of regional development can be explained by reference to key region-based innovations.[36] Technical innovation and economic change in the regions are seen as a cumulative process of evolution, building upon successive advances, which Freudenberger and Mensch call 'generative regional growth'. This process is not self-sustaining, however, but relies on 'a favourable climate for improvement and achievement' in the cultural, social and political as well as economic environment.[37]

The problem with all these approaches, like the Schumpeterian account of the long waves which they rely on, is that they implicitly see technology itself as independent of the wider social context within which it develops. While some of the authors referred to above *do* see technical change as dependent upon catalytic social and political forces, they do not relate the *nature and form* of that technology to the nature of the wider social forces. It is for this reason that Marxists analyse technology as but one factor within the capitalist labour process. The latter represents the conjunction, not only of the technical means of production, but also of the social relationships of capitalist production which rest fundamentally on the exercise of power by the owners of capital over the workforce. Technology is not 'neutral' but is an instrument whereby that power is exercised. Technology is not limited simply by scientific possibilities. It is also constrained by working practices, even by whole cultures. During the Industrial Revolution, for example, the transition from dispersed, workshop production to concentrated, mechanised factory systems did not arise spontaneously from the possibilities raised by the radical scientific advances of the period. On the contrary, new norms of working life had to be actively constructed by the factory owners and often met with active resistance from the workforce.[38] In all periods of capitalist development technology has been shaped by the need to construct and reconstruct fresh forms of organisation, supervision and discipline in the labour process.

However the approach adopted in this book is not only counterposed to the Schumpeterian perspective of the long waves. It also takes issue with several key components of Mandel's reformulation. Mandel has ably demonstrated how what he calls the 'objective' laws of capitalist development give rise to the long waves, accounting for the latter's origin and inevitability. However, he introduces the 'subjective' forces of human agents, of social and political conflict, only at selected points in his approach. He does not systematically relate the abstract dynamics of the long waves to the concrete processes of social conflict through which these dynamics actually occur.

Since Mandel's *Late Capitalism* was first published in 1972 debates in Marxist economic and social theory have stimulated widespread rejection of deterministic or 'capital logic' stances that interpret phenomena solely in terms of the logical imperatives of capital, laws of accumulation or whatever. On the negative side the 'value controversy' has demonstrated the limitations of abstract theoretical frameworks in the explanation of concrete processes of capitalist socio-economic development.[39] With more positive implications the revival of interest in the capitalist labour process has stressed how the technological development of industrial capitalism is not some self-contained process of logical advance but a terrain of social struggle, of class conflict and negotiation.[40]

The only Marxist attempt, of which I am aware, to apply the long-wave thesis to the study of regional development is the recent work by Michael Dunford and Diane Perrons, who draw heavily on a labour-process interpretation of the long waves.[41] These authors reject the conventional stress on technology in industrial change, substituting an analysis which relates regional industrial development to the historical evolution of the capitalist labour process from semi-agricultural workshop production to the factory system and to modern, mass production and assembly. In my view, however, Dunford and Perrons tend to employ the long-wave approach only as a convenient historical framework within which they are better equipped to analyse the different systems of capital accumulation which form the focus of their study. They do not systematically relate the process of uneven regional development to the causes of the long waves. The strength of these authors' analysis is its interpretation of regional development as an arena of social conflict and contest between the attempts of the capitalist class to mould local communities and workforces to the technical requirements of capital accumulation, on the one hand, and the resistance of regional populations to that process, on the other.

This brings me to the final, and perhaps most important, purpose of this study of long waves and regional development. A recurrent theme throughout this work is that the pattern of regional development is not a predetermined outcome of technical advance or global economic forces. On the contrary it is a fluid process in which regional social and political forces are to some extent able to exert a relative autonomy in shaping their own destinies. The theory of long waves has too often been interpreted as a fatalistic and predictive theory of regular, fifty-year cycles in which twenty-five years of slump follows twenty-five years of boom as surely as night follows day. This study seeks to show that the nature and turning-points of the long waves have been the outcome of social conflict rather than of predestined forces beyond human influence. Each historic turning-point of the long waves has witnessed the rise of new social and political forces. Regionally-based political and social movements, like the Manchester Chartists and free-traders of the 1830s and 1840s or the Birmingham-based social imperialists in the late nineteenth century, promoted and championed the particular course of regional, national and sometimes international development which characterised the ensuing historical period.

The British economy and society once again stands at a historic turning-point in a pattern of development whose future course remains far from certain. Many observers in the late 1970s predicted that the deepening recession would generate fresh 'regional crises' and new forms of regional social unrest in response to the international economic crisis and the collapse of the post-war political consensus.[42] The Scots and Welsh nationalist movements, the steel strike of 1979–80, the sporadic inner-city riots of 1981, the coalfield strike of 1984, the reconstructed local government movement of the 1980s and other examples besides are all, in different ways, symptomatic of those economic and political upheavals. In my view the historical analysis presented in this work helps to provide an appreciation of the historic significance and possibilities of these contemporary phenomena.

The Structure of this Study

Chapter 1 examines a variety of different long-wave theories, comparing and contrasting the price-cycle approach of Kondratieff and Rostow, the technical innovation account proposed by Schumpeter and the contemporary Neo-Schumpeterians, the capital over-accumulation model generated by Forrester and the Marxist interpretations of Trotsky and Mandel. Each of these perspectives draws on different evidence in support of different theoretical explanations which amount to very different conceptions of the long waves.

Chapters 2 and 3 evaluate these alternative theories, focusing upon their interpretations of technical change and short-term economic cycles within the long waves. It is argued that each long wave constitutes a distinctive historical period characterised by different technical and social systems of production and by different forms of short-term fluctuations. Each wave is the outcome of historically variable combinations of factors which produce varied and uneven experiences of development, not least at the regional scale.

Chapter 4 draws on British regional employment data from the decennial Census to show how each long wave has been associated with the rise and fall of different industrial sectors, how these sectoral patterns have taken different courses in different regions and how these are reflected in successive historical phases of regional inequality.

Chapters 5 and 6 examine in more detail the pattern of regional industrialisation in Britain from the Industrial Revolution to the First World War. Chapter 5 shows how the long waves of national economic development were based upon very different regional experiences, stressing in particular how expansionary growth in some regions was frequently combined with stagnation and decline in others. Chapter 6 goes on to argue that the evolving pattern of British regional industrialisation can only be understood in the context of the unique social character of British capitalism and its internal divisions. Social and political contests were frequently fought over regional interests. The outcomes of these regional disputes sometimes determined, not only the course of uneven regional development, but also the long-term pattern of national and even international economic development.

Chapter 7 draws on a variety of statistical studies to show how the 'regional problem' formed during the interwar depression was not a static state of spatial imbalance, but entailed a dynamic, cyclical dimension. The long post-war boom after 1945 involved a particular pattern of regional economic fluctuations. Changes in the structure of these fluctuations in the mid-1960s heralded the end of the post-war expansion and the arrival of a fresh depressive long wave involving new forms of interregional economic imbalance. Chapter 8 examines the nature of this turning-point in the course of national economic development and the new spatial inequalities that have emerged since the late 1960s.

The concluding section summarises the chief results of this study and discusses their implications for an assessment of future prospects for uneven regional development in a fifth Kondratieff upturn.

Part I
Long Waves of Capitalist Development

1
Theories of Long Waves: From Kondratieff to Mandel

Introduction

All proponents of the theory of long waves acknowledge the existence of alternating long-term phases of relative expansion and contraction in the historical development of industrial capitalism. But the nature of the long waves, their origins and appearance, has been the subject of wide-ranging debate.

In its 'pure' form, as proposed by Kondratieff himself, the long waves are seen as a commodity price cycle in which the pace of economic development is regulated by relative movements of input and output production prices. The recent revival of interest in the long waves draws heavily on Schumpeter's work in which the waves are related to the innovatory product cycles of successive leading industrial sectors. Another approach, chiefly associated with Jay Forrester, explains the waves through cyclical imbalances in the supply of and demand for capital equipment in production. The Marxist approach proposed by Ernest Mandel views the waves as distinct historical periods whose nature and causes must be explained in relation to specific historical conjunctions of factors rather than to any self-reproducing cyclical dynamic. This chapter reviews each of these perspectives in turn.[1]

I Price-cycle Theories: Kondratieff and Rostow

It was in commodity price data that the long waves were first discovered and it is this statistical indicator which provides the strongest support for the notion of regular, long-term cycles in economic activity. Figure 1.1 shows a wholesale price index for the

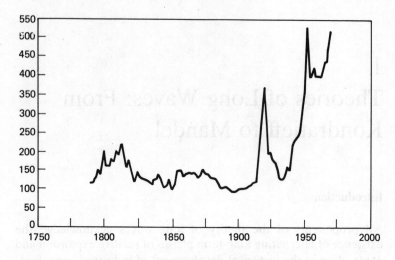

FIGURE 1.1   *UK Wholesale Price Index, 1790–1970 (1900=100)*
SOURCE   Cleary and Hobbs, 1983, p. 166.

UK from the late-eighteenth century to 1970. As Cleary and Hobbs point out: 'The eye has no great difficulty in picking out a 50–60-year periodic movement in prices with peaks in the 1810s, the 1860s and the 1920s'.[2] While the series ends at 1970 to prevent the inflation of the past decade overshadowing earlier price movements, the price rises of the 1970s would be consistent with a fourth peak in the 1980s.

1. *Kondratieff's Theory of Long Cycles*

The notion of long waves in capitalist development is normally associated with the work of the Russian economist Nikolai Kondratieff (sometimes spelt Kondratiev or Kondrat'ev), published in a series of articles between 1922 and 1928. The theory has a longer history, however, dating back to the Russian Marxist Parvus in the 1890s and subsequently taken up by the Dutch economists Van Gelderen and De Wolff.[3] But it was Kondratieff's presentation of the long waves which constituted the most advanced version of the theory, assuming a prominent position during economic debates in the newly formed USSR of the 1920s.[4]

Statistical presentation Kondratieff's earliest work consisted almost entirely of statistical presentation, employing a nine-year moving average to eliminate short-term cycles and random deviations from the empirical data to reveal long-term cyclical movements in economic indicators of capitalist development.[5] The most complete statistical indicators he produced were indices of commodity prices in England, France and the USA, although he reinforced his conclusions with a range of other indices such as quotations of interest-bearing securities, wages in England, French foreign trade, and mineral consumption and production in both England and France. From this statistical evidence Kondratieff identified two and one-half long waves, each wave consisting of one cycle of upswing and one of downswing, between the years 1780 and 1920. The periodicity and duration of these long cycles are described in Table 1.1.

Kondratieff was extremely cautious in ascribing cyclical significance to these waves of economic activity, asserting only that 'on the basis of the available data, the existence of long waves of cyclical character is very probable'.[6] However, he felt justified in stating his suspicion that the long waves were an inherent tendency of capitalist development both by the regularity of the cycles revealed in his own data and by his discovery in early 1926 of the work of Van Gelderen and De Wolff which had hitherto been unknown to him. Kondratieff was well aware of the implications of his theory for the whole analysis of capitalist societies:

> we believe ourselves justified in saying that the long waves, if existent at all, are a very important and essential factor in economic development, a factor the effects of which can be found in all the principal fields of social and economic life.[7]

In an attempt to relate the long waves to these wider effects, Kondratieff listed the main social, economic and political features which accompanied each phase. According to Kondratieff, cycles of upswing were preceded by profound economic changes, most importantly changes in productive technology, the extension of the global capitalist economy to new territories and changes in gold production and monetary circulation. Most major wars, social upheavals and revolutions occurred during cycles of upswing.

TABLE 1.1   *Periodicity and Duration of Kondratieff's Long Cycles*

Long wave	Direction of cycle	Period	Duration of cycle	Duration of wave
I	Upswing	1789–1814	25 years	60 years
I	Downswing	1814–49	35 years	60 years
II	Upswing	1849–73	24 years	47 years
II	Downswing	1873–96	23 years	47 years
III	Upswing	1896–1920	24 years	–
III	Downswing	1920–	–	–

During expansionary phases the short-term business cycle was characterised by intense booms and short depressions, vice versa during cycles of downswing in which agricultural sectors tended to suffer from particularly acute depressions.

However, Kondratieff's investigation of these phenomena amounted to no more than a simple inventory of recurring coincidences of observable features. He made no attempt to assign causal relationships to these features, nor was his purpose to do so. For Kondratieff the movements of the long waves could not be attributed to such 'external' factors, but were regulated by internal necessities inherent to capitalist economic development.

A 'tentative explanation'   In one of his last papers, delivered in 1926 and published jointly with his collaborator Oparin two years later, Kondratieff provided, with his customary caution, a 'first attempt to give a tentative explanation of the long cycles'. Deriving a concept of long-term capitalist equilibrium from his reading of Alfred Marshall, Kondratieff argued that:

> The wavelike fluctuations are processes of alternating disturbances of the equilibrium of the capitalistic system; they are increasing or decreasing deviations from the equilibrium levels.[8]

These deviations, according to Kondratieff, were caused by the cycle of replacement of long-term fixed capital assets in production necessitating large-scale investment activity. Borrowing the idea from Marx that business cycles were caused by the need for periodic reinvestment of funds in fixed capital with a limited economic life, Kondratieff distinguished between normal cycles of fixed capital replacement and extraordinary waves of investment in what we would today call infrastructure – large plants, railways, canals, buildings – together with investment involved in the adaptation of the labour force to new skills and techniques. These extraordinary investments combined to extend the whole basis of capitalist production. Kondratieff thereby introduced a hierarchy of alternate types of capital investment, differentiated by their production period, their durability or economic life and the scale of investment required for their introduction. For Kondratieff:

> The material basis of the long cycles is the wear and tear, the replacement and the increase of the fund of basic capital goods, the production of which requires tremendous investment and is a long process. [9]

Cycles of upswing in capitalist development were characterised by an acceleration of investment, shifting the direction of development above the equilibrium course or 'trend line'. In the cycles of downswing investment slowed down, shifting the course of capitalist development back towards the equilibrium level and below it. The long waves were part of an overall process of cumulative capitalist growth since 'the equilibrium level itself changes in the process of cyclical fluctuations, and shifts, as a rule, to a higher level'. [10]

Having related the long waves to the cycle of replacement of certain basic capital goods, Kondratieff went on to explain why the process of investment took a cyclical rather than a continuous course by introducing Tugan-Baranowsky's theory of 'free loanable funds'. Large investments required large sources of loanable funds. This was dependent upon the fulfilment of four conditions – a high propensity to save, low interest rates, institutional availability of funds and low prices conducive to both capital investment and savings from incomes. By identifying the relationship between these four factors and the rate of investment Kondratieff sought to explain the cyclical discontinuities in the investment process itself.

During the phase of upswing, Kondratieff argued, loanable funds were accumulated in excess of current investment, provided by savings from those social groups whose real incomes rose with the relatively low price level. The duration of the phase of expansion, based on new fixed capital investment, was limited by both rising interest rates on capital borrowing (due to rising demand for funds) and the actual shortage of funds as capital stocks became depleted, together with rising prices which militated against any substantial replacement of funds from savings. The upper turning-point thus appeared as a result of over-investment relative to capital resources but the lower turning-point remained unexplained. Kondratieff's presentation of the cumulative historical process shows how conditions *favourable* to expansion develop. But he failed to point out precisely what factors cause the actual turning-point from contraction to expansion.[11]

Contemporary criticisms It is clear that Kondratieff did not consider this outline to be an adequate or full theoretical analysis of the statistical evidence for the long waves. But he was never permitted to complete it. In 1928 he was removed from his position as head of the Moscow Business Research Institute. In the autumn of 1930 he was arrested as an alleged leader of an illegal anti-government 'Peasants' Labour Party' and deported to Siberia without trial where, like so many of his contemporaries, he subsequently 'disappeared'. The 1929 edition of the official Soviet Russian Encyclopedia referred to his work on the long waves with the single sentence: 'This theory is wrong and reactionary.'[12]

However, in the intervening period between the consolidation of Communist power in the new Soviet state and the Stalinist thermidor, Kondratieff's work gave rise to an intense and often vehement debate among Soviet economists. In the young and vulnerable USSR, perspectives on the future development of the external capitalist world were of more than mere academic interest; they were of imminent concrete political concern.

Kondratieff, with the exception of perhaps one critical collaborator, Oparin, stood alone in defence of his findings, isolated even within his own Institute, against a barrage of criticism. George Garvy has provided an extensive account of these critiques, which

ranged in character from a polemical denial of the political implications of Kondratieff's work (Sukhanov, Granovsky, Svetlov) to
more rigorous analysis of his methodology (Bogdanov) and testing
of his empirical findings (Guberman, Gerzstein, Eventov).[13] Generally the existence of extended movements in capitalist economic
development was not disputed, although Kondratieff's statistical
presentation of these movements – both his methodology and his
detailed findings – received intense criticism. Oparin provided a
comprehensive alternative presentation based on a reworking of
the data through a different statistical technique (an eleven- in-
stead of nine-year moving average). The most serious criticisms
were addressed to Kondratieff's use of the concept of capitalist
equilibrium. For Kondratieff the long-term economic movements
were of cyclical character, the regular and inevitable result of the
interplay of forces inherent to capitalist economies. Critics, on the
other hand, argued that the turning-points were not brought about
by an inevitable succession of logical cycles, but were caused by
social and political factors operating independently of any internal
economic dynamic.

2. Rostow's 'Stages of Economic Growth'

Kondratieff's primary contribution to the long-wave thesis was his
compilation of statistical evidence for long-term swings in commodity prices rather than his theoretical account of these movements. In so far as Kondratieff *did* attempt a 'tentative
explanation', he attributed the price movements to a more fundamental process of growth, decay and replacement of productive
fixed capital and its effects on the supply of and demand for
investment funds. As described below, later theorists in the
Schumpeterian tradition have more forcefully argued that the
process of technical change in production is a prime causal factor
in the long waves. This section considers the contribution of
W. W. Rostow, who, more than any other theorist, has interpreted the long waves as a price cycle and pointed to the commodity price movements as *in themselves* a key causal element of
the waves.

Stages of growth and the Kondratieff price cycle In his early work
on *The Stages of Economic Growth* Rostow postulated that all

societies follow a similar pattern of economic development through five distinct stages: first, the pre-industrial 'Traditional Society'; second, a stage in which the 'Preconditions for Take-off' are established; third, the 'Industrial Take-off' when economic growth becomes a normal feature of society; fourth, the 'Drive to Maturity' in which industrialisation and growth are consolidated in the economy; and fifth, the age of 'High Mass Consumption', following some sixty years after the take-off, in which the benefits of industrialisation accrue to the mass of the population in higher living standards and provision of services.[14]

In his later magnum opus on *The World Economy* Rostow focused on the transitions between these stages through sectoral data for a range of both developed and Third World economies.[15] The Kondratieff cycle was presented as the central mechanism behind these transitions, based on technological revolutions which transform the economic organisation of society, raising it to a new stage of development. Thus, in the case of Britain, Rostow identifies the years from 1783 to 1830 as the stage of industrial take-off based on the cotton textile revolution. The drive to maturity was divided into two phases (a feature unique to the British experience), the first from 1830 to 1870 in which the railways replaced cotton as the leading sector, the second from 1870 to 1913 based on the rise of steel and seeing the origins of electric power, motor-vehicles and the chemicals industries. From 1920, according to Rostow, the British economy achieved the stage of high mass consumption with the expansion of the motor, electrics, plastics and synthetics sectors. This stage proceeded weakly in the interwar years and accelerated in the post-war period which witnessed the growth of state welfare and the increasing tertiarisation of the economy.[16]

Rostow's explanation   Rostow's explanation of the Kondratieff cycle focuses on the prices of food and raw materials relative to the prices of industrial products, the cyclical phases of upswing and downswing corresponding to periods of relative shortage or abundance of foodstuffs and raw materials. Changes in relative prices underlie the shifts in income distribution, spatial and sectoral directions of investment, trends in interest rates, real wages and overall price levels which Rostow sees as the characteristic statistical indicators of the long waves. 'Why', Rostow asks, 'were these cycles so long compared, for example, to conventional business cycles which averaged, say, nine years?':

> The answer seems to lie in the fact that the opening up of new sources of food and raw materials required substantial periods of time. . . . The lags involved in responding to a relative rise in food or raw material prices, and the fact that the response often required the development of whole new regions, led to an overshooting of world requirements and a period of relative surplus. A relative fall in the prices of food and raw materials then followed. This trend persisted, gradually slowing down, until expanding world requirements caught up with the excess capacity and stocks generated in a Kondratieff upswing.[17]

Contradictions of the price-cycle approach In the above statement Rostow seems to confuse the two distinct cycles – that of industrial production and that of the production of raw materials and food – by presenting them as one. His exposition of the food and materials price cycle is quite straightforward. High prices stimulate expanded production leading to an over-abundance of food and materials which in turn depresses prices, reducing production, leading to a relative shortage, higher prices and so on. His explanation of the industrial product cycle is more subtle. Food and raw material inputs constitute a substantial part of the cost prices of industrial products, either directly through consumption in the production process or indirectly by determining wage levels. Therefore, periods of high food and material prices will stimulate industrial innovation – technological advance and territorial expansion – in the quest for cheaper alternative sources of inputs to the production process. As the demand for these *new* inputs of food and materials rises, so their prices increase, stimulating a further round of innovation.

It is apparent that Rostow fails adequately to integrate these two cycles together in his explanation of the 'Kondratieffs'. First, it is unclear how the price cycle of *old* food and raw materials, the input of the previous phase of industrial expansion, can affect the subsequent industrial cycles when these former inputs have been superseded by *new* sources. Second, if there *is* a relationship between the price cycles of industrial products and of food and raw materials in Rostow's account, then it must surely focus on the stimulus to technological innovation provided by the phase of high food and material prices. Yet Rostow seems to introduce technological advance as a factor affecting the long waves almost as an afterthought. For Rostow it is the cycle of relative commodity price levels which constitutes the central endogenous mechanism which causes the long waves, technological innovation entering as an exogenous, secondary factor. The two are each awarded an independent dynamic:

> The rhythm of the great technological innovations did not conform systematically to the rhythm of relative prices for basic commodities; but the rise and fall of the great innovations did leave their marks on relative price movements. The story of the Kondratieff cycles must be told, then, by weaving together the impulses imparted to the world economy by periods of relative scarcity or overabundance of food and raw materials with the saga of technological change.[18]

Rostow's explanation cannot be accepted as an advance on previous theories; in fact in one sense it represents a regression. Rostow's price-cycle explanation resembles an initial thesis proposed by Kondratieff which the latter quickly abandoned (since it did not withstand the test of empirical evidence) in favour of the 'capital investment cycle' account outlined above. Rostow's approach leads him to absurd conclusions in his analysis of recent economic experience. According to Rostow the 'price revolution' of 1972–7, the reversal of the terms of trade between raw material and manufactured good producers brought about by the sharp rise in oil prices, marks the beginning of a 'fifth Kondratieff upswing' since it will stimulate industrial expansion based on alternative energy sources, raw materials and products.[19] The idea that the world economy is presently enjoying a long wave of expansionary growth – and has been since 1972 – is an absurdity which makes no sense of economic performance over the past decade.

II Technical Innovation and Sectoral Growth-cycle Theories: Schumpeter and the neo-Schumpeterians

The price-cycle theories of Kondratieff and, more recently, Rostow both recognise technological changes in industrial fixed capital as an important feature of the long waves. But these two authors award differing degrees of emphasis to this factor. In the case of Rostow, technical change is seen as a consequence rather than a cause of the price cycle. Kondratieff, on the other hand, saw the cycle of technological adaptation as the ultimate origin of the statistical price movements through the impact of technical changes on flows of investment funds.

However, Kondratieff was, quite literally, physically prevented from pursuing this analysis beyond his first tentative suggestions. This step was left to Joseph Schumpeter in the 1930s, who explained the long waves as the outcome of discontinuities in the entrepreneurial process of technical innovation. Schumpeter's more recent followers have extended his analysis by relating the waves to the product and process cycles of successive leading industrial sectors.

1. Schumpeter's Theory of Technical Innovation and 'Creative Destruction'

In his classic study of *Business Cycles* Schumpeter constructed a multicyclical model of capitalist development based on the interrelationship between a range of cycles of varying duration which he named after the main researchers with which they were associated: the $3\frac{1}{2}$-year Kitchin cycle, the Juglar cycle of 9–10 years and the 55–year 'Kondratieffs'.[20] The publication of Schumpeter's work in 1939 gave rise to a debate among American economists in which similar issues were discussed as had been raised a decade earlier by Kondratieff's Russian antagonists. The most important areas of debate were: first, the significance of Schumpeter's statistical evidence; second, the relationship of the long cycles to external factors such as wars; and third, the issue of whether the long waves were true cycles or might be more appropriately labelled 'epochs' of capitalist development.[21]

For Schumpeter, as for Kondratieff, the long waves were an internal regulator of capitalist development. However, in his earliest works Schumpeter rejected the notion that economic development could be defined simply in terms of changes in savings or investment patterns. For Schumpeter such factors were *exogenous* to the process of economic development. They were an inherent feature, not of the economic, but of the demographic process, saving and investment tending to rise naturally over time with the increase of population. For Schumpeter the term 'development' in the economic sense implied a qualitative shift in the nature of production, not mere quantitative changes in the level, rate of increase or distribution of wealth.[22]

Technical innovation This qualitative change is described in Schumpeter's concept of technical '*innovation*', the establishment of a new productive function. Applying this formulation to his study of business cycles Schumpeter argued that innovations did not appear continuously but in clusters of frantic entrepreneurial activity involving new 'combinations' of products and means of production – new commodities, new productive techniques, the opening-up of new markets, the utilisation of new raw materials and the sectoral reorganisation of parts of the economy. Examples of such combinations were found in the 'Technological Revolutions' of the nineteenth century, proceeding not by a steady, continuous process of advance, but by a discontinuous pattern of fits and starts. Concentrations of intense entrepreneurial innovation were separated by long periods of consolidation of previous advances with no major new innovative activity.

It was this discontinuous process of innovation which Schumpeter identified as the basis of the long 'Kondratieff cycles' of upswing and downswing in capitalist development. The Industrial Revolution in Britain was the first of these cycles from the 1780s to 1842 based on iron-smelting, steam power and the mechanisation of the Lancashire cotton industry. The second 'Kondratieff' from 1843 to 1897 was based on the generalisation of the steam motor, the railways and steel. The third cycle, running from 1898, saw the rise of electric power, chemicals and the internal-combustion engine, reaching its completion in the 1930s at the time Schumpeter was writing. All these changes were preceded by clusters of innovation in the work of the great industrial entrepreneurs – Darby's iron-ore-smelting process, Watt's steam engine, Bessemer's steel-making process, the engineering feats of the Brunels and Stephensons in shipbuilding, bridge construction and railways, Edison's commercial electricity projects and Ford's mass-production techniques, to name just a few of the more memorable individuals.

It should be apparent from this list that Schumpeter drew an important distinction between 'innovations' and 'inventions'. Innovative combinations were not dependent upon the instigation of radically new scientific advances or inventions. It was quite possible for the application of new innovative combinations to proceed without inventions, while inventions as such need not necessarily give rise to innovations or have any economic consequences. For Schumpeter it was innovation itself, stimulated by the drive of individual enterprising capitalists, which constituted the endogenous factor that caused the successive long cycles in economic development.

The process of 'creative destruction' The relationship of Schumpeter's explanation of the long waves to that of Kondratieff is somewhat ambiguous. On the one hand, Schumpeter's formulation seems to echo Kondratieff's emphasis on the discontinuous clustering of basic technological investments which revolutionise the production process on a cyclical basis. But, on the other hand, Schumpeter did not attribute his cycles of innovation to *objective* economic mechanisms of supply of and demand for capital funds, in the manner of Kondratieff, but to *subjective* factors inherent to the entrepreneurial psyche. For Schumpeter, economic development had a self-generating effect – innovation breeding innovation – until the spread of new innovative combinations became generalised throughout the economy. This had a dampening impact on the psychological spur to innovate until such time as individual capitalists were again captured by entrepreneurial fever, leading to a fresh period of accelerated innovation. Schumpeter characterised the cyclical course of capitalist development as a *'process of creative destruction'* where the destructive disruption of capitalist development was a necessary, functional prerequisite for the creative renewal of development in a fresh long cycle of expansion.[23] Economic development could not proceed through a linear, continuous course. It was necessary for some industries, sectors or markets to disappear in order to stimulate new innovations, reconstructing the economy on a new, higher plane of development.

2. The neo-Schumpeterian Revival

With the onset of the post-war boom after 1945 the theory of long waves entered a phase of relative neglect. A theory which suggested that depression would follow boom as surely as night follows day failed to excite much interest among economists at a time when the industrialised countries were enjoying a prolonged, and apparently indefinite, period of growth and prosperity. Schumpeter himself had been doubtful of the predictive capacity of his theory. The theory had long since disappeared (along with Kondratieff!) from the Marxist and Soviet literature. While Rostow developed his stage theory of economic growth during the 1950s it was not until nearly two decades later that he sought to integrate his theory with the historical movements of the Kondratieff price cycle.

However, with the slowdown of growth since the late 1960s and the international recessions of the mid-1970s and early 1980s there has been a significant revival of interest in the long-wave perspective. Economists and other observers have been drawn to the theory in increasing numbers as comparisons between the contemporary period of economic stagnation and its historical precedents have become progressively more striking. As the Marxist economist Mandel wryly observes, there may be long waves in theories of long waves![24]

Further evidence: Mensch's research on the clustering of basic innovations   The recent revival of interest in the Schumpeterian long-wave thesis owes much for its inspiration to the research of the West German economist Gerhard Mensch.[25] This researcher has examined the pattern of technological change and economic development over the past two centuries, identifying clusters of 'basic' innovations – defined as innovations which create a new market or industry – around the years 1770, 1825, 1885 and 1935.

Several critics of the technical change explanation of business cycles have drawn attention to the fact that the association between economic fluctuations and technological progress does not necessarily confirm the notion that business cycles stem from a discontinuous pattern of technical innovation. As Aldcroft and Richardson put it, the idea that cyclical upturns in the economy are led by investment in new industries and technologies is 'consistent with virtually any explanation of cycles, and cannot be used as support for the view that cycles are essentially fluctuations due to innovational activity'.[26] In his review of Schumpeter's *Business Cycles*, Kuznets wrote in 1940 that the former's account of the long waves remained to be substantiated by empirical evidence of intensified innovatory activity in the years of depression preceding an expansionary Kondratieff led by new industrial products and processes.[27] Some thirty-five years later, Mensch's findings provided this missing empirical ingredient.

In Mensch's view the peak of an expansionary wave tends to be followed by what he calls a 'technological stalemate' where 'improvement innovations' and 'pseudo-innovations' merely modify the existing framework of industrial technology. But as the recessionary wave deepens, more radical 'basic innovations' increase in frequency via an 'accelerator mechanism' which reduces the time lag between scientific inventions and their application in technical innovations. Hence the deep troughs during the depressive waves provide a stimulus to the subsequent recovery.

Subsequent neo-Schumpeterian researchers have by no means unconditionally accepted Mensch's statistical findings and explanatory account. George Ray stresses, in opposition to Mensch's view, that it is not the precise *nature* of the innovation (improvement, pseudo or basic) which directly causes the expansionary upturns.[28] Rather it is the *diffusion* of an innovation through the economy and, more pertinently, the *speed* of this diffusion which is crucial to providing the expansionary trigger.

In the first major critical survey of Mensch's findings, a research team at the University of Sussex Science Policy Research Unit have similarly taken issue with Mensch's results.[29] Freeman, Clark and Soete have conducted a parallel attempt at dating the appearance of basic innovations using Mensch's data sources. They found no strong correlation between any clusters of innovations and the depressed phases of the long waves, concluding that Mensch's findings are based on a highly subjective and arbitrary dating procedure. However, for Freeman *et al.* it is not the precise date of the introduction of a new technological process or product which is important; it is the subsequent diffusion of the innovation and its potential to generate what they call a 'new technological system'.

Technological systems and sectoral growth cycles   Freeman *et al.* disagree with Mensch's emphasis on the statistical clustering or 'swarming', as Schumpeter put it, of basic innovations as the key factor in economic development. They argue that it is not the *number* of disparate innovations but their *interrelationship* in technology systems involving a high degree of inter-firm product and process linkages which stimulates economic rejuvenation. Freeman *et al.* perceive this interpretation of the swarming process as more akin to Schumpeter's own use of the term.

Freeman *et al.* argue that the phases of origin, development and degeneration of technological systems correspond to the successive movements of alternate long waves. The evolution of leading industries and technologies is spread across four stages. These are:

(i) the depressive phase of a Kondratieff in which embryonic and experimental features of the new industry/technology begin to appear in competition with the declining sectors whose development lay in an earlier wave;

(ii) the boom period of the ensuing expansionary Kondratieff in which the new industry/technology becomes a leading sector with substantial employment growth and secondary effects on other industries and services;

(iii) the stagflationary turning-point where the former rapid growth of the sector gives way to consolidation and rationalisation involving intensive competition, increasing capital concentration and slower employment growth;

(iv) the ensuing depressive wave with a slowdown in output and investment, falling employment levels and over-capacity.

This interpretation of the long waves as a reflection of successive phases in the life-cycles of different products, processes and industrial sectors has been more fully developed by Van Duijn.[30] For Van Duijn, as for Mensch, clusters of basic innovations are the major force triggering long economic fluctuations. The particular contribution of Van Duijn, however, has been to construct an analytical model of the way in which the impetus imparted by these innovatory triggers is diffused through the economy. Drawing on earlier studies of product life-cycles, Van Duijn argues that basic innovations give rise to new industrial sectors which develop according to an S-shaped pattern through successive phases of introduction, growth, maturity and decline as illustrated in Figure 1.2. Van Duijn then introduces Forrester's multiplier/accelerator model to show how leads and lags in demand for and supply of fixed capital equipment required by the new industrial sectors lead eventually to an excess accumulation of capital stock. This fixed capital over-accumulation, combined with the levelling-off of de-

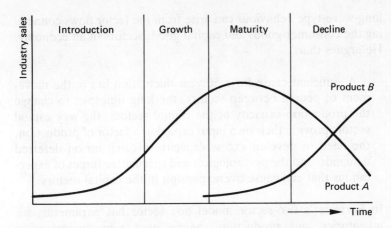

FIGURE 1.2 *A Simple S-shaped Product Life-cycle Model*

SOURCE Van Duijn, 1983, p. 23. Reproduced by permission of Van
Gorcum Publishers.

mand as the leading industrial sectors approach the end of their
life-cycle, dampens the scale and pace of economic development
and marks the beginning of a depressive long wave. Forrester's
over-accumulation model is considered in more detail in the following section.

III A Fixed Capital Over-accumulation Theory: Forrester's 'System Dynamics' Model

The System Dynamics account of the long waves developed by a
research team at the Massachusetts Institute of Technology
headed by Professor Jay Forrester is, by its nature, perhaps the
most esoteric explanation of the phenomenon.[31] The MIT team
have developed a computerised 15-sector System Dynamics National Model of the US economy which shows that the simulated
interaction between production sectors can give rise to three
different types of economic fluctuation. These are very similar to
the 3–7-year business cycle, the 15–25-year Kuznets cycle and the
45–60-year Kondratieff cycle perceivable in the workings of real
industrial economies.

Forrester describes how computer simulations suggest that

long-wave-type behaviour can arise from the factor flows connecting the consumer-goods and capital-goods sectors of an economy. He argues that:

> A sufficient cause for a 50-year fluctuation lies in the movement of people between sectors, the long timespan to change the production capacity of the capital sectors, the way capital sectors provide their own input capital as a factor of production, the need to develop excess capacity to catch up on deferred demands, and the psychological and speculative forces of expectations that can cause overexpansion in the capital sectors.[32]

In Forrester's two-sector model one sector has parameters for inventories and production change over time typical of a consumer-durables sector. The other is a typical capital-goods sector. The consumer-durables sector orders capital equipment from the capital-goods sector and has labour readily available. The capital-goods sector also has easy access to labour, but orders its capital equipment from its own output.

Given this structure an increase in consumer demand will lead the consumer-goods sector to increase its employment and productive capacity. Labour is readily available but the supply of capital equipment will be dependent upon the expansion of the capital-goods sector. The response of the capital-goods sector to the demand for new equipment from its customers in the consumer-durables sector will be limited by the need of the capital-equipment sector to first replenish and expand its *own* fixed capital stock.

In the System Dynamics model the basic origin of the long waves lies in the tendency of the capital-goods sector towards overproduction. At the end of a depressive wave the capital stock of both capital and consumer sectors will be badly depleted given the low level of demand and output in the economy. An upturn in demand, stimulating recovery, will require a rapid expansion of the capital-goods sector which must replenish the capital stock not only of the consumer sector but also of its own productive operations. The rate of expansion required to fill the depleted pool of fixed capital in an acceptable time period (Forrester gives twenty years as an example) will be greater than can be sustained once the pool has been replenished. At this point of maximum capacity the capital-goods sector will over-expand and be compelled to retrench. Other factors, such as business attitudes towards innovation and risk-taking or the efforts of governments to sustain an expansionary phase through monetary reflation, will tend to accentuate the fluctuation.

IV Marxist Theories: Trotsky and Mandel

Leon Trotsky's 'curve of capitalist development' is not a theory of long waves; indeed, it was presented partly to counter Kondratieff's theory during the 1920s. None the less, it is included in the review of long-wave theories here for two reasons. First, it provides an example of the critique advanced by several Marxist (as well as non-Marxist) theorists who argue that the phenomena referred to as long waves are not internally regulated cycles. Rather, they are historical periods whose turning-points are determined by exogenous social and political forces such as wars and revolutions. Second, Trotsky's critique provides a useful introduction to the contribution of Ernest Mandel, who argues that the long waves can be conceived of as the unity of both endogenous economic mechanisms and exogenous social and political factors which combine together to determine the path of capitalist development.

1. *Trotsky's Curve of Capitalist Development*

The bitter, even vindictive, antagonism which Kondratieff's theory provoked among his contemporaries has been briefly referred to above in the discussion of the Russian economist's account of the long cycles. The hostility to Kondratieff's theory stemmed not only from academic disagreements, but also, and more importantly, from much deeper political conflicts. Kondratieff adopted a quite conservative role in the debates on Soviet industrialisation and economic planning for the transformation of Russian society. He disagreed strongly with the Gosplan (State Planning Commission) over the pace of industrialisation and the policy of curbing the private sector of the economy. In a bitter attack on the Kondratieff group in 1927, Zinoviev went so far as to describe what he called 'Kondratievshchina' as 'a complete ideology of the new bourgeoisie'.[33]

In the early years of the USSR the new Bolshevik leadership did not expect their country to stand isolated from the rest of the globe for long, but were optimistic about the prospects for socialist revolution elsewhere. For the leaders of the Communist International, as Trotsky proclaimed in 1921, 'with the imperialist war we entered the epoch of revolution, that is, the epoch when the very mainstays of capitalist equilibrium are shaking and collapsing'.[34] For Kondratieff, on the other hand, the world economic crisis of 1920–1 following the disruptions of the First World War was not exceptional. Placed in the historical context of the long waves the crisis was a necessary step towards the restoration of capitalist equilibrium rather than the preliminary stage of its imminent collapse.[35]

The concept of capitalist equilibrium   Trotsky's major disagreement with Kondratieff was over the latter's use of the concept of capitalist equilibrium. At first sight it appears that their interpretations of the concept were not dissimilar. In his report on the world economic crisis to the Third Congress of the Comintern in 1921 Trotsky argued:

> Capitalist equilibrium is an extremely complex phenomenon. Capitalism produces this equilibrium, disrupts it, restores it anew in order to disrupt it anew, concurrently extending the limits of its domination. . . . Capitalism thus possesses a dynamic equilibrium, one which is always in the process of either disruption or restoration. But at the same time this equilibrium has a great power of resistance, the best proof of which is the fact that the capitalist world has not toppled to this day.[36]

Trotsky's view of the way in which the cyclical movements of the capitalist economy were blended with the long-term dynamics appears to echo that of Kondratieff:

> In periods of rapid capitalist development the crises are brief and relatively superficial in character, while the booms are long-lasting and far-reaching. In periods of capitalist decline,

the crises are of prolonged character while the booms are fleeting, superficial and speculative.[37]

In his presentation of empirical data Trotsky's division of capitalist development into successive historical periods was roughly similar to Kondratieff's divisions between the long cycles.[38] However, at this point the similarity ends.

The curve of development In his discussion of the 'curve of capitalist development' Trotsky explicitly rejected Kondratieff's notion of a smooth, regular transition from one phase of development to another. For Trotsky capitalism's 'moving equilibrium' was periodically interrupted at clearly defined turning-points, altering its slope. This curve of capitalist development was conditioned, not by internal forces, but by external, 'superstructural' (social and political) features which were relatively autonomous from the internal tendencies of capitalist economies. The notion of long cycles obscured the distinction between short-term cyclical fluctuations in capitalist economies, in the sense with which Marx discerned them, and the distinct historical periods in the evolution of capitalism and its social relationships:

> One can reject in advance the attempts by Professor Kondratiev to assign to the epochs, which he calls long cycles, the same 'strict rhythm' which is observed in short cycles. This attempt is a clearly mistaken generalisation on the basis of a formal analogy. The periodicity of short cycles is conditioned by the internal dynamics of capitalist forces, which manifests itself whenever and wherever there is a market. As for those long (fifty-year) intervals of the capitalist curve, which Professor Kondratiev hastily proposes to call cycles, their character and duration is determined not by the internal play of capitalist forces, but by the external conditions in which capitalist development occurs'.[39]

2. *Mandel's Reformulation: Asymmetric Waves forming Specific Historical Periods*

The unique contribution of Mandel to the theory of long waves is his attempt to link an orthodox Marxist account of the inherent crisis-prone tendencies of capitalist development with an account of the exogenous social and political processes of class conflict which bring these internal economic mechanisms into play. Mandel characterises the resulting historical periods of economic, social and political development as 'asymmetrical waves' whose turning-points are determined by the articulation of both endogenous and exogenous forces and not as strict cycles wholly regulated by internal economic mechanisms.

Explaining the downturns: the falling rate of profit thesis   In his magnum opus on *Late Capitalism*, Mandel takes his starting-point for the analysis of the long waves in the fundamental 'laws of motion' of capitalism.[40] From an orthodox Marxist viewpoint a theory of long waves in capitalist development must be a theory of long-term fluctuations in the capitalist rate of profit. In the Marxist theoretical framework the accumulation of capital is a process of self-expansion of capital values through the medium of human labour power. The exploitation of the workforce at the point of commodity production generates a social surplus product, that is a product over and above that whose equivalent is received by workers in the form of wages. This is embodied in commodities as surplus value and is ultimately realised through the sale of commodities at the market and returned to the capitalist owners in the form of profits, the fundamental motor of accumulation.

The accumulation of capital is a contradictory process, continually reproducing barriers to its development. Expansionary accumulation occurs through the growth of the productive forces at capital's disposal under the stimulus of inter-capitalist competition. Put simply, inter-capitalist competition leads to a drive to mechanise the production process, increasing the stock of fixed capital by replacing labour with machines and thereby driving up the productive yield on labour power. To use the Marxist terminology there is a tendency to replace value-creating 'living' labour in production with fixed capital equipment embodying value created by previously expended 'dead' labour, i.e. there is a tendency to expand the 'constant capital' elements of the commodity production process (machinery, raw materials, etc.) relative to the 'variable capital' elements (labour power). The standard Marxist formula for the value components determining the capitalist rate of profit is $r = s/(c + v)$, where r is the rate of profit, s is surplus value produced, c is constant capital expended and v is variable capital expended in a given turnover period of commodity production. Obviously, if s and v remain static then an increase in c or, more pertinently an increase in the 'organic composition of capital' ratio c/v, will lead to a fall in r. It is this rising organic composition of capital which brings Marx's Law of the Tendency of the Rate of Profit to Fall (TRPF for short) into effect, exerting a downward pressure on the capitalist rate of profit and consequently upon the rate of accumulation.[41]

In the theoretical framework of orthodox Marxist economics there is thus a well-founded reason why an initial phase of expansionary accumulation should give way to one of stagnation or contraction. Mandel takes this explanation a step further by showing how the pace of accumulation can be subjected to *short-term* cyclical fluctuations.

Marx himself described a number of countervailing tendencies which could offset the falling rate of profit arising from his general law. Mandel argues that the relative influences of the general law on the one hand, and its counteracting influences on the other, fluctuate with the movements of the short-term business cycle. Given any particular level of development of capitalism's productive forces, i.e. a particular state of technological advance, then an increase of investment in new fixed capital relative to additional labour during the upturn of the cycle will bring the law of TRPF into effect. The resulting over-accumulation of fixed capital and falling rate of profit leads to a downturn in the cycle. The destruction of parts of the fixed capital stock during this phase (plant closures, idle machines, etc.) will tend to reduce the organic composition of capital in the economy and revitalise the rate of profit. This in turn will stimulate increasing capital investment, and so the cycle begins anew.

Successive cycles of investment do not merely replace or enlarge the fixed capital stock at its former level of technological development. Rather each round of investment involves incremental advances in new technology. Incremental technical advance adds either directly or indirectly to the forces counteracting the falling rate of profit. This may arise directly through increases in the level of labour productivity, i.e. the rate of surplus value s/v, revitalising profitability in the branch of production concerned. It may also occur indirectly through a cheapening of raw materials, plant and machinery produced in the capital-goods sector (which Marxists refer to as Department I of the economy) and supplied to other sectors; or by a cheapening of wage goods produced in the consumer-goods sector (Department II) which contribute to the determination of the wage–price of labour power in both sectors. These factors stimulate the expansion of accumulation through reconstruction of fixed capital at a higher level of technical productivity until a further threshold of overproduction is reached, shifting the cycle into a fresh phase of decline.

Mandel goes on to argue that the movements of the short-term cycle involve imbalanced growth between the capital-equipment and consumer-goods sectors of the economy in response to their differential rates of profit. During the upswing in the cycle demands for means of production in the consumer-goods sector raise both the output and the rate of profit of their suppliers in the capital-equipment sector. Investment funds therefore tend to flow towards the capital-goods sector where, in the short term, above-average rates of profit can be achieved. During the downswing, although overproduction and falling profit rates are felt first in the consumer-goods sector, these problems are more powerfully experienced in the capital equipment sector as the impacts of overproduction filter back throughout the economy. This leads to flows of investment funds towards the consumer goods sector. The overall cycle of industrial production, and the development of its different sectors, is therefore regulated by successive movements in the rate of profit:

> The entire capitalist industrial cycle thus appears to be the consequence of accelerated capital accumulation, over-accumulation, decelerated capital accumulation and under-investment. The rise, fall and revitalisation of the rate of profit both correspond to, and command, the successive movements of capital accumulation.[42]

Each successive phase of expansion in the industrial cycle is generated through a renewal of the productive forces which revitalises the rate of profit and extends the material basis of the accumulation process. However, Mandel goes on to argue that this process of incremental economic rejuvenation cannot continue indefinitely. Given any particular level of technological development of the productive forces, there are inherent *technical* limits on the extent to which incremental advances in productivity can be extracted as a means of overcoming periodic crises of falling profitability. Over several successive cycles the opportunities for counteracting the tendency towards a falling rate of profit will eventually be exhausted. Hence, Mandel argues, the contradictions inherent to the inner logic of the accumulation process mean that a long wave consisting of several short cycles whose main undertone is one of expansion must *of necessity* eventually give way to a long wave of contractive tonality.

Explaining the upturns: the role of surplus profits   In Mandel's account the law of TRPF which works through a tendency towards capital overaccumulation provides a sufficient explanation for the upper turning-points of the long waves. But the crucial point for Mandel is that there is no similar internal economic mechanism which can explain the turning-point of the long waves from contraction to expansion. At this point for expansionary accumulation to proceed anew it is necessary for the mass of fixed capital to undergo a large-scale process of reconstitution or 'Technological Revolution'. This raises the level of development of the productive forces to a higher plane, opening up new opportunities for profitable investment and setting in motion a fresh phase of the industrial cycle with an underlying tonality of expansion.

As a long wave of expansion gives way to one of contraction, crises of excess capital become increasingly prolonged and acute in comparison to crises during the preceding expansionary wave. Why is this excess capital only eventually relieved in one particular phase of crisis during the contractive long wave rather than in others when the pressure for a radical regeneration of the productive forces may be equally intense? For Mandel the answer is that the revolutionary renewal of the productive forces can only take place *following* an extraordinary upsurge in the capitalist rate of profit on a generalised scale.

At this point in his explanation Mandel introduces the concept of above-average 'surplus profits' in the capitalist economic framework. These surplus profits generally arise wherever a particular enterprise or sector enjoys monopolistic access to certain advantageous factors which place it in a superior position with respect to its competitors. This can occur through monopolistic access to factors of production such as cheap labour, cheap raw materials or advanced productive technology. Surplus profits can also occur through the structural or institutional framework, for example where marketing and distribution networks enable an enterprise or sector to speed up its investment turnover cycle by avoiding stockpiling of goods awaiting sale.

In Mandel's view the long waves of capitalist development have been triggered by three main sources of surplus profits. The long waves in Continental Europe from 1848, and in Britain from about fifty years earlier, were fuelled by surplus profits arising from the monopolistic access of rising capitalist manufacturing industry to pre-capitalist agricultural regions providing sources of cheap labour and materials. The long wave from the late nineteenth century drew on surplus profits generated by the imperialist expansion of the developed capitalist economies into colonial markets, vigorously protecting their monopoly over particular colonial territories through trade barriers and military aggression. The long boom following the Second World War was fuelled by surplus profits accruing to the giant corporations through their monopoly over the most productive techniques relative to the more backward sectors in the developed economies and to the under-industrialised neo-colonial countries.

The intervention of social and political forces   In Mandel's view different historical combinations of surplus profits have triggered the expansionary turning-points of the long waves. However, Mandel goes on to argue that these expansionary triggers have not arisen through any endogenous mechanism of capital accumulation. On the contrary, Mandel stresses that the upward turning-point can only emerge through the intervention of exogenous social and political forces which combine to permit a dramatic rise in the rate of profit and bring the internal mechanisms of accumulation back into play.

Mandel argues that the mid-nineteenth-century upturn in European capitalist development was triggered by the 1848 Revolutions, which opened up the potential for new markets. These in turn stimulated sweeping technological changes such as the boom in railway construction which was instrumental in achieving market penetration. The expansionary wave from the late nineteenth century to the outbreak of the First World War was achieved at the cost of colonial wars and intense inter-imperialist rivalry. Capitalist recovery after 1945 was founded on a combination of factors including the long years of depression in the inter-war period, the experience of fascism and war, and the Cold War of the McCarthy years in the USA which, Mandel argues, shattered the physical and ideological foundations of labour resistance permitting rapid increases in productivity and falling real wages.

Thus, Mandel argues that the long waves must be conceived of as distinct historical periods representing the unity of capitalism's internal mechanics with the intervention of externally motivated factors. Once set in motion the endogenous economic laws of capitalist development will inevitably dissolve an expansionary period into one of crisis-ridden stagnation. But these same endogenous mechanisms cannot in themselves restore the upward path of accumulation:

> the emergence of a new expansionist long wave cannot be considered an endogenous (i.e. a more or less spontaneous, mechanical, autonomous) result of the preceding depressive long wave, whatever the latter's duration and gravity. Not the laws of motion of capitalism but the results of the class struggle of a whole historical period are deciding this turning point. What we assume here is a *dialectic of the objective and subjective factors of historical development*, in which the subjective factors are characterised by *relative autonomy*; that is, they are not predetermined directly and unavoidably by what occurred previously in regard to the basic trends of capital accumulation, the trends in transformation of technology, or the impact of these trends on the process of labor organization itself.[43]

It is this point which chiefly distinguishes Mandel's position from that of the American Marxist, David Gordon.[44] The work of Gordon closely resembles that of Mandel, with its stress on the articulation between economic laws of motion and the class struggle in the explanation of the long waves. But, for Gordon, class struggle or the 'social conditions of accumulation', as he puts it, is *itself* an endogenous factor determined by economic imperatives arising from the preceding long wave. In Gordon's analysis class struggle follows a cyclical path determined by economic movements such as the impact of fluctuations in employment levels on organised labour's wage-bargaining power or the effect of periodic technical changes on the level of labour's resistance to new working practices.

For Mandel, on the other hand, class struggle *cannot* be seen as a mechanical outcome of conditions in the preceding period. It is a response to material conditions as they are perceived through the intermediate filter of human consciousness. Class struggle is a fluid, living process in whose analysis the whole cumulative history of human experience must be brought to bear. Moreover, by its very nature, class struggle is the manifestation of contradictions in economic and social relations. It is not a monolithic outcome of predetermined, fatalistic forces. For Mandel the course of capitalist development through the long waves cannot be explained solely by capitalism's internal laws. The decisive turning-points of the long waves which usher in each fresh phase of expansionary development can only be explained by reference to specific historically variable configurations of factors: 'any single-factor assumption is clearly opposed to the notion of the capitalist mode of production as a dynamic totality in which the interplay of *all* the basic laws of development is necessary in order to produce any particular outcome'.[45]

Conclusion

This chapter has described a variety of approaches to the theory of long waves. The approaches all adopt different conceptions of the waves, draw on different sources of empirical evidence and propose different theoretical explanations. The alternative perspectives are not simply competing explanations of the same phenomenon since they disagree markedly on the nature and definition of the phenomenon to be explained. The price-cycle approach sees the waves as strict cycles evidenced by regular long-term fluctuations in commodity prices. The association of wars, revolutions and other social upheavals with the turning-points of each wave is cited by critics as refutation of this conception of the waves as internally regulated economic cycles. A Marxist like Mandel, on the other hand, sees the waves as historical periods representing the interaction of internal economic mechanisms with social and political forces. For Mandel the social upheavals marking each historical turning-point provide evidence *for* the long-wave thesis according to his interpretation.

In my view Mandel's approach is the most useful for my purposes precisely because it provides a cohesive framework within which to combine many of the factors which other authors have concentrated on, such as internal economic mechanisms and technological change as well as social and political forces, rather than focusing on one factor to the exclusion of others. However, this is not to say that Mandel's approach is without some serious problems, nor that the other perspectives have nothing to offer, as is argued in the next two chapters.

2
Long Waves, Technological Change and the Capitalist Labour Process

Introduction

Having described the major approaches to the theory of long waves Chapter 2 takes a more critical and analytical look at some of the strengths and weaknesses of these approaches. This review focuses upon the role of technological change in capitalist economic development, arguing that all the major theories of long waves adopt an over-deterministic interpretation of this factor – a deficiency to which the Marxist approach proposed by Mandel is no exception.

The last chapter provided a survey of different long-wave theories as a prelude to examining ways in which the approach can enlighten our understanding of regional industrial development in capitalist economies. But before we can apply the theory of long waves to regional analysis, or to any other subject for that matter, we are faced with a thorny problem: which theory?

Most authors who have sought to integrate a theory of long waves within their own particular field of inquiry have tended to opt for whichever approach seems to best fit their academic tradition or political persuasion. Economists like Rothwell and Zegveld with an interest in the effects of technical change on employment are drawn to the Schumpeterian perspective which has most to say about technological aspects of the long waves.[1] Socialists like Friend and Metcalf, on the other hand, are more interested in the political aspects of unemployment whereby capital stamps its authority over the 'industrial reserve army of labour' and hence take on board Mandel's framework to the exclusion of others.[2]

In my view this is a shortsighted, and ultimately negative, way of seeking to introduce new explanatory frameworks into a field. It implicitly assumes that one theory has everything to offer and its competitors nothing – a proposition which needs to be justified, or at least explicitly recognised, rather than assumed without question. Moreover, as well as enjoying the advantages of applying one theory to a particular field, this approach is in danger of imitating the theory's weaknesses, especially where the theory concerned is simply taken as the definitive long-wave thesis without critical evaluation.

Cross-fertilisation of the alternative long-wave theories is not facilitated by the very different theoretical traditions and political standpoints they represent, by the different methodologies and terminologies they employ and by the different historical contexts in which they were developed by their respective authors. It is not the purpose of this work to produce a definitive theory of long waves. I do not profess to academic neutrality and as a socialist I am attracted to many aspects of Mandel's account. However, I believe that an evaluation and comparison of the alternative long-wave theories reveals several points of contact, and some of agreement, which can help to strengthen both the long-wave thesis in general and its application to my own field of inquiry in particular.

I   Conceptions of Technological Change and Capitalist Instability

1. *Problems of the Schumpeterian Approach*

Several of the theories reviewed in Chapter 1 acknowledge technological change as an important feature of the long waves. Kondratieff saw the radical renewal of fixed capital infrastructure as a determinant of the strength and periodicity of each successive expansionary movement. Rostow argues that the long waves must be understood by weaving together the commodity price fluctuations with the process of technological advance and development. Mandel sees periodic technological revolutions as sponsors of the far-reaching rejuvenation of capitalism's productive forces which carries forward each long wave. But only the Schumpeterian

approach looks to the process of technological change and innovation as *in itself* the key causal factor behind the long waves and
their turning-points.

Schumpeter related the long waves to discontinuities in the
innovatory activities of particular entrepreneurs who pioneered
the qualitative changes in the nature of industrial production
which he equated with the process of economic development. As
Kaldor put it, however, 'the trouble with Schumpeter's theory is
that it is descriptive rather than analytical'.[3] By proposing direct
causal chains between entrepreneurial activity and economic
development, Schumpeter reduced the dynamics of capitalism
solely to the psychological make-up of individual capitalist entrepreneurs and their pioneering spirit of innovation. To paraphrase
Marx, 'Innovate, innovate!' is the Moses and prophets of Schumpeter's capitalists.[4] Schumpeter neglected to set the innovation
process within its wider material context. In his account individual
capitalists seem to innovate purely for the novelty rather than
because of their need, as individuals, to establish technical superiority over competitors and their requirement, as a social class, to
extend their ownership and control over the labour process.

This critique has been most forcefully advanced by Marxist
opponents of the Schumpeterian theory. From this standpoint
Paul Mattick argues that Schumpeter 'developed a kind of heroic
theory of business fluctuations, seeing in them the dynamic of the
capitalist system'.[5] The mechanism of capitalist development is
'embodied in a type of person who, tormented or blessed by
creative unrest, breaks by self-willed activity through the cycle of
static equilibrium'.[6] Mandel argues that Schumpeter failed adequately to account for the innovatory clusters which mark the
phase preceding each expansionary wave.[7] In Mandel's view this
problem can only be resolved by relating the acceleration of
innovative activity to the upturn in actual or expected rates of
profit which form the material incentive for investment in new
productive technology.

In defence of the Schumpeterian perspective, Freeman, Clark
and Soete deny that Schumpeter based his interpretation on the
misconception of an autonomous dynamic of entrepreneurial
energy, ignoring the importance of the rate of profit.[8] They argue
that 'by definition' Schumpeter's concept of innovation embodied
this factor and that Schumpeter explicitly saw innovation as the

means for opening up new opportunities for profitable investment. It is debatable whether Schumpeter saw capitalists' quest for profits as the underlying motive for innovation. But he undoubtedly failed to relate *shifts* in the pace and scale of innovatory activity to shifts in profitability or profit expectations.

For their own part Freeman *et al.* concede that technological innovation and diffusion 'may well be' supported by the movements in the rate of profit described by Mandel; that there 'may well be' additional causal factors arising from the differential development of the wage-goods and capital-goods sectors as emphasised by Forrester and by Mandel; and that such approaches are 'probably right' in perceiving shifts in general profit rates as an important determinant of the long waves' turning-points.[9] However, as Freeman *et al.*'s indecisive approach to such issues illustrates, the neo-Schumpeterian contribution to the long-wave thesis has been chiefly concerned with examining the detailed pattern of innovation in industrial production as one mechanism governing the course of economic fluctuations. It has fallen to other theorists to investigate the relationship of this factor to other forces generating instability in the capitalist economic framework.

2. *Technological Determinacy in the Marxist Account*

In my view the emphasis placed by Mandel on shifts in capitalist profitability as a fundamental stimulant to fluctuations in other indicators of economic development represents an important advance over the Schumpeterian perspective. Given the central place occupied by this factor within Mandel's account, it is perhaps surprising that some other Marxists should have accused Mandel of reducing the long waves to changes in productive technology. Erik Olin Wright, for example, is sympathetic to Mandel's theory, but takes issue with what he interprets as Mandel's view that 'the pivotal characteristic of each phase of the history of capitalism, and the decisive transformations which set in motion new long waves of accumulation, centre on technology'.[10] This criticism seems to me to be utterly without foundation since Mandel emphatically denies that technological changes set in motion the long waves, assigning this causal role to exogenous social and political forces which stimulate an upturn in the rate of profit.

With regard to the upturns of the long waves the allegation of technological determinacy in Mandel's account is quite invalid. However, regarding Mandel's explanation of the downturns in development and his account of the basic origin of economic fluctuations, I believe that the criticism contains a kernel of truth.

Mandel sees the cyclical course adopted by the Law of the Tendency of the Rate of Profit to Fall (law of TRPF) as the fundamental origin of the long waves in capitalist development. In Mandel's view it is the tendency towards capital over-accumulation through the growth of the technical means of production relative to human labour which ultimately depresses the rate of profit, bringing about the swing from an expansionary long wave to one of stagnant or contractive accumulation.

In recent years, largely if not exclusively under the influence of the so-called 'neo-Ricardian' school within economics inspired by the work of Piero Sraffa, the Marxist value framework in its entirety has been subjected to a number of logico-mathematical critiques.[11] A number of specific criticisms have been levelled at Marx's law of TRPF in particular.[12] It has been argued that:

(i) The law reduces the determination of capitalist profits to changes in productive technology (equated with changes in the organic composition of capital) neglecting the influence of class struggle on profits through the determination of the wage rate.

(ii) The law assumes a certain kind of technical change (labour-saving) as the sole motor force of expansionary accumulation, ignoring other forms of technical advance.

(iii) The law assumes that changes in the 'technical composition' of capital (i.e. *physical* quantities of labour and fixed capital employed) can be equated with changes in the 'organic composition' (i.e. the *values* of the physical components).

(iv) The law ignores the inherent effect of a changing organic composition of capital, c/v, on the rate of surplus value, s/v. Marx assumes a stable s/v and rising c/v in his presentation. But increases in the productivity of labour implied in a rising c/v must involve a rising s/v, an increasing intensity of exploitation of labour with the production of relative surplus value, cancelling any downward influence on r of the rising c/v.

(v) The so-called 'law' is therefore not a tendency at all. The combination of tendency (rising c/v) and counter-tendency (rising s/v, cheapening of c and v elements, etc.) might be turned on its head and called the 'law of the rising rate of profit' with the rising c/v awarded only the status of a counter-tendency.

In my view the logico-mathematical critique of the law of TRPF has devastating implications for the law as it has traditionally been interpreted by orthodox Marxist economists, bringing into question the whole basis and purpose of Marxist value analysis. The law cannot be conceived as an empirical tendency that can be proven by 'transforming' national accounts into value equivalents in order to calculate movements of capital's organic composition and the rate of surplus value and thereby to demonstrate a tendential fall in the rate of profit.[13] Nor is it sufficient to argue that the law is an abstract formulation which is not directly perceivable in the workings of real capitalist economies, but which none the less lies behind concrete movements in profit rates and other empirical indicators.[14] The Sraffian critique has not only demonstrated that there is no logical quantitative connection between Marxist value categories and concrete economic components such as wages, prices and profits. The critique has also shown that the alleged quantitative relationships between the value components themselves, including the effects of a rising organic composition of capital upon the value formula for the rate of profit, are logically inconsistent.

3. *Capitalist Instability and the Over-accumulation Thesis*

The 'value controversy' over the 'transformation problem' in Marxist economic theory seems destined to continue *ad infinitum*, some might say *ad nauseam*.[15] It is pertinent to note that while a range of fresh interpretations have been proposed to defend the valid analytical use of Marxist value *categories*, no one has ever convincingly challenged the logical rigor of the Sraffian critique of value *quantities* as, indeed, many Marxists are quite prepared to acknowledge.[16] In my view Marx's law of TRPF is unacceptable as a quantitative account of fluctuations in capitalist profit magnitudes.

However, a rejection of the quantitative value theory of profit determination does not imply a rejection of the tendency towards over-accumulation as the basic source of capitalist instability. On the contrary the over-accumulation thesis is far from unique to the orthodox Marxist perspective and has been proposed by a range of theorists, none of whom adhere to any quantitative theory of value. At around the same time as Schumpeter was developing his theory of 'creative destruction' Michal Kalecki was arguing that over-investment in fixed capital was the basic origin of instability and crises in capitalist development.[17] This resulted, not from any mysterious underlying law of capital accumulation, but simply because as soon as one group of capitalists invest in advanced productive technology they render the older productive methods of their competitors technologically and economically inferior, undermining profitability and expansion in the less-productive enterprises:

> Investment considered as capitalists' spending is the source of prosperity and every increase of it improves business and stimulates a further rise of spending for investment. But at the same time investment is an addition to the capital equipment and right from birth it competes with the older generation of this equipment. The tragedy of investment is that it calls forth the crisis because it is useful. I do not wonder that many people consider this theory paradoxical. But it is not the theory which is paradoxical but its subject – the capitalist economy.[18]

The accumulation of capital is a contradictory process in which the development of some enterprises, industrial sectors or national economies is frequently combined with the relative decline of others. The succession of leading industries, technologies and national economies which dominated each alternate long wave of capitalist development gained their superiority by exerting their competitive advantage over others. Schumpeter explained the cycle of 'creative destruction' in terms of discontinuities in the psychological spur to technical innovation. For the reasons discussed above I do not believe that this can be taken as an adequate explanation since it fails to relate the motives for innovation to more fundamental characteristics of the capitalist economic framework and its inherent instability.

In contrast to Schumpeter's account Forrester has suggested that psychological factors, such as the level of business confidence, may accentuate economic fluctuations, but do not constitute the ultimate origin of the long waves. In Forrester's view the long waves can be related to a tendency towards imbalanced growth of the consumer-goods and capital-equipment sectors of production. During an upsurge in fixed capital investment, the capital-goods sector must expand at a sufficient rate and on a sufficient scale to satisfy demand for new equipment, not only in the consumer-goods sector, but also in the capital equipment sector itself. The eventual satisfaction of this demand leaves the capital goods sector in a position of relative over-expansion, exerting a dampening effect upon the pace of industrial development until the build-up of demand for new fixed capital stimulates a further wave of expansion.

Forrester's account resembles that of Mandel, who also stresses the disproportionate growth of the capital-goods and consumer-goods sectors, or 'departments' in the Marxist schema, as a key mechanism underlying economic fluctuations. But as Mandel takes pains to point out, his explanation differs from that of Forrester in one important respect.[19] In Forrester's model the backlog of pent-up demand for capital equipment at the threshold of an expansionary turning-point is sufficient to propel the fixed capital sector and the economy as a whole into a fresh expansive wave. For Mandel, on the other hand, such endogenous economic mechanisms can only be set in motion by the intervention of exogenous social and political factors which raise the rate of profit and profit expectations.

4. *The 'Exogenous Variable': Economic Fluctuations and Class Struggle*

By relating the upward turning-points of the long waves to historically variable combinations of social and political factors, Mandel claims to have accomplished a dialectical unification of the objective and subjective factors of historical development.[20] In Mandel's view the short-term cyclical fluctuations of economic development within each wave occur through the internal economic contradictions of capital accumulation. They occur *regardless* of such secondary effects as the impact of employment fluctuations on workers' bargaining strength and hence on wage rates and profitability.

This point is important to Mandel's thesis since one of his prime objectives is to show that the long waves are an inevitable product of competitive relationships *between capitalists* (rather than between capitalists and workers) who perennially sow the seeds of their own destruction by over-accumulating fixed capital. This internal contradiction inevitably generates conditions, not only of economic crisis, but also of social and political turmoil. At this point only the victory of capital over labour in decisive social struggles can re-create the conditions for renewed expansionary accumulation. However, the outcomes of these historic turning-points are not predetermined by endogenous, inter-capitalist economic relations. They remain the subject of an indeterminate process of social and political conflict. The political implication of this analysis is that the class struggle may not only select a new course for capitalist development, but may also select a path of development which is not capitalist at all. For Mandel the inner contradictions of capitalism inevitably create and re-create the conditions for a socialist transformation of society.

By this means Mandel sees his approach as a synthesis of the long, internally regulated cycles of development identified by Kondratieff and others with the historical epochs of development seen by Trotsky as the outcome of an externally determined international class struggle. However, in my view the 'class struggle' as interpreted by Mandel is a rather strange phenomenon which emerges every fifty years or so to fulfil its historic role before sinking into the background where it patiently waits for capitalism's internal 'laws of motion' to pursue their inevitable path.[21] A similar criticism of Mandel's thesis has been made by Bob Rowthorn, who objects to Mandel's stress on the suddenness of the upheavals which mark each expansionary turning-point.[22] In Rowthorn's view it is not the speed of the shift in development which is important, but rather its far-reaching, radical nature. The radical changes which usher in each fresh wave of expansion need not necessarily occur through a sudden upheaval, but may equally emerge through a long process of development, perhaps spanning one or two decades.

Of course, Mandel is well aware that social and political conflict is as endemic to a class-divided capitalist society as are the contradictory mechanisms of capital accumulation. By stressing the inevitability of economic fluctuations and crises *within* the long waves regardless of social and political intervention Mandel is not denying the importance of the latter. Rather, his purpose is to show that even in a perfectly harmonious capitalist society where the owners of capital met with no resistance from workers in their effort to restructure production, introduce new technical processes of work organisation or depress employment levels and wage rates, the process of inter-capitalist competition would *still* lead to contradictions and crises.

As I have pointed out above, however, the Marxist interpretation is not the only perspective which sees periodic crises as inevitable within the capitalist economic framework. In Forrester's model, which assumes unimpeded access to labour inputs of the right quantity and quality and at the right price, the disproportionate supply of and demand for fixed capital equipment between capital producers and consumers *still* generates periodic crises of overaccumulation.

Both Forrester and Mandel have in different ways shown theoretically how, everything else remaining equal, inter-capitalist economic relations will be sufficient to generate fluctuations in economic development. But in reality, social, political and economic relationships in capitalist societies are far from equal. Capitalists and wage-workers enjoy highly unequal degrees of control and ownership over production . The capitalist class, by definition, exercises ownership over capital and the means of production and will seek to maintain maximum control over the conditions under which they hire labour power and set that labour to work. The working class for its own part will attempt to maximise the wage received for the expenditure of their labour and to contest the conditions under which it is employed. The history of capitalist industry has been one of continual, day-to-day conflicts between the attempts of the capitalist class to extend their power over the labour process, on the one hand, and the struggles of labour to resist their subordination to capital, on the other.[23]

In my view, by excluding the influence of social and political forces upon the short-term cycle of development within each long wave, Mandel devalues the most important, indeed unique, contribution which the Marxist theoretical framework can bring to an understanding of the long waves. The Schumpeterian perspective has ably demonstrated how the long waves unfold through the generation and regeneration of successive technological systems. Forrester's System Dynamics model has demonstrated how the cycle of technological advance and replacement of industrial fixed capital provides the basic source of long-term fluctuations and instability in the capitalist economic structure. But neither of these perspectives is equipped to examine the process of technical change and capitalist development as a *social* process involving the reproduction, not only of the physical or technical means of production, but also of the social relationships between capital and labour which accompany them.

So far in this chapter I have argued that an account of the long waves in terms of technological advance and the uneven development of industrial sectors is far from unique to the Marxist perspective. By explaining these factors as the outcome of the abstract, ill-specified and logically inconsistent law of TRPF, Mandel's account of the long waves tends to confuse rather than clarify the process of technical change and uneven economic development. In my view the most important contribution which a Marxist analysis can make to the theory of long waves is to relate the physical processes of technical and industrial change to the social structures within which these processes occur. The remainder of this chapter investigates ways in which this might be accomplished, drawing on recent Marxist contributions to the study of the capitalist labour process.

II   Technological Systems and the Capitalist Labour Process

1. *The Limits of a 'Technical' Analysis*

I have described above how recent Sraffa-inspired studies have demonstrated that the *quantitative* theory of value in Marxist economics is logically inconsistent and hence unacceptable as an account of the determination of prices, profits and other quantitative economic categories. For some economists influenced by the Sraffian critique this renders the Marxist value system redundant as a tool of economic and social analysis.[24] In reply others have argued that the interpretation of Marxist value analysis as a proto-mathematical economic model of prices and profits is a false one. Diane Elson acknowledges that the Sraffian critique is undoubtedly correct within its own terms, but goes on to argue that the object of Marx's theory of value was not prices but *labour*.[25] The object of value analysis is *not* to show how the combination of different magnitudes of labour and capital inputs to production determines a particular output level and profit rate. The Sraffian dated-labour analysis performs that task quite adequately. Rather, the object of value analysis is to analyse the character of labour in capitalism and to show why labour takes the forms it does.

The Sraffian economic system, as well as the theories of long waves advanced by Kondratieff, Forrester and others besides, equate the development of industrial capitalism with the growth and advance of the technical forces or physical means of production at its disposal. But the physical process of expansion and adaptation of capitalism's technical forces is simultaneously a process of reproduction and transformation of the *social* relationships within which the technical process takes place and, indeed, make production possible at all.

In this regard the Marxist approach offers much deeper insights into the economic process than its competitors. In Schumpeter's account of the long waves, new technological systems develop through the entrepreneurial individuality of industrial innovators. The implications of radical technological advance in terms of the far-reaching transformation of working conditions and practices, which may involve the rise of whole new modes of social existence, are neglected. In Forrester's computer simulation, the intersectoral movement of labour is schematised as just another paradigmatic variable. In the Sraffian world of mathematical logic and rigor there may be two different technological systems simultaneously yielding the same rate of profit and there is no reason why, having once adopted one particular productive technique, a capitalist enterprise should not revert to another. Indeed, the Sraffians see the 'switch in methods of production' as one of the most important insights of their approach.[26]

In the Marxist account, on the other hand, it is precisely the transformation of the social relationships in production which makes such technological advance irreversible. For example, the transition in the nineteenth century from a fragmented system of small-scale workshop production to a centralised system of large-scale, mechanised factory production involved radical changes in managerial techniques and working conditions. This transformation was not simply a logical response to technical possibilities. It involved the development of whole new cultures of working life and managerial practices. Old skills and habits were lost on the part of the capitalist owners and managers as much as on the part of the workforce. Where relatively backward sectors or subsectors employing primitive productive techniques still survive in the British economy today, they do so because they are frequently paralleled by particular managerial and working cultures. Evidence suggests that a whole new clothing subsector has grown up in the inner urban areas of the West Midlands in recent years based on several hundred Asian-owned workshops and small factory units.[27] These clothing firms are often characterised by outdated techniques, low value and poor-quality premises, sweatshop working conditions and low wages. The owners have little management experience. The workforce, predominantly composed of Asian women, have little, if any, experience of working conditions and regulations which would be considered normal in other manufacturing sectors. The whole subsector is held together by tightly knit social relationships based on cultural and family ties.

Such examples serve to illustrate the complex links which bind the development of productive techniques with the framework of social relationships within which production occurs. Recent contributions to Marxist economic theory have stressed this inseparable link between the social relationships and technical forces of production at their meeting-point in what is referred to as the 'capitalist labour process'.

2. The Structure of the Capitalist Labour Process

The basic structure of the labour process in capitalist production has been described by Christian Palloix whose stylised model of the labour time components in a working day is reproduced in Figure 2.1.[28] The line T represents the total duration of the working day. Tv is the time devoted to value-creating commodity production, i.e. the total working day less the unproductive time spent in breaks, machine change-overs, breakdowns, workers' washing-up time, etc. Tn is the 'socially necessary labour' time

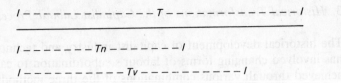

FIGURE 2.1 *Representation of the Labour Time Components in a Working Day*
SOURCE Palloix, 1976, p. 49.

required for the reproduction of labour power, the product of which is received by workers in the form of wages. The difference between Tv and Tn is 'surplus labour' time over and above that which is socially necessary, the product of which is appropriated by the capitalist owners in the form of a social surplus product. The rate of return on capital deployed in production is a reflection of the yield on labour power represented by the ratio of surplus labour to necessary labour expended, i.e. $(Tv - Tn)/Tn$.

These internal components of the capitalist labour process provide a set of structural limits within which the possibility and potential for capitalist profits is constrained. The rate of return on capital can be increased by altering the relationships between these labour time components. This can be achieved through three methods.[29]

Method I involves reducing the difference between T and Tv. This can be done by eliminating breaks; by exercising greater work discipline to reduce time spent 'idling' on the job; or by fragmenting the production process into discrete tasks, reducing the time spent in changing between jobs.

Method II involves increasing T and with it the value-creating labour time component Tv, while leaving Tn unchanged. This can be pursued by simply increasing the hours of the working day.

Method III involves reducing Tn. This can be achieved by raising productivity in the consumer-goods sectors, thereby reducing the price of goods required for the reproduction of labour power and which are paid for out of wages; or by fragmenting the production process into routine tasks, reducing the skill requirements of labour and depressing the value commanded by labour power.

3. *Historical Transformations of the Capitalist Labour Process*

The historical development of capitalist industry and technology has involved changing forms of labour's subordination to capital achieved through various combinations of the three methods for increasing the yield on labour power just described. Marxists commonly refer to a number of distinct historical phases in the transformation of the labour process in industrial capitalism. These are the labour processes associated with manufacture, machinofacture, Taylorism/Fordism and neo-Fordism.

Manufacture   The rise of industrial capitalism in the period from the mid-sixteenth to the eighteenth centuries was associated with the development of a manufacturing system of production. Workers were brought together from fragmented domestic units into workshops where they were subjected to the increasing exercise of direct capitalist control and discipline over the labour process (Method I) together with an increase in the length of the working day (Method II). The fragmentation of production into rhythmical stages (Method I) also reduced the skill requirements of labour (Method III).

Machinofacture   The period of machinofacture in the nineteenth century involved the wholesale reconstitution of the labour process in factory locations. The instigation of routinised machine production led to greater efficiency and control over production (Method I). The employment of large numbers of women and children working long hours for low wages led to a massive upsurge in the opportunities for increasing the yield on labour power through Methods II and III.

Taylorism and Fordism   The term 'Taylorism' refers to the work of Frederick W. Taylor in the late nineteenth century who pioneered the introduction of 'time and motion' studies in American factories.[30] The term 'Fordism' was first coined by Gramsci to denote the spread of assembly-line processes in the 1920s, pioneered by the Ford Motor Company.[31] The instigation of Taylorism and Fordism has involved the ruthless subordination of labour to flow-line assembly processes of production (Method I). Deskilling and the growth of cheap, mass-produced consumer goods have greatly extended the scope for Method III.

Neo-Fordism The contemporary trend towards neo-Fordism represents a continuation of these twentieth-century trends with the prospect of an unprecedented degree of intensification of the labour process through the 'white heat' of the scientific and technological changes since the late-1960s. The characteristics of neo-Fordist labour processes are discussed in more detail in the next section.

4. *The Labour Process as a Historical Variable*

Recent analyses of neo-Fordist tendencies in contemporary capitalism have shed considerable light, not only on an emerging new form of organisation in industrial production, but also on the historical nature of the capitalist labour process in general. In *Capital*, volume I, Marx himself examined the changes in the capitalist labour process which accompanied the transitions from pre-industrial domestic or workshop production to industrial manufacture and machinofacture.[32] He isolated a number of characteristics of this historical process.

First, Marx identified the transition from the 'formal' to the 'real' subordination of labour to capital in production. In the pre-industrial period the labour process took place in fragmented locations at a distance from the capitalist owners where workers exercised a degree of autonomous control over the performance of their labour. While workers were formally subordinated to capitalist control due to their positions as wage-labourers, they did not experience this as an all-pervasive and oppressive feature of their lives. With the concentration of production into large, mechanised factory units, however, the labour process became directly regulated both by human supervisors and by the machine-tempo of mechanised production. This involved whole new modes of labour discipline and working practices, most notably the imposition of a strictly structured working day.

Second, Marx showed how the development of a centralised and mechanised production system involved an increasingly intensified labour process with greater stress laid upon the extraction of what he called 'relative' as opposed to 'absolute' surplus value. In the more primitive phases of industrial development the chief obstacle to the expansion of capitalist manufacture was the small size of the industrial working class. Capitalist strategies were focused on drawing larger numbers of workers into wage-dependence, increasing the absolute quantity of surplus value extracted from workers in the commodity production sector. With the transition to mechanised manufacture the major capitalist imperative became one of increasing the relative amount of surplus value produced per worker by intensifying the technical productivity of the labour process.

Third, Marx argued that the increasing mechanisation and routinisation of labour, in combination with the centralisation of production into large-scale manufacturing units, led to the deskilling of the workforce, destroying the old craft-based specialisms and agglomerating the labour force into a relatively homogenous class of factory recruits. Capitalism alienated workers from the products of their labour by substituting a labour process based on production of commodities destined for exchange at the market for the economic system based on production for direct consumption or use. The intensification of production alienated workers from their labour power itself. With the loss of skill or craft-based distinctions the workforce lost control over their own labour.

These themes in Marx's nineteenth-century writings were taken up by Harry Braverman, who saw the introduction of scientific management and Fordism in the twentieth century as further evidence of capitalism's historic tendency to fragment the labour process and degrade work as an activity.[33] More recent Marxist contributions to what has been commonly referred to as the 'labour-process debate' have identified newly emerging forms of industrial organisation which run counter to the earlier examples of twentieth-century Fordism. Christian Palloix argues that recent neo-Fordist adaptations of the labour process in some industrial sectors, notably the motor industry, have involved a degree of *re*centralisation in production and *re*skilling of the labour force.[34] In some European car plants, for example, the formerly fragmented continuous assembly-lines have been divided into separate productive units encompassing a number of flow-line processes where the workforce exercise a degree of self-supervision and responsibility for quality control.[35] This reconstitution of the labour process is seen by Palloix as an attempt to overcome the inherent technical and other contradictions of Fordism. The division of formerly continuous production lines into disaggregated units overcomes certain technical problems of production, such as the potential for bottlenecks to develop due to machine breakdowns or stoppages. At the same time the delegation of certain supervisory or other skilled functions to the assembly workforce leads to a degree of 'job enrichment', combatting the notorious boredom and alienation of assembly-line work which frequently leads to unacceptable levels of absenteeism, poor or uneven production quality and even sporadic industrial sabotage.

Such recent research has led several Marxist theorists to question the whole notion of a historic tendency towards deskilling and productive fragmentation in capitalist industry. Tony Elger, for example, argues that the phenomenon of deskilling cannot be seen as a general characteristic or long-term tendency of capitalist development.[36] Rather, it can only be understood as a product of particular conditions prevailing at particular times. In a detailed examination of the historical evolution of capitalist management strategies since the Industrial Revolution, Andrew Friedman draws a distinction between two strategies which he refers to as 'direct control' by capital over the labour process as opposed to the delegation of 'responsible autonomy' to the workforce.[37] In Friedman's view there has been no ongoing historic tendency for responsible autonomy to be withdrawn in favour of direct control. There is always a certain tension between these two strategies. The form of managerial strategy prevalent in different industries in different times and places varies in accordance with a number of factors, not least of which is the continuous process of bargaining and conflict over the labour process between management and workforce.

This last point introduces the most important criticism which has been levelled at Braverman's thesis. In the latter's account changes in the form of the labour process involving new forms of labour's subordination to capital are interpreted as an inevitable outcome of capitalism's unyielding tendency to expand its productive forces. Several critics have objected to this view of the labour process as a simple outcome of 'capital logic'. Stanley Aronowitz, for example, argues that the technical forces and social relationships of capitalist production have rarely developed harmoniously.[38]

They generally run into contradiction. In Aronowitz's view the capitalist labour process is a contested terrain reflecting the attempts of capital to mould the workforce to the technical needs of production countered by the capacity of labour to resist the new forms of subordination to capital implied by these technical requirements. The historical evolution of the capitalist labour process is not a history of technical logic but of social struggle.

5. *Class Struggle over the Labour Process*

These criticisms of Braverman's account of the capitalist labour process are similar to those I have made of Mandel's long-wave thesis. Both Braverman and Mandel are concerned with explaining the growth and development of capitalism's technical forces. Braverman is primarily concerned with the way in which different managerial strategies, particularly Taylorist scientific management, have been developed to further capitalism's technical advance. Mandel is more interested in the underlying value dynamics of technical change and their effects on cyclical movements in the rate of profit. But the approaches of both these authors share two important common features. First, they see the motor of technical change as capitalist profitability in terms of the need of particular enterprises to strive for competitive superiority over others. Second, they see the process of technical advance as a one-way process of capital achieving new ways of subordinating labour to the technical needs of production.

As outlined above, this kind of 'capital logic' approach has been extensively criticised in recent years. It has been argued that technical change is not just a means whereby individual capitalists compete over markets and profits with others. It is also a process whereby the capitalist class *as a whole* exerts its power over labour in production. Moreover the ability of capital to exercise control over the labour process is not predetermined or guaranteed. Capitalist managers must continually strive to develop new means of subordinating labour to capital in order to combat the forms of resistance developed by labour to confront and challenge that subordination. Technical change and the capitalist labour process can only be understood as an *historical* process of ongoing development and conflict.

Andrew Friedman's analysis of 'class struggle at work and

monopoly capitalism' provides a fine example of this interpretation.[39] Friedman argues that the development of different capitalist industries in different local areas must be interpreted as a social process of evolving class conflict over the labour process rather than as a simple process of technical advance. Friedman is particularly concerned with the way in which different managerial strategies in different historical periods have exploited divisions within the working class by skill, sex and race to further capital's control over production. In Friedman's view the development of the capitalist labour process in Britain can be divided into five historical periods involving different forms of management strategy and worker resistance. Friedman makes no reference to any theory of long waves in his account of these historical phases. However, his dating of the phases of conflict over the labour process is remarkably similar to the turning-points which other authors have related to the long waves of industrial capitalist development. Friedman himself notes how the scale and pace at which new forms of managerial strategy and worker resistance emerged was bound up with changing conditions of international economic development. For example, Friedman remarks that the 'dislocating effects' of the rise of manufacture upon workers in domestic or workshop production and in agriculture were masked during the years of relative prosperity from the 1780s to the end of the Napoleonic Wars.[40] Worker revolt in the form of machine-breaking, riots and mass demonstrations became more intense with the arrival of what other authors would call the 'first Kondratieff downturn' from the 1820s to the late 1840s. Similarly falling profitability during the Great Depression of the late nineteenth century was a key stimulus to the early experiments in scientific management involving the exercise of new forms of managerial authority and the instigation of fresh forms of work organisation.[41]

A 'labour perspective' of the Kondratieff waves   Friedman's periodisation of phases in the development of the industrial class struggle provides a useful historical framework in parallel to the dominant theories of long waves which conceive of capitalist development in terms of economic growth and technical change. More recently Ian Benson and John Lloyd have introduced what they call a 'labour perspective' on the Kondratieff long waves complimentary to the more usual 'economic perspective' proposed by Schumpeter and his later followers.[42] Benson and Lloyd argue that the progress of the labour movement, like that of technology and the long waves of economic development, has involved alternating phases of construction, destruction and reconstruction:

> The progress of the Kondratiev waves has shaped the development of the labour movement, and it is in the history of the labour movement that the discontinuous nature of technological change can be seen most clearly. Its very essence is one of alternating advance and retreat; of gains secured, eroded and restored; of organisations formed, degenerating and reformed. Here we find the periods associated with steam, rail, electricity and electronics notable for the introduction of new words into our vocabulary to articulate novel social events: luddism, unemployment, technological and now structural unemployment.[43]

In Benson and Lloyd's view it is not so much the discontinuous clustering of technical innovations stressed by the Schumpeterians which determines the pattern of the long waves. Rather, it is the ebb and flow of class struggle over industrial organisation and technological change which both shapes and is shaped by the long waves. Benson and Lloyd's chief objective is to propose a practical labour and trade union politics to cope with the upheavals of the 'Scientific-Technical Revolution' since the 1960s rather than to conduct an academic inquiry into the historical long waves. None the less, the long-wave thesis colours the whole of their analysis, particularly through the stress they lay upon the *uneven* development of labour-movement politics in different industries and national economies.

Benson and Lloyd argue that different sections of the international labour and trade union movements have developed different responses to industrial and technological change in different countries and in different historical periods. None the less, these divergent experiences correspond to a cohesive pattern of development spanning the long waves. Within the leading industrial sectors of the leading national economy during each wave will generally be found the most advanced forms of labour responses to the new forms of industrial organisation. The leading industries and national economies of each long wave introduce new labour processes which subsequently become a norm for other sectors and countries. Similarly, the labour movements in the leading national industries pioneer new forms of conflict over the labour process which frequently, but by no means always, form new models which are followed by other national labour movements.

Thus, during the two nineteenth-century long waves it was the British labour movement, in the most advanced industrial economy, which developed the most advanced responses to the dislocations of working-class life brought on by the spread of manufacture and machinofacture. With the loss of British capitalism's international leadership in the twentieth century, the locus for the evolution of the modern labour movement shifted to the US. Here the growth of 'science-based industry', where the norms of Taylorism and Fordism were most developed, created what Benson and Lloyd call the 'collective worker', enmeshed in a new institutionalised, legalistic process of formal collective bargaining with the science-based corporations.

While Benson and Lloyd confine their attention to the development of different forms of labour and trade-union activity at the national scale, I will argue later that this uneven development of social and political responses to industrial and wider economic change is equally evident at a subnational or regional scale. Moreover, this process is not confined to the working-class labour and trade-union movements, but is also represented in the uneven development of different regionally based sections of the British ruling class and their political movements.

Conclusion

The recent revival of the theory of long waves has been strongly associated with renewed interest in technological change as a factor in economic development. While the importance of technical change can be readily acknowledged I have suggested that it should not be viewed in isolation from its wider social context and purposes. Marxist critics have strongly objected to the idea that technological change causes the long waves. Mandel's approach provides an attractive alternative to the technical innovation approach by stressing the link between internal economic mechanisms and external social forces in determining the course of capitalist development.

Closer examination of Mandel's thesis, however, reveals that Mandel too relies on a technological-deterministic view of the manner in which the long waves unfold. Mandel employs the orthodox Marxist over-accumulation theory to explain the processes which lead to the degeneration of an expansionary wave into a contractive one and the pressures which subsequently mount within the economic system for a radical regeneration of the productive forces in a fresh wave of expansion. Framed in terms of the growth and advance of capitalism's technical forces, the over-accumulation thesis fails fully to consider the accompanying social relationships which, first, make production in capitalism possible at all and which, second, circumscribe the forms that production assumes.

This problem with Mandel's account is shared with other capital over-accumulation theories of long waves, most notably Forrester's System Dynamics model. But Mandel's approach is doubly disappointing because, in my view, the great strength of the Marxist theoretical framework is its interpretation of economic change and development as a social process embodying relationships of power and authority. A variety of theoretical frameworks can be drawn on to support the basic over-accumulation theory of capitalist instability. But only the Marxist approach is equipped to fully examine the social and political processes embodied in the accumulation of capital. Mandel's interpretation fails to fully exploit the potential insights of the Marxist perspective.

I have proposed that by examining the conjunction of capitalism's technical forces and social relationships of production at their meeting-point in the capitalist labour process we are better able to understand the changing nature of the different productive systems (manufacture, machinofacture, Fordism, etc.) which characterise industrial development in each historical long wave. Most importantly this perspective demonstrates how the long waves unfold through historical processes of social change and conflict rather than in accordance with some pregiven pattern of technical change.

3
Long Waves, Capitalist Crisis and the Business Cycle

Introduction

The last chapter proposed an interpretation of economic development and technical advance as a process of social change and conflict, closing with a description of Benson and Lloyd's 'labour perspective' of the long waves. In my view, however, it is not sufficient to simply graft a social conflict or labour perspective on to the more conventional technical account of the long waves in order to extend the theoretical advances made by the latter. I have argued that the development of capitalism's technical forces and social relationships are indissolubly linked. A theory of the capitalist labour process does not 'stand alone', but has important implications for our understanding of the cyclical process of technical advance.

Chapter 2 argued that the cycle of capital accumulation involves not only a periodic rejuvenation of capitalism's technical forces, but also a parallel transformation of the social relationships engaged in those forces. Chapter 3 now goes on to show how the development of capitalism's social relationships has a reciprocal effect upon the historical course adopted by capitalism's accumulation cycle.

I Class Struggle in the Business Cycle

Chapter 2 criticised Mandel's account of fluctuations in capital accumulation through the 'tendency of the rate of profit to fall' on the grounds that this approach neglects the influence of the social relationships of production, and of conflict within these relationships, upon the cycle of development. In Mandel's view the process of technical development, involving an expansion of fixed capital relative to labour in production, is sufficient to bring about cyclical fluctuations regardless of the implications of this process for employment or wage levels. But workers are bound to accept neither reductions in employment levels nor changing working conditions for those who remain in employment. Moreover, even if the workforce *did* accept such a reorganisation without resistance, far-reaching changes in the technical constitution of production require equally radical transformations of social relationships at the workplace. These transformations do not occur spontaneously. They involve the introduction of new forms of work discipline and supervision which present problems *from the viewpoint of capital* as well as labour. This section looks at ways in which some authors have attempted to introduce what might be called a 'class-struggle dimension' to business cycle theory.

1. *Political Business Cycles*

A number of socialist theorists have attempted to relate the ebb and flow of class struggle to cyclical fluctuations in economic activity. In his seminal paper of 1943 Kalecki argued that economic fluctuations were in part a reflection of what he called 'political business cycles'.[1] In Kalecki's view state regulation of economic fluctuations through demand management policies varies according to the balance of political pressure exerted upon governments by the capitalist class, on the one hand, and by 'the masses', to use Kalecki's term, on the other. The balance of class influence, and hence the form and direction of government economic policy, tends to oscillate with the phases of boom and recession in the business cycle. At the end of a boom phase during which conditions of full employment have been created, capitalists are unable to tolerate the enhanced bargaining power of labour. Consequently they will exert political influence on governments to enact deflationary policies leading to recession and rising unemployment. This in turn stimulates labour to put pressure upon governments, whether through industrial militancy or through the ballot box, to adopt reflationary policies aimed at curbing the recession and restoring full employment.

Kalecki's article was addressed to the short-term business cycle.

However, Michele Salvati has argued that, given the long time-lags involved in policy action, employment responses and policy reaction, Kalecki's thesis may be more relevant to the long-term trends in industrial relations described by authors like Phelps Brown.[2]

Criticisms of the 'political business cycles' interpretation   A number of criticisms can be made of Kalecki's 'political business cycles' approach. First, most modern Marxists would object strongly to the assumption underlying Kalecki's approach that the state is in some way a neutral arbiter of class interests which simply reacts to whichever political force happens to be in the ascendancy. While few would today subscribe to the classical Marxist view of the state as a simple instrument of capital, the state in capitalism remains a specifically *capitalist* state operating within certain structures which constrain the degree of responsiveness of the state apparatus and political structures to the demands of labour.[3]

Second, Kalecki's interpretation adopts a very simplistic view of political consciousness and influence as directly determined by economic conditions in general and the level of unemployment in particular. This approach neglects the way in which changing economic conditions are manifested in changing ideologies and political perspectives. It is difficult to see, for example, how Kalecki's theory might explain the re-election of the Conservative government in 1983 whose first four years in power had seen unemployment more than double.

Third, Kalecki's approach seems to see economic cycles as artificially induced by government macroeconomic policies in response to political swings. Of course, most theories of economic fluctuations see business cycles as the outcome of certain tendencies towards instability inherent to the capitalist economic fabric itself. Indeed, in other articles Kalecki himself pointed to over-investment as the root cause of cyclical fluctuations.[4]

Fourth, the business cycles described by Kalecki occur within a static process of development. While Kalecki sees business cycles as alternate swings from boom to slump, many other authors draw attention to the important qualitative changes in the process of economic development which are brought about in the course of successive cycles, most notably the process of technical change and advance. The implications of these dynamic processes of change are not considered in Kalecki's theory. Yet the process of technical change clearly has important impacts on employment levels, competitive relationships between firms, industrial structures and other factors which influence the nature and form of economic policies.

Finally, Kalecki's theory is highly specific to a particular period of capitalist development, namely the post-war period of Keynesian demand management. Kalecki was certainly far-sighted in his anticipation of the way in which 'full employment' would come to dominate economic policy and perceptions of economic performance. But the idea of state regulation of economic fluctuations, a social democratic political system and the concept of full employment itself bear little relevance to capitalist development throughout the eighteenth and nineteenth centuries and, indeed, seem to be becoming decreasingly pertinent in the present decade.

2. *Wage Bargaining and Unemployment*

Several Marxist authors have attempted to relate business cycles to the impact of unemployment fluctuations and phases of class conflict in quite different ways to Kalecki. Most importantly they have related unemployment and class conflict *directly* to the inherent cyclical tendencies of the capitalist economic structure without recourse to any theory of state economic policies as a mediator between class interests and economic fluctuations. The idea that rising unemployment during the depressive phase of a cycle tends to discipline labour and facilitate the ensuing upturn is quite a common one in Marxist business-cycle theories. David Gordon's use of this interpretation to explain the lower turning-points of the long waves has been briefly referred to above in Chapter 1.[5] A more sophisticated version of this kind of approach has been provided by Andrew Glyn and John Harrison, who introduce the concept of 'scrapping' as a regulator of technical change and economic cycles.

'Scrapping' and technical change Glyn and Harrison adopt a fairly traditional Marxist stance in arguing that the pace and direction of capital accumulation is a function of capitalist profitability, which in turn is governed by the levels of wages and technical productivity.[6] Wages are not solely determined exogenously by the outcome of labour militancy in pay disputes. In Glyn and Harrison's view wages are partly determined within the ac-

cumulation cycle itself by the effects of technical change upon employment levels. They argue that, in a phase of low unemployment or relative labour shortage from the standpoint of capital, new investments in new productive units must recruit labour by offering higher wages than their competitors in the older lines of production. In the new production lines these wage rises eat into the increased profits brought on by the increased productivity of the more technically advanced investments. At the same time capitalist owners in the older production lines are forced to offer higher wages, and therefore accept lower profit margins, in order to compete for labour supplies with the new investments.

This wage spiral eventually leads to what Glyn and Harrison call the 'scrapping' of old lines of production whose profits are not partially insulated from the effects of rising wages by the advantages of superior productivity held by the newer production lines. This scrapping leads in turn to the displacement of labour from the older sectors of production, raising unemployment and putting pressure on the labour force to accept jobs at lower wage levels. This leads to a revitalisation of profitability and prepares the ground for the next cyclical round of investment.

Limitations of the 'wage-bargaining' approach Glyn and Harrison's approach overcomes several of the criticisms of Kalecki's theory, outlined above. These authors relate unemployment fluctuations and class conflict to the inherent instabilities of capitalist development. They integrate this perspective with a theory of technical change through their novel use of the 'scrapping' concept. They do not rely on any notion of a class-neutral state artificially inducing economic fluctuations in response to competing political pressures. However, in my view their approach mirrors an important deficiency of Kalecki's work which limits the usefulness of the Glyn and Harrison thesis for my purposes.

Glyn and Harrison's account is intended to analyse a highly specific subject-matter, namely the relative decline of British capitalism during the post-war period of full employment, rather than to construct a general theory of capitalist fluctuations. Except for a few industries demanding highly skilled labour it is difficult to see how Glyn and Harrison's wage-bargaining mechanism works during the 1980s when the 'relative labour shortage' of the 1950s and 1960s has been overtaken by relative superabundance.

3. *Principles of an Alternative Approach*

In my view the highly historically specific nature of Glyn and
Harrison's approach indirectly supplies an important clue towards
solving the problem of relating social and political factors to
economic fluctuations. The social framework of class relationships
within which capitalist production occurs is not a static or timeless
structure. I have suggested in Chapter 2 that different capitalist
industrial and technological systems have relied on very different
forms of social relationships to accomplish commodity production.
Marxists commonly equate these different social relationships with
the historical periods of domestic/workshop production, manufacture, machinofacture, Fordism and, lately, neo-Fordism. These
alternate systems of social relationships are created by capital to
serve the requirements of production. Yet, at the same time, they
impose certain social structural constraints upon the possibilities
for production – constraints which may in fact become contradictory with respect to production's technical requirements.

The remainder of this chapter adopts an approach which analyses the forms and causes of economic fluctuations by placing them
within the social structural context in which they occur. In my view
particular cycles of accumulation can only be understood within
their particular historical context. Any theory which purports to
provide a general or panhistorical account of cyclical fluctuations
in capitalist development can do no more than point to a few very
basic and abstract characteristics of the capitalist economic system
that offer the potential for economic instability. Such a general
theory of capitalist instability is certainly a vitally necessary tool of
analysis. But it cannot in itself meet the needs of an historical
analysis, such as a theory of long waves, which by its nature is
concerned with concrete manifestations of capitalist instability
whose appearance varies in time and space.

II Marxist Theories of Capitalist Crisis

The concept of economic crisis occupies a pivotal position in
Marxist thought. It could be argued, to put it crudely, that the
whole of Marx's economic writings were devoted to demonstrating

that the capitalist economic system relies on a process of class exploitation in production, a process whose internal contradictions and crisis tendencies inevitably sow the seeds of its own destruction, providing the objective preconditions for a socialist transformation of the economy and society. Not surprisingly, therefore, the concept of capitalist crisis has been the focus of wide-ranging analysis and debate among Marxist theorists. A number of alternative interpretations of Marx's own crisis theory have been proposed, as well as a smaller number of more independent Marxist crisis theories.

1. Crises in the Circulation of Capital

So far the only Marxist theory of capitalist economic crisis to which I have referred is the capital over-accumulation thesis which draws on Marx's Law of the Tendency for the Rate of Profit to Fall (TRPF). Given my own interest in the phenomenon of economic fluctuations, my reasons for concentrating upon this particular variant of Marxist crisis theory are threefold. First, in my view the law of TRPF is the most fully developed theory of crisis in Marx's own work and, today at least, is the nearest we have to an orthodox Marxist crisis theory. Second, the law of TRPF has been widely interpreted as a theory of cyclical fluctuations where the term 'crisis' refers to one particular phase of the cycle rather than to a linear descent of capitalist economies into chronic breakdown or some other permanent rupture of economic development. Third, for these same two reasons the law has been adopted by Mandel as a basic explanatory framework and I have naturally devoted a large measure of attention to this author, who remains the foremost modern Marxist proponent of the theory of long waves.

The structure of capital circulation   The capital over-accumulation thesis, or law of TRPF, relates capitalist economic crises to over-investment in fixed capital in production. But the process of production forms only one sphere in the overall process of capital accumulation. Marx conceived of capital accumulation as a process whereby value circulates through alternate stages of production and consumption linked by exchange and distribution.

During this process of circulation, value itself takes different material forms corresponding to money, commodities and productive capital.

The basic motor of capital accumulation is the generation of surplus value. But surplus value does not have any 'pure' form; it is embodied in physical quantities of money, commodities and capital. Surplus value is created in the sphere of production through the exploitation of labour power in combination with the technical means of production. A social surplus product is produced in the form of commodity outputs from production. These commodities are distributed to the consumption market where they are exchanged for their monetary equivalents. The surplus value thus realised is exchanged by the capitalist owners for fresh commodities – labour power, materials and equipment – which are brought together in the next round of production. Marx conceived of the accumulation cycle as the unity of three circuits of money capital, commodity capital and productive capital.

The harmonious course of the accumulation process is clearly dependent upon the various commodity inputs and outputs of production being produced in strict proportion and at exchangeable prices in order to balance supply with demand.[7] In *Capital*, vol. ii, Marx described the process of interaction between production and consumption in different sectors of the economy by means of his 'reproduction' schemas.[8] These showed what would today be called an 'input–output matrix' of economic development based on equilibrium exchanges of commodities between the fixed capital- and consumer-goods sectors of production. The capital-equipment and raw-materials sector (or 'Department I' in Marx's schema) produced inputs to the production processes of both its own industries and the industries of the consumer-goods sector (Department II). The latter sector produced consumer goods for the reproduction of labour employed in both itself and the raw materials and equipment industries. The equilibrium of the circulation process was maintained through the expansion of production and consumption in equivalent proportions.

'Disproportionality' and 'underconsumption' theories of crisis
Marxist economists during the early twentieth century attached a great deal of importance to Marx's reproduction schemas, seeing in them the most comprehensive account of how capitalist econ-

mies worked and the potential for economic crises within the capitalist system. The most influential interpretations were the 'disproportionality' and 'underconsumption' theses. While there were many variations within these two schools of thought it is possible to discern a number of basic features of each approach.[9]

The disproportionality approach, whose more memorable adherents included Rudolph Hilferding and Nikolai Bukharin, saw the origins of capitalist crises in the general instability of anarchic, unplanned accumulation.[10] Individual capitalist owners, driven by market competition, are incapable of planning their investments with regard to the capacity of the market as a whole. In the myriad of individual investments which constitute the capitalist system a harmonious exchange between different producers and consumers can scarcely be maintained. The capitalist economy is therefore continually in peril of breakdown.

The disproportionality theorists attributed crises to the inherent irrationality of an unplanned market economy driven by private gain. The Soviet economist Bukharin took this perspective to its logical conclusion in arguing that, by substituting a centrally planned system of 'state capitalism' for the market system of allocation, crises could be abolished within the capitalist economic framework. The under-consumption theorists, on the other hand, related crises to the fundamental structure of an economic system based on exploitation of labour in production. According to this perspective capitalists continually strive to increase the productivity of their investments by securing an ever-increasing quantity of surplus value relative to the value they pay out as wages to the workforce whose exploitation generates surplus value. This rising rate of surplus value, based on an increasing intensity of labour exploitation, is contradictory from the viewpoint of the economy as a whole. Surplus value is not produced for its own sake. For accumulation to be successfully reproduced surplus value must be *realised* at the market and reinvested in production. But it can only be fully realised if there is sufficient demand for the commodities within which it is embodied, i.e. if it is matched by an equivalent purchasing power from consumers. The balance of production and consumption cannot be maintained since the value of commodities produced is constantly increasing relative to the value commanded by labour. In other words, the purchasing power of wage-earners will tend to diminish in proportion to the value of commodities put up for sale at the market and an increasing share of the commodities will remain unsold. This structural tendency towards under-consumption means that a proportion of the surplus value generated in the economy will fail to be realised and fail to contribute towards the renewal and expansion of accumulation.

The most forceful proponent of the under-consumption thesis was Rosa Luxemburg.[11] She suggested that this structural contradiction of capital accumulation grew increasingly acute with the epoch of 'monopoly capitalism' in the late nineteenth century. This historical period was marked by an increasing intensity of exploitation brought on by advanced mechanisation in large productive units. The resulting pressure placed upon the realisation of surplus value led to deepening competition and an urgent struggle to open up fresh markets for commodity consumption. In Luxemburg's view this constituted the economic basis for imperialist expansion from the developed capitalist heartlands to new colonial markets marked by the intensification of inter-imperialist rivalries which precipitated the First World War.

2. *'Profits Squeeze' Theories of Crisis*

The under-consumption theory concurs with the capital over-accumulation thesis is so far as it sees capitalist crises originating in the sphere of production through an increasing intensity of labour exploitation accompanying labour-saving technical change. The capital over-accumulation thesis suggests that the resulting pressure on the rate of profit can be resolved, at least temporarily, within the economic system through structural changes brought about by the crisis itself. The under-consumption thesis, in contrast, proposes that the obstacle to accumulation cannot be resolved internally but generates pressure for an external solution via imperialist expansion.

The more recent 'profits squeeze' perspective suggests, in common with the over-accumulation thesis, that crises in capitalist development involve a tendency for the rate of profit to fall. However, unlike the over-accumulation and under-consumption theories, the profits squeeze perspective does not attribute pressure on the rate of profit to technical change or an increasing intensity of labour exploitation. Rather, the profits-squeeze thesis sees the falling rate of profit as the result of the increased bargaining strength of organised labour and consequent upward trend of wage costs which are deducted from profits.

In an influential book on the post-1945 decline of British capitalism as a global power, Andrew Glyn and Bob Sutcliffe argued that the already weakened competitive position of British capital was accentuated by the post-war strength of the labour movement.[12] In the struggle for market shares British companies were unable to pass on increasing wage costs to consumers by increasing prices since this would have undermined sales in a situation where British firms were already losing ground in export markets and were being undercut in the domestic market by relatively cheap foreign imports. Hence, British companies were obliged to meet rising wage costs by reducing profit margins. In effect British capital was caught in a cleft stick. On the one hand, companies were in a weak position to resist wage claims since prolonged strikes would reduce output and stocks, lead to default on deliveries to buyers who would turn to alternative sources and further cut British firms' market share. On the other hand, by meeting increasing wage costs out of profits British companies reduced their retained earnings which could have been invested in modern equipment to combat the deteriorating price competitiveness which constituted the source of 'the critical condition of British capital', as Glyn and Sutcliffe put it in an earlier article.[13]

Glyn and Sutcliffe's analysis pointed to a *secular* deterioration of the rate of profit in Britain. In the USA, Raford Boddy and James Crotty sought to develop a similar profits-squeeze perspective into a business-cycle theory.[14] According to these authors successful pay struggles on the part of labour during the upswing in the cycle brought about an erosion in profits. At this point 'the rise in unemployment engineered by the capitalists and acquiesced in and abetted by the state' reduced labour's bargaining strength and restored profit rates to their former level.[15] There are obvious parallels here between Boddy and Crotty's view and Kalecki's theory of 'political business cycles', discussed above.

In a more recent work, Andrew Glyn and John Harrison have developed Glyn's earlier work with Sutcliffe into a theory of technical change in the business cycle.[16] Unlike Boddy and Crotty, these authors do not explain the rise of unemployment in the downward phase of the cycle as arising from the perverse intentions of capitalists and the state. Rather, they see unemployment fluctuations as a reflection of the cycle of technical change and the scrapping of old production lines. Glyn and Harrison's thesis has been described in more detail earlier in this chapter as one example of the way in which a 'class-struggle ingredient' might be added to a capital over-accumulation perspective on technical change and the business cycle.

III   Capitalist Crisis as a Historical Variable

Debates over the nature and causes of capitalist crises continue to occupy a central place in Marxist economic theory. Sadly, these exchanges have generally been conducted in very insular terms. Proponents of the various positions, particularly the over-accumulation and under-consumption theorists, have frequently resorted to quotations from Marx's work to 'prove' the validity of their approach as the true legacy of Marx while original empirical analysis has been strikingly rare.

Marx himself is not overly helpful in this respect. Makoto Itoh is not alone in having discovered in Marx's work 'two different types of theory which are not easily reconciled with each other'.[17] On the one hand we find the over-accumulation or 'excess capital' theory in Marx's writings. Proponents of this approach frequently refer to Marx's comment in the *Grundrisse* that the law of TRPF is 'the most important law of modern political economy'.[18] On the other hand, we find elements of an under-consumption or 'excess commodities' theory of crisis in Marx's work. Advocates of this interpretation are equally fond of quoting Marx's statement in *Capital*, vol. iii, that: 'The ultimate reason for all real crises always remains the poverty and restricted consumption of the masses as opposed to the drive of capitalist production to develop the productive forces as though only the absolute consuming power of society constituted their limit.'[19] In reply the over-accumulation theorists point to Marx's explicit rejection of an under-consumption theory of crisis in *Capital*, vol. ii: 'It is a sheer tautology to say that crises are caused by the scarcity of effective consumption, or of effective consumers. The capitalist system does not know of any other modes of consumption than effective ones.'[20]

This kind of quasi-theological argument by quotation and counter-quotation seems to me a fruitless way of developing a Marxist account of capitalist crises. Certainly it is useful to establish Marx's own position as a starting-point for further inquiry. But even if a definitive theory of capitalist crisis *could* be uncovered in Marx's nineteenth-century writings this would not necessarily establish its validity. Nor would it eliminate the need to extend and adapt the basic theory in order to take account of the far-reaching changes in the workings of capitalist economies that have taken place since Marx's time.

In response to the crisis debate in Marxist economics a number of modern theorists have refrained from siding with one position against another. Rather they have taken the approach of seeking ways to integrate the different perspectives within a broader, essentially *historical* account of crises in capitalist development.

Erik Olin Wright argues that if the various interpretations of capitalist crises are each treated as 'total explanations', sufficient to explain the appearance of every crisis at any time and in any place where the capitalist economic system prevails, then the competing crisis theories are indeed mutually incompatible.[21] However, Wright argues, if the alternative theories are conceived of as explanations for *particular* crises in particular periods of capitalist development, it is possible to integrate the different approaches within a theory of 'historical transformations of capitalist crisis'.

A chronology of crises and crisis theories   In my view the various Marxist crisis theories are *not* all intended to be 'total explanations'. In chronological order Marx developed his capital over-accumulation/law of TRPF thesis in the context of nineteenth-century liberal or competitive capitalism whose development took a course of fairly regular cyclical fluctuations overshadowed by an unprecedented growth and advance of industrial capitalism's productive forces.

The boom–crisis cycle of the nineteenth century led to the progressive concentration of capital into fewer hands as the larger, technically superior enterprises engulfed their smaller, less-efficient competitors. The emergence of giant corporations with the arrival of twentieth-century 'monopoly capitalism' formed the context within which theorists like the German Social Democrat

Hilferding developed and applied their theories of capitalist disproportionality. It was Hilferding who coined the term 'finance capital' to describe the fusion of industry and finance into large, monopolistic units.[22] The threat to accumulation posed by the disproportionality of individual capitalist investments would become increasingly severe, the argument ran, as each disproportionate investment became progressively larger. The crisis of one key industry, such as coal or steel, would inevitably propel the whole capitalist system into breakdown.

At around the same time under-consumption theorists like Luxemburg argued that the structural crisis of the developed capitalist economies could be resolved externally through the export of surplus commodities to colonial markets. Although not generally recognised as a crisis theory as such, Lenin's *Imperialism* was addressed to the same kind of issues as Luxemburg's work.[23] Whereas Luxemburg saw the export of surplus *commodities* as the chief characteristic of imperialism, Lenin argued that colonialist mercantilism was only the advance guard of a more important movement towards the imperialist export of *capital*.

The deepening economic and military conflicts between imperialist capitals, which culminated in the first World War, corresponded with a hitherto unprecedented degree of state intervention in capitalist economies. This trend was accelerated by the demands of the First-World War economy and was consolidated with rearmament in the 1930s and the 'Total War' of 1939–45.[24] With the arrival of an increasingly corporatist and state-regulated capitalism in the post-1945 period, some Marxists have contrived new explanatory frameworks to tackle the new forms of relationship between the state, capital and labour that have accompanied this stage of capitalist development.

Glyn and Sutcliffe's 'profits squeeze' thesis has been one of the more influential treatments of the undermining of capitalist growth by the pressure of full employment. Some of the most original and innovative Marxist contributions to contemporary crisis theory have looked beyond the economic realm to examine the effects of changing social relationships in the spheres of the state, ideology and political life. James O'Connor has shown how the modern state plays an important role in maintaining the social and economic infrastructure for capital accumulation.[25] But the growth of social welfare, economic, military and other state expenditure places an increasing burden on the private sector. In a period of slow-down in capitalist growth, the need for state expenditure runs into contradiction with the ability of the private sector to withstand the strain on the economy's resources, generating what O'Connor calls a 'fiscal crisis of the state'.[26]

Several West German sociologists, most notably Claus Offe and Jürgen Habermas, have developed more subtle theories of the way in which crisis tendencies in the economic sphere may be displaced to the political and ideological terrains.[27] In particular they have shown how the ability of the state to maintain social cohesion in social democratic societies may be undermined by the breakdown of a number of mechanisms, bureaucratic and administrative as well as economic, leading to what Habermas calls a 'legitimation crisis' of the social system.

The important point here is that all of these crisis theories are both addressed to, and a reflection of, the specific historical circumstances in which they were developed. Marx himself was concerned with uncovering the most fundamental characteristics of capitalism and the potential for crises within the economic system. Subsequent theorists have been more concerned with examining different forms of crisis at different times in capitalist development. The Japanese economist Itoh suggests a similar interpretation when he argues that: 'A reading of Luxemburg's *The Accumulation of Capital*, Hilferding's *Finanzcapital*, and Lenin's *Imperialism*, in that order, shows that with the establishment of the stages theory of imperialism Marx's crisis theory fell more and more into disuse as a direct starting-point.'[28]

In my view the various crisis theories are *not* in fact alternative explanations of capitalist crises, but more or less complimentary accounts of different forms of crises in capitalist development. I say '*more or less* complimentary' because this interpretation does not exclude the possibility that each crisis theory may suffer problems within its own terms of reference. Following this approach the task of constructing a Marxist theory of crisis ceases to be one of evaluating competing alternatives, adopting one and excluding all others. Rather the task becomes one of identifying the *historical links* between these different forms of crisis to show how it is that one form evolves into another.

IV   Historical Transformations of Capitalist Crises

It was suggested in Chapter 2 that the development of industrial capitalism has involved changing forms of the conjunction between the technical forces and social relationships of production in the capitalist labour process. It is the historical transformations of the *labour process*, rather than changes in technology, which form the hub of the process of industrial development, since it is only through the achievement of new forms of social subordination of labour to capital in production that the introduction and diffusion of new technical products and processes is accomplished. Some authors refer to the long wave of steam power, the railway wave, the motor-vehicle wave and, lately, the microelectronics wave. In contrast to this perspective I prefer to characterise the long waves in terms of their emergent social relationships of production. Following this approach I have referred to the long waves of manufacture, machinofacture, scientific management and Fordism, and the most recently developing phase of neo-Fordism.

1. *Regimes of Accumulation*

In an influential book Michel Aglietta has taken this labour-process interpretation a step further.[29] In Aglietta's view the labour process at the point of production cannot develop in isolation from the structural forms of the much broader accumulation process as a whole. The latter encompasses the processes of consumption, distribution and exchange as well as production. The changing structure of production and its social relationships involves corresponding changes in the structures of all other spheres of accumulation.

Aglietta distinguishes between two periods of capitalist development which, in order to describe the totality of the processes involved, he calls 'regimes of accumulation'. The latter are defined as modes of production and distribution of surplus value which secure changes in the conditions of production, consumption and the development of the labour process in such a way as to provide a set of structural economic and social relationships appropriate to the needs of expansionary accumulation.

Aglietta calls the primary phase of industrial capitalist development the 'regime of extensive accumulation'. This regime involves the extensive extraction of 'absolute surplus value' by expanding the absolute size of the industrial working class. The chief social structural adaptation of this regime is the spread of the *wage-labour norm* by which an increasing proportion of the population come to depend for their existence upon selling their labour to capitalist owners rather than upon self-employment or semi-subsistence agriculture.

The second phase of development corresponds to what Aglietta calls the 'regime of intensive accumulation', based on an expanding role for the production of 'relative surplus value' in the economy. In this regime the emphasis of accumulation is placed not so much upon increasing the absolute level of surplus value that can be produced, but upon raising the relative level which can be extracted from each unit of labour. This involves an intensification of the labour process through the techniques of scientific management and Fordism. The major social structural characteristic of this regime is the growth of the *mass consumption norm* to match the enormously expanded productive capacity of the economy.

This interpretation of capitalist development has far-reaching implications for our understanding of crises in capitalist development. Put simply, Aglietta argues that there is an inherent tendency towards disproportionality in the economy through the over-accumulation of capital in one or more industrial sectors whose productive capacity is not matched by an equal capacity for consumption in other sectors. In Aglietta's view the basic crisis tendency of capitalist economies is the tendency towards the uneven development of production and consumption. Aglietta argues that the 'tendency towards uneven development is a macro-economic feature of the law of accumulation' which 'can only be neutralised by social transformations that depend on the evolution of the class struggle'.[30] The term 'macroeconomic' is important here since by 'class struggle' Aglietta means much more than the isolated gains of capitalists over workers in individual conflicts. Rather, the harmonisation of production and consumption depends upon the long-term development of whole new conditions of life which Aglietta sees as centring upon the wage-labour and mass consumption norms of capitalist societies.

The development of industrial capitalism is structurally constrained by the development of these two social norms. The regime of extensive accumulation can only develop through the spread of the wage-labour norm. This regime can only evolve into a regime of intensive accumulation through the consolidation of a mass consumption norm. In this context Aglietta objects to what he considers to be the one-sided perspectives of neo-classical and Marxist economic theories. Neo-classical economics has focused upon theories of capitalist equilibrium, or theories of *reproduction*. Marxist economics, on the other hand, has been preoccupied with theories of capitalist crisis, or theories of *rupture*. Aglietta seeks to integrate both these aspects through his theory of capitalist *regulation*. The reproduction or harmonious development of capitalism is limited by the prevailing social structural norms. The historical development of capitalism can only be achieved, therefore, by a periodic rupture of these norms giving rise to new social relationships of production and consumption. The fluctuating course of accumulation is regulated by the social relationships which bind together the various components of the accumulation process.

2. *Transformations of Crisis*

In my view this perspective of regulation enables us to link the interpretation of capitalist crises as historically variable, proposed above, with the historical account of transformations in the capitalist labour process presented in Chapter 2. Changes in the technical organisation of the labour process depend upon changes in the social relationships of production and consumption. These same social relationships restrict the range of possible forms of accumulation. When the requirements of accumulation conflict with those constraints, i.e. when the social structures and relationships begin to function as obstacles to the further advance and development of accumulation, then it can be said that accumulation has run into structural contradiction or crisis. At this point the only way for capital accumulation to renew its development is to break down the social structural obstacles to its advance and to open up a new range of possibilities and options – which will include fresh restrictions and obstacles.

Following this kind of approach, Erik Olin Wright has suggested that the development of industrial capitalism can be divided into a series of historical stages, each characterised by certain structural constraints on accumulation generating pressure for structural solutions to these problems.[31] The rest of this section elaborates on Wright's description.

Primitive accumulation (in Britain during the eighteenth century) The chief constraint on capitalist development during the period of primitive accumulation was the limited absolute size of the social surplus product that could be appropriated from the wage-earning class. This was a symptom of the relatively small size of the working class. It also reflected the relatively primitive level of development of the technical forces of production and the social relationships embodied in the labour process.

Capitalist development in Europe and the north-eastern USA was substantially fuelled by the appropriation of cheap raw materials and labour (slaves) from colonial and peripheral territories. Social and institutional barriers to industrial expansion in the capitalist heartlands generated pressure for the reconstitution of the conditions of wage-labour characteristic of centralised manufacture.

Manufacture (in Britain from the late eighteenth century to the 1830s) The wage-earning class grew in size as the site of production shifted from domestic and workshop locations towards concentrated factory units. Whereas workers' incomes had formerly been frequently supplemented by agricultural and horticultural production, workers and their families were now totally dependent upon wage-labour for their existence.

The chief constraint upon the growth and advance of manufacture was the relatively low intensity of labour exploitation, i.e. the limited yield per unit of labour power, symptomatic of the continued high unit costs of employing labour. This created a stimulus towards labour-saving technical innovation which depressed wage costs in three ways: first, by reducing the labour input required for each unit of output; second, by permitting the threat of unemployment to discipline the wage-dependent class; and third, by cheapening the prices of manufactured goods and hence the wage required by workers for their reproduction.

However, the real wages commanded by workers were not only determined by the balance of demand for and supply of labour. They were also geared to fluctuations of agricultural prices. In the absence of a fully developed working-class market for capitalistically produced consumer goods, the conditions of pre-capitalist or semi-capitalist agricultural production continued to act as a major constraint upon capitalist industry through their effect upon food prices which remained a central determinant of wage costs. The subordination of agriculture to capitalist manufacture became a key imperative for the further development of capital accumulation, generating antagonisms between industrial capital and landed interests. In Continental Europe this frequently erupted into bitter conflicts over the 'land question'. In Britain, where the technical revolutionisation of agriculture had preceded the development of industrial manufacture, the conflict between industrial capitalists and landed gentry was more sharply focused upon the artificially high prices of domestic agricultural prices maintained by tariff barriers to grain imports.

Machinofacture   (in Britain from the 1840s to 1890s) The far-reaching growth and development of capitalism's technical forces wrought by the Industrial Revolution in Britain set in motion the fairly regular cycle of capital accumulation which characterised economic fluctuations during the nineteenth century. As well as the continuing drive to expand the size of the working class there was increasing pressure to revolutionise the production and transportation of fixed capital equipment and raw materials. This was evidenced by the growth of mechanised heavy industry on the iron- and coal-fields to meet the expanding requirements of the manufacturing sector. The extraordinary booms and slumps in railway investment added a speculative dimension to the cycle of industrial accumulation and over-accumulation.

Monopoly capitalism and imperialism   (in Britain from the 1890s to 1930s) The enormous liberation of capitalism's technical and productive potential brought about by the Second Industrial Revolution, strongly evident in Germany and the USA as well as in Britain, was countered by the tendency for production to expand beyond the capacity of domestic consumption. Intensive competition for markets led to the increasing concentration and centralisation of capital into large, corporate enterprises. The constraint on consumption was broken down by increasing the exports of commodities to foreign markets, generating a marked expansion of foreign trade. The continuing drive to access cheap sources of raw materials was manifested in the imperialist export of surplus capital to colonial territories to set up new productive units.

Imperialist expansion ceased to function simply as a solution to structural constraints on accumulation, i.e. under-consumption, within the developed capitalist economies, but effectively internationalised that constraint. The expansion of production on a global scale led to acute international competition for markets and growing inter-imperialist rivalries over colonial spheres of influence. This process reached its cataclysm in the inter-imperialist war of 1914–18 followed by the great under-consumptionist crises of the 1930s. The latter was preceded by acute speculative pressures, especially in the USA, as surplus capital was switched from industry towards investment in property and financial assets until the bubble burst in the crash of 1929.

Advanced monopoly capitalism (post-1945) The unprecedented degree of state involvement in the years preceding and during the Second World War was consolidated in the post-1945 period. State expenditure on rearmament and public works formed the foundation for post-war Keynesian demand management of advanced capitalist economies through a growing public sector of nationalised industries together with the governmental and welfare apparatus. The post-war boom was marked by relatively stable capitalist development as the boom–bust cycle of the earlier epoch gave way to a growth cycle of speed-up and slow-down.

The major constraints on accumulation during the post-war period were the increasing collective strength of the working class engaged in a corporate bargaining system and the growing economic burden of state expenditure. These pressures combined to generate the acute price inflation in the late 1960s and throughout the 1970s for which there was no historic precedent during peacetime.

The slow-down of growth in the late-1960s and early-1970s prompted increasing international competition accompanied by a wave of mergers and take-overs as the giant multinational corporations cemented their dominance of world markets. This involved the increasing internationalisation of productive capital as the multinationals decentralised production towards markets for cheap and poorly organised labour in the Third World.

The structural constraints on accumulation in the developed

capitalist countries have only recently begun to be tackled as the austerity of the 1970s has given way to the deepest international slump since the 1930s. The return of mass unemployment has weakened the resistance of organised labour to the reorganisation of production and promoted a 'new realism' in pay determination. At the same time monetary restraint, prompted by spiralling inflation since the oil price shocks of the mid-1970s, has been accompanied by economic and political pressure to slow down the growth of public expenditure and reopen sections of public sector industry and the welfare apparatus to private enterprise.

V   Historical Metamorphoses of the Business Cycle

The preceding discussion has moved some considerable way from the initial concern with theories of long waves in Chapter I. I have criticised theories which reduce the long-term fluctuations of capitalist development to single factors or to panhistorical mechanisms sufficient to explain every wave and its turning-points. It has been suggested that both the upper and lower turning-points of the long waves can only be fully understood in their particular historical context. The radical advancements of capitalism's technical forces that marked each expansionary long wave also entailed equally radical upheavals in the social relationships underlying capital accumulation. These social relationships formed the basis of different sets of structural constraints or crisis tendencies acting upon accumulation as well as providing different possibilities for their resolution. It is in this sense that the long waves can be conceived of as qualitatively distinct historical periods of industrial capitalist development and not just as quantitative fluctuations in economic trend indicators.

However, this conclusion raises a basic question regarding the purpose of a theory of long waves. If the waves can be more accurately described as distinct historical periods, why confuse matters by calling these periods 'long waves'? It may be recalled from Chapter 1 that Trotsky rejected Kondratieff's thesis partly on these grounds. Most if not all Marxist economists, including the classical theorists whose various crisis theories have been discussed above, distinguish between a number of distinct periods of capi-

talist development. Depending upon their particular interpretation
they variously label these periods primitive or petty commodity
production; liberal or competitive capitalism; monopoly capitalism
or imperialism; advanced capitalism, late capitalism or state monopoly capitalism. Yet comparatively few Marxist economists have
drawn upon any theory of long waves in constructing such period-
isations. We do not have to be 'long wavists', let alone Marxists, to
acknowledge the existence of alternating historical periods of
advance and retrenchment in capitalism's development. With the
particular exception of the late-nineteenth-century Great Depression, there is a general consensus among economic historians
that capitalist development has involved successive phases of
change followed by consolidation whose dating roughly corresponds to the phases which other observers equate with the long
waves.[32] Others, notably Landes, acknowledge the historical phases
while explicitly denying the validity of any long-wave explanation.[33]
On a more positive note one school of French historians have
drawn on the long-wave framework as a setting for their analysis of
what they refer to as 'conjunctural waves' of social and political
change.[34] But it should be noted that this school are concerned
with very broad, epoch-spanning movements and remain highly
sceptical about any notion of 'turning-points' which, of course,
have been the focus of debates among adherents of the long-wave
thesis.

What then, if anything, can a long-wave perspective add to our
understanding of these historical periods? So far I have analysed
the long waves in terms of historical transformations in the labour
process, transformations in the forms of capitalist crises, and
transformations in the social relationships of accumulation which
underlie these movements. I have used the term 'transformation'
to emphasise the dominant characteristics which distinguish one
historical period from another. But, of course, these transformations do not occur overnight. Moreover, the dominance of one
particular form of accumulation in any one period does not pre-
clude the existence of others. Having described the key differences
between each period the next task for a historical analysis is to
examine their *continuity*: to show the process whereby one form of
accumulation evolves into another.[35] Here we are dealing, not
with the sharp contrasts implied by the term 'transformation'; but

with incremental changes which can be more accurately labelled a process of *transition*. In this regard I believe that the long-wave thesis can provide useful insights.

1. *Long Waves and the Business Cycle: Some Empirical Evidence*

In the purest sense of the term there is no such phenomenon as a 'Kondratieff cycle'. Taking the strongest statistical indicator of the movements we cannot discern a fifty-year cycle in commodity price movements. The long cycles are in fact groups of shorter cycles, the net result of whose upswings and downswings yields a certain underlying long-term movement. Several proponents of the long-wave thesis, including Kondratieff himself as well as Mandel, have suggested that one characteristic which distinguishes the expansive from the contractive phases is a change in the duration and amplitude of the short-term cycles within each wave. It is argued that during expansionary phases the short-term cyclical booms are both stronger and longer than the downturns. During the contractive waves, on the other hand, the cyclical downturns are deeper and more durable than the upturns.

However, detailed empirical studies of business cycles over the past two centuries have revealed more complex quantitative relationships between the peaks and troughs of successive cycles as well as longer-term changes in the structure of economic fluctuations. Derek Aldcroft and Peter Fearon, for example, have identified twenty-four cycles in UK industrial production between 1785 and 1913 with an average duration of 5.3 years.[36] The length of individual cycles varies widely, however, from two to ten years. The shorter, minor cycles were mostly confined to the earlier part of this period, from 1785 to 1836, after which cycles tended to be longer with an average duration of 6.4 years. This increase in the average length of cycles from the late-1830s onwards is confirmed by Aldcroft and Fearon's analysis of fluctuations in UK gross national product (GNP) from 1836 to 1913. A total of eleven cycles are observable during this period with an average length of seven years, varying individually between three and eleven years in duration. For both industrial production and GNP, the amplitude of cycles remained remarkably consistent until 1913. This pattern was broken during the interwar years, however, when cycles were both longer and more intense than those throughout the preceding century.

What support, if any, does this empirical analysis of business cycles in the UK economy provide for the long-wave interpretation? Aldcroft and Fearon themselves are very doubtful of the existence of any such long waves in economic fluctuations. None the less, the changes in the historical patterns of fluctuations which they identify in their data would seem to provide qualified support for the view that business cycles since the late eighteenth century can be grouped into several fairly distinctive periods: short and frequent cycles, averaging three to four years, punctuating econ- omic development during the first half of the nineteenth century; longer cycles with a periodicity of six to ten years marking the second half of the nineteenth century and early twentieth century; and equally durable, but significantly more intense, cycles from 1920 to the Second World War. As for the period since 1945, Aldcroft and Fearon note that, until the early 1970s at least, post-war fluctuations in the UK took the form of 'growth cycles' in which the former cyclical slumps were replaced by periodic phases of slower growth without the pronounced troughs which had been a feature of economic instability for the previous 150 years.[37]

However, the durations and amplitudes of successive cycles certainly do not fall into convenient historical blocks in the manner in which a proponent of the long-wave thesis like Mandel would have it. As Friend and Metcalf put it, there is a certain 'unreal symmetry' about the way in which Mandel generalises some of the alleged characteristics of the long waves.[38] It is too great a gener- alisation to say that all cycles within the expansionary waves entail long, intense booms and short, less-marked downturns or that cycles in the contractive periods have hesitant upturns and more durable, intense slumps. Empirical evidence suggests that each cycle has its own distinctive structure and character which cannot be simply subsumed within epoch-spanning general patterns of fluctuation.[39]

This is not to say that the short-term cycles are unrelated one to another. While reflecting the influence of particular causal factors each cycle takes place within the context of broad changes in economic structures which both generate the potential for insta- bility in the first place and to a large extent determine the historical form of that instability if not its precise conjunctural character.

2. *Cyclical Metamorphoses: Decisive and Indecisive Crises*

The last statement brings us back to the discussion of historical transformations in the internal crisis tendencies of capital accumulation. The evolution of the social structural framework for accumulation imposes certain limits and possibilities for capitalist development. It is only by confronting those limitations at the point of crisis that accumulation breaks down obstacles to its development, opening up fresh possibilities and simultaneously establishing a new social structure of limitations.

By 'point of crisis' is meant the downward phase of the business cycle. Historical transformations in capitalism's underlying crisis tendencies have involved what Makoto Itoh calls 'metamorphoses' of the capitalist business cycle.[40] It is through incremental changes in the form and causes of the short-term cyclical fluctuations that the longer-term and more far-reaching cumulative transformations are achieved. But the process of transformation is not simply one of continuous or steady evolutions. Rather, it involves an uneven course of fits and starts in which some industrial cycles are of qualitatively greater significance than others. Most cyclical crises are of a relatively *indecisive* nature, serving only to reproduce the underlying crisis tendencies of the preceding period. But a few crises are of a much more *decisive* significance, marking the arrival of a qualitatively new period of cyclical fluctuations involving fresh forms of crisis tendencies in accumulation. It is in this sense that I believe it is possible to refer to long waves and turning-points in the historical development of capitalism's cyclical course.

In Itoh's view the tendency towards periodic phases of over-accumulation of industrial fixed capital was the basic cause of economic fluctuations from the major crisis of 1825 to the crisis of 1874. The capitalist business cycle during this period was pre-eminently an industrial (mining, manufacturing and construction) cycle of accumulation, over-accumulation, physical destruction and renewal of capitalism's productive forces. Cycles in the financial sphere were organically linked to the industrial fluctuations. From the last quarter of the nineteenth century, however, the financial sector became increasingly separated from industry and took on a relatively autonomous cyclical dynamic. The cycle of accumulation ceased to be regulated internally through the periodic destruction or depreciation of excess productive capital and financial surpluses. The tendency towards over-accumulation was relieved externally through the imperialist export of surpluses. Industrial over-accumulation, the basic origin of capitalist instability, was supplemented by under-consumption tendencies and the susceptibility of the economic cycle to financial shocks. All these tendencies combined after the First World War to bring about the acute cyclical troughs of the interwar depression, beginning with the industrial crisis of 1921 followed by the financial crash of 1929.

The relative stability of Western capitalist development after 1945 contrasted markedy with the fluctuations of earlier periods. But this relative stability was achieved at the expense of increasing state expenditures which, in combination with other factors, ultimately led to what Itoh calls the 'inflational crisis of world capitalism' during the 1970s.[41] Since the international recession of 1974–5, and especially since the sharp slump beginning in 1979, the symptoms of prolonged economic depression have become only too familiar with relatively low levels of industrial output, periodic financial crises, the reappearance of mass unemployment and the continuing threat of entrenched inflationary pressures. Whether future economic historians will interpret the 1979–81 slump as the decisive crisis which swept away the preceding order, or as merely the forerunner to an even deeper international slump, remains to be seen.[42]

Conclusion

The last two chapters have suggested that the theory of long waves can be developed into a historical framework for economic and social analysis by weaving together perspectives of the course of the long waves, the overall historical periods of capitalist development, the short-term cycles which occur within each wave and the evolution of the labour process which marks each phase of industrial and technological transformation. The development of industrial capitalism can be divided into three historical periods. These are the period of competitive capitalism, consisting of two long waves from the late eighteenth to the late nineteenth century; the imperialist long wave from the late nineteenth century to the Second World War; and the post-war long wave of late capitalism.

Business cycles during competitive capitalism took the form of a fairly regular cycle of industrial boom and slump. The increasing relative autonomy of financial fluctuations from the industrial cycle after the 1850s led to speculative manias and crashes which ushered in the imperialist era. Business cycles during late capitalism have, the most recent recession excepted, hitherto been characterised by relatively less severe downturns coupled with inflationary pressures.

Cyclical crises during each wave are indecisive in the sense that they are of insufficient impact to sweep away social, economic and political obstacles to capitalist regeneration. The upward turning-points of the long waves presume a decisive crisis which has the function of transforming the social and economic structure, preparing the path for a fresh and durable phase of renewed economic expansion. These decisive crises involve social upheavals hinging upon the transformation of the capitalist labour process.

The two long waves of competitive capitalism were marked initially by the appearance of the manufacturing system of production, involving the growth of the industrial working class, and subsequently by the rise of machinofacture which entailed the increasing subordination of the workforce to machine-regulated production through an intensive division of labour. The imperialist long wave witnessed the origins of scientific management and Fordism involving the increasing routinisation of assembly-line production and the beginnings of a mass-consumerist capitalism. These norms of capitalist social relationships were consolidated during the post-war period, marking the achievement of a regime of intensive accumulation. A simple guide to the historical inter-relationship between all these different features of the long waves is shown in Figure 3.1.

In my view, there is no single panhistorical theory capable of explaining each long wave and the cyclical fluctuations within them. But this does not mean that we are forced to examine each wave or short-term cycle as a unique and individual event. I would not agree with Aldcroft and Richardson's view of British economic fluctuations between 1870 and 1939 that: 'Changes in the relative influence of the main causal factors over time and the obvious irregularity of shocks of quite different magnitude suggests that the remarkable constancy in periodicity and amplitude of British business cycles over this period was largely accidental.'[43] I have

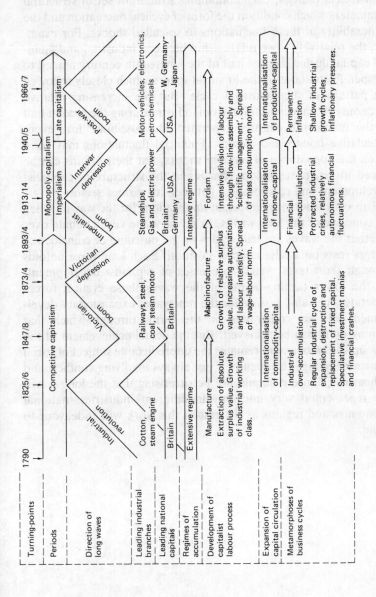

FIGURE 3.1 *Schematic Representation of the Major Features of the Long Waves and Their Historical Sequence*

argued that industrial capitalism has developed through a number of historical periods, each containing a different set of structural parameters which condition the form of cyclical fluctuation and the vulnerability of these fluctuations to so-called shocks. For example, the relatively close relationship between industrial and financial capital during the first half of the nineteenth century tended to dampen fluctuations in the financial sphere which closely followed the pattern of the industrial cycle. But the increasing relative autonomy of financial capital from industry during the second half of the nineteenth century generated the possibility for severe speculative booms and slumps. Financial fluctuations may have taken the appearance of random shocks, but their origins can be traced to far from random changes in the structure of capitalist development and relationships between its various sectors.

This conclusion has important implications for the way in which we conceive of the long waves. In my view the vexed debate over whether the waves are true cycles or the outcome of coincidental factors rests on a false counter-position. Each long wave unfolds through short-term cyclical processes of capitalist development. At the lower turning-points of the waves these cyclical forces generate a certain *pressure* for the renewal of expansionary development and set constraints on the forms through which that turning-point can be achieved. But the actual achievement of the new upward movement remains the unpredictable subject of social structural change, frequently if not always involving conflicts and upheavals. Hence it should not be surprising that the long waves are represented very unevenly in different industries, national economies and regions as the rest of this work will endeavour to show.

Part II
Long Waves of Regional Development in Great Britain: A Description of the Pattern

4
Regional Industrial and Employment Change, 1841-1971

Introduction

The remainder of this work examines the British experience of uneven regional development since the Industrial Revolution in the light of the perspective on the long waves of capitalist development presented in Part One. Later chapters provide a somewhat fragmented historical account and analysis of uneven regional development over the course of the long waves, focusing upon the major features of each historical period. Chapter 4 provides an empirical background to the later analysis by providing a more unified account of the changing pattern of uneven regional development in Britain across the historical long waves.

While the main focus of this chapter is empirical in nature, this is allied to two more analytical objectives. These are, first, to demonstrate that there is some empirical basis for identifying long waves in *industrial* activity and that the long waves are not confined merely to commodity price data; and, second, to show that there is an important *regional dimension* to the long waves of industrial change and development deserving of further analysis.

I Analysing the Patterns

As discussed in Part One of this work the statistical evidence for long waves has been intensively investigated at the national and international scales. At the subnational or regional scale, in contrast, there have to my knowledge been no attempts to assemble statistical indicators of long waves in economic activity on a systematic and comparable basis. This chapter seeks to initiate the process of filling this deficiency using the only continuous statistical series of economic activity available at the regional and sectoral levels, namely employment data from the decennial Census of Population between 1841 and 1971 recently made more accessible by C. H. Lee's invaluable compilation.[1]

1. *Limitations of the Employment Data*

Lee has recalculated employment data since the 1841 Census on the basis of the modern English, Welsh and Scottish counties or administrative areas constituted on 1 April 1974. The regional data referred to throughout this chapter are for the British economic planning regions as defined on that date and illustrated in Figure 4.1. To minimise problems of sectoral, spatial and temporal comparability over such a long period of time, Lee provides two continuous data series. Series A covers the period 1841–1911, series B the period 1901–71. For the sake of graphical clarity all the figures in this chapter use series A data for the period 1841–1911 and series B for 1921–71 except for Figure 4.7, which shows overlapping data from both series.

Before proceeding it is necessary to add a note on the limitations of the employment data for my purposes. Lee's series cover the period 1841–1971 at ten-year intervals with the exception of 1941 due to the war-time suspension of the Census. They therefore span only the three most recent long waves and do not include the wave represented as the late-eighteenth- and early-nineteenth-century Industrial Revolution. Moreover, the data series do not allow for any precise dating of the turning-points of the long-term movements in employment, showing only the decade during which, say, a particular series switched direction from expansion to contraction rather than the exact year of this change in trend. This provides difficulties in relating the employment series to the long waves which, of course, do not conveniently change direction in the Census years. All the graphs of the employment data in this chapter carry vertical reference lines showing the turning-points of the long waves. For my purposes these lines are located at the Census year *immediately preceeding* the actual turning-points of the long waves given by Mandel's dating.[2] A comparison between the actual turning-points of the long waves and these employment series reference years is provided in Figure 4.2.

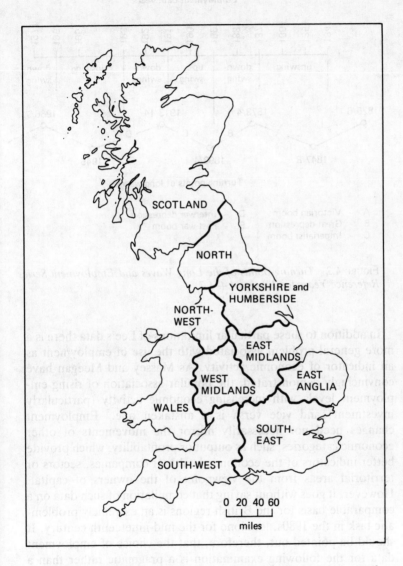

FIGURE 4.1 *Standard British Economic Planning Regions since April 1974*

SOURCE Based on Central Statistical Office map.

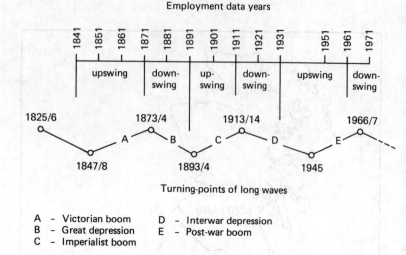

FIGURE 4.2   *Turning-points of the Long Waves and Employment Series Reference Years for Figures 4.4–4.7*

In addition to these particular limitations of Lee's data there is a more general problem associated with the use of employment as an indicator of economic activity. As Massey and Meegan have convincingly demonstrated, the popular association of rising employment levels with increasing economic activity (particularly investment) and vice versa is a mistaken one.[3] Employment changes need not necessarily mirror the movements of other economic categories, such as output or profitability, which provide better indicators of the economic health of companies, sectors or territorial areas from the viewpoint of the owners of capital. However, it goes without saying that compilation of such data on a comparable basis for the British regions is an extremely problematic task in the 1980s, let alone for the mid-nineteenth century. It should be pointed out, therefore, that the choice of employment data for the following examination is a pragmatic rather than a preferred one. Employment data may not be the most suitable for my purposes, but it is the best available.

2. *Sectoral Growth Cycles and Patterns of Employment Change*

As described in Chapter 1, several recent studies of long waves, technological change and employment patterns have related the long waves of economic activity to sectoral growth cycles of development. Van Duijn, for example, argues that the typical pattern of development of an industrial sector takes the form of an S-shaped curve corresponding to the upward and downward movements of the long waves.[4] Following a similar approach, Freeman, Clark and Soete suggest that a typical sector-cycle is spread across three long waves of development.[5] These are a 'main carrier' wave in which the sector plays a leading part in generating employment growth sandwiched between the downward phase of a preceding wave, in which the sector experiences its embryonic development, and the upward phase of a subsequent wave where the sector ceases to lead and enters a period of relative decline and job losses.

A stylistic graph of this 'carrier' pattern of sectoral development is shown in Figure 4.3 (a). If the successive leading sectors of a national economy were to conform to this abstract model of development then the long-term picture of sectoral employment change over three long waves might be expected to resemble the stylistic interpretation shown in Figure 4.3 (b). Here each fresh long wave is associated with a new carrier sector, the economic development process following a course of sectoral 'replacement' at the junctions between the long waves.

A glance at the actual pattern of sectoral employment change in a national economy shows that in the British case there has been no such simple replacement process. Figure 4.4 exhibits a much more complex and diverse pattern of employment change than can be schematised in any one abstract model of sectoral development. But the pattern by no means defies interpretation through the long-wave framework. As a descriptive aid I have classified the range of sectoral patterns into four main types. These are illustrated in Figures 4.3 (a)–(f).

(i) The '*carrier*' pattern has been described above where the rapid employment growth of a sector is largely confined to one expansionary wave followed by a phase of rapid decline in the succeeding wave of contraction. Over several

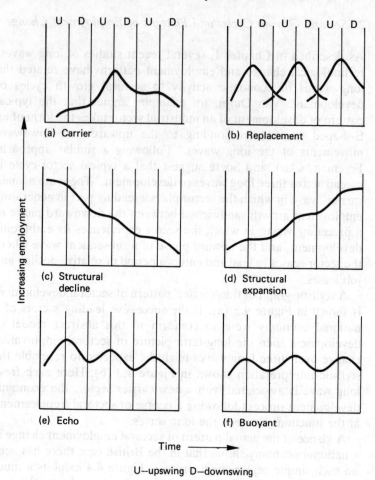

FIGURE 4.3 *Schematic Typology of Sectoral Employment Patterns over three Long Waves of Economic Development*

long waves there may be a succession of leading carrier-type sectors exhibiting an overall process of '*replacement*' of the leading sector.

(ii) The patterns of '*structural decline*' and '*structural expansion*' follow a secular trend spanning the long waves. Such patterns reflect long-term changes in the nature of advanced capitalist economies, notably the decline of agricultural employment and growth of service sectors.

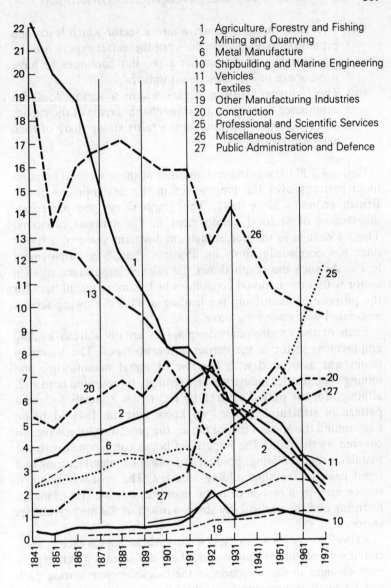

1 Agriculture, Forestry and Fishing
2 Mining and Quarrying
6 Metal Manufacture
10 Shipbuilding and Marine Engineering
11 Vehicles
13 Textiles
19 Other Manufacturing Industries
20 Construction
25 Professional and Scientific Services
26 Miscellaneous Services
27 Public Administration and Defence

FIGURE 4.4 *Great Britain: Percentage Shares of Total National Employment (Males and Females) for Selected Industrial Sectors, 1841–1971*

(iii) The '*echo*' pattern occurs where a sector which leads one expansionary long wave does not thereafter experience the rapid decline of the carrier type, but continues to have some share of the subsequent upturns.

(iv) The '*buoyant*' pattern occurs where a sector does not experience the dramatic swings characteristic of the carrier and echo types, but maintains a fairly stable share of each expansionary wave.

Figure 4.4 illustrates the combination of these sectoral employment patterns over the long waves in the development of the British economy since 1841. The graph shows the *percentage distribution* of sectoral employment in the national economy. Thus, a change in the percentage employment share of a sector does not necessarily imply an absolute change in employment levels. As such the graph shows the *relative* importance of each sector within the national economy which is more useful here for the purpose of identifying the leading or fastest-growing sectors associated with each long wave.

Each of the expansionary long waves entails a fresh leading employment sector of the carrier and echo types. The Victorian boom was associated with the rise of metal manufacture and mining. The textiles industry is also strongly represented here and, although for the period covered by Figure 4.4 it mostly follows a pattern of structural decline, we know that the 1841–61 phase represented the apex of its rise during the preceding long wave not covered by the data. The imperialist boom corresponds with the sustained rise of mining, gradual expansion of manufacturing and rapid peak of the shipbuilding industry. The post-war boom is represented by a revival of metal manufacture, the rise of manufacturing and the particularly strong growth of the motor-vehicles sector.

As well as these carrier-type sectors whose appearance is associated with particular long waves, there are sectors which experience changes in the direction of their development during each wave. Chiefly respresentative of this more buoyant pattern are the miscellaneous services and construction sectors, which maintain a share of each expansionary phase.

Patterns of structural decline and structural expansion are followed by the agriculture and professional services sectors respectively. Agriculture tends to follow the steepest downward path during the depressive phases of the long waves, pausing in its decline during the phases of expansion. The professional services sector, on the other hand, experiences the most rapid expansion during the boom phases, with its course interrupted temporarily in the downward phases of the long waves.

II   Regional Employment Structures, 1841–1971

The complex combination of different sectoral employment patterns at the national level tends to mask the overall ebb and flow of the long waves. While there is a clear association between each wave and the phases of expansion and contraction of employment in different sectors, there is no immediately striking pattern of sectoral replacement in the national data. But, just as different national sectors follow different paths of development, so there are varied sectoral patterns in the regional employment series shown in Figures 4.5 (a)–(j). These series show that the same industries frequently do not follow the same patterns of development in different regions. Moreover, the combination of industries which follow similar patterns within a region reveals much about the nature of that region's industrial development and its relationship to the long waves of development in the national economy.

The regional series, like the national data presented above, are percentage figures showing the trend of each sector relative to employment in the regional economy as a whole. In addition, they represent the *percentage deviation* of the regional share of employment in a sector *above* the national share, providing a crude measure of each regional sector's significance within the national as well as the regional economy.

A comparison of the regional series shows the historical predominance of the north–south division in the regionalisation of the British economy. The northern industrial regions exhibit the most pronounced carrier-type patterns of employment change. The southern regions show more buoyant patterns, relatively immune from the dramatic swings of sectoral fortunes which characterise their northern counterparts.

The *South-east* region exhibits the most prominent combination of buoyant sectoral patterns. While there is some carrier-type

FIGURE 4.5 *Great Britain: Regional Employment in Selected Industrial Sectors, Percentage Points Deviation above the National Employment Share of each Sector, 1841–1971*

Sectors shown are those with a deviation of at least 1 per cent above the national share at any time during this period.

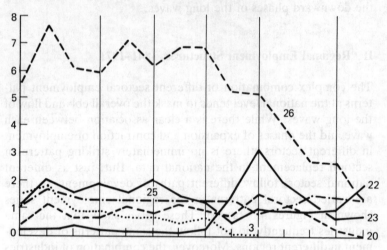

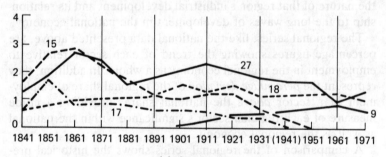

(a) South-east

3	Food, Drink and Tobacco	20	Construction
9	Electrical Engineering	22	Transport and
15	Clothing and Footwear		Communication
17	Timber, Furniture, etc.	23	Distributive Trades
18	Paper, Printing and	25	Professional and
	Publishing		Scientific Services
		26	Miscellaneous Services
		27	Public Administration
			and Defence

FIGURE 4.5 *Great Britain: Regional Employment in Selected Industrial Sectors, Percentage Points Deviation above the National Employment Share of each Sector, 1841–1971*

Sectors shown are those with a deviation of at least 1 per cent above the national share at any time during this period.

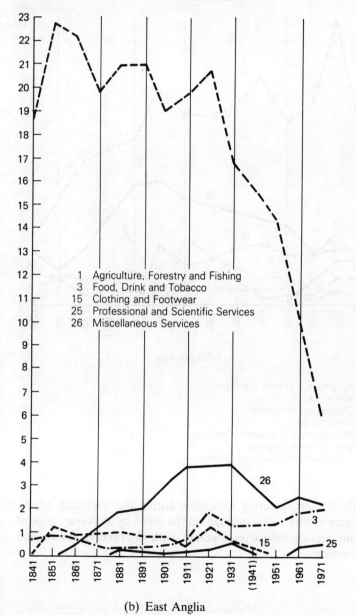

1   Agriculture, Forestry and Fishing
3   Food, Drink and Tobacco
15 Clothing and Footwear
25 Professional and Scientific Services
26 Miscellaneous Services

(b) East Anglia

FIGURE 4.5 *Great Britain: Regional Employment in Selected Industrial Sectors, Percentage Points Deviation above the National Employment Share of each Sector, 1841–1971*

Sectors shown are those with a deviation of at least 1 per cent above the national share at any time during this period.

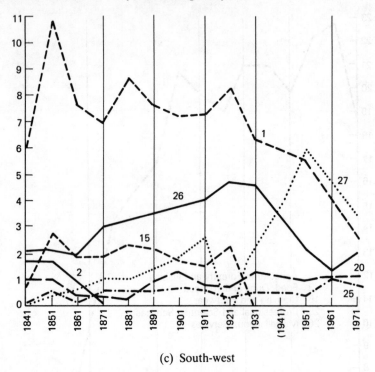

(c) South-west

1   Agriculture, Forestry and Fishing
2   Mining and Quarrying
15 Clothing and Footwear
20 Construction
25 Professional and Scientific Services
26 Miscellaneous Services
27 Public Administration and Defence

growth of manufacturing industries during the Victorian boom, the region is dominated throughout the series by a diverse range of buoyant service industries together with distributive trades and construction.

FIGURE 4.5 *Great Britain: Regional Employment in Selected Industrial Sectors, Percentage Points Deviation above the National Employment Share of each Sector, 1841–1971*

Sectors shown are those with a deviation of at least 1 per cent above the national share at any time during this period.

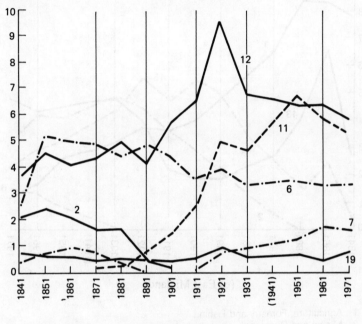

(d) West Midlands

2 Mining and Quarrying
6 Metal Manufacture
7 Mechanical Engineering
11 Vehicles
12 Metal Goods not elsewhere specified
19 Other Manufacturing Industries

In *East Anglia* and the *south-west*, on the other hand, the miscellaneous services sector follows a carrier pattern which peaks in the interwar years. Both regions remain dominated until quite recently by agriculture which, unlike the pattern of structural

FIGURE 4.5 *Great Britain: Regional Employment in Selected Industrial Sectors, Percentage Points Deviation above the National Employment Share of each Sector, 1841–1971*

Sectors shown are those with a deviation of at least 1 per cent above the national share at any time during this period.

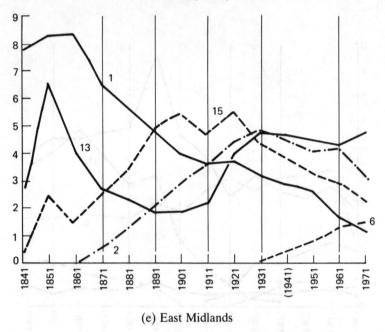

(e) East Midlands

1   Agriculture, Forestry and Fishing
2   Mining and Quarrying
6   Metal Manufacture
13 Textiles
15 Clothing and Footwear

decline evident at the aggregate national scale, follows an echo-type pattern with some significant revitalisation during each upturn until the post-war boom. The main difference between the two agricultural regions lies in the performance of their manufacturing industries. The East Anglian sector follows a buoyant pattern, dwarfed in relative importance by agriculture and services. In the south-west, on the other hand, the mining and manufacturing (clothing and footwear) sectors in the nineteenth century are more significantly represented. They play a carrier-type role in the two expansionary upturns with mining reaching its

Figure 4.5 *Great Britain: Regional Employment in Selected Industrial Sectors, Percentage Points Deviation above the National Employment Share of each Sector, 1841–1971*

Sectors shown are those with a deviation of at least 1 per cent above the national share at any time during this period.

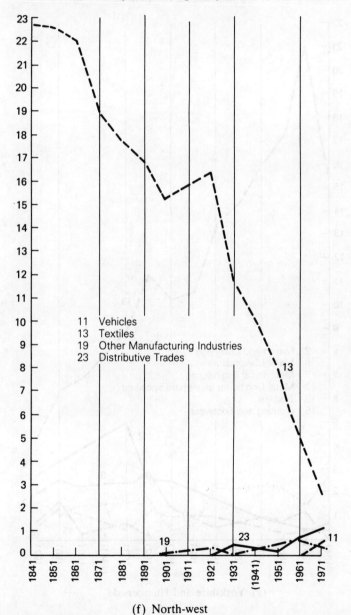

11 Vehicles
13 Textiles
19 Other Manufacturing Industries
23 Distributive Trades

(f) North-west

118

FIGURE 4.5 *Great Britain: Regional Employment in Selected Industrial Sectors, Percentage Points Deviation above the National Employment Share of each Sector, 1841–1971*

Sectors shown are those with a deviation of at least 1 per cent above the national share at any time during this period.

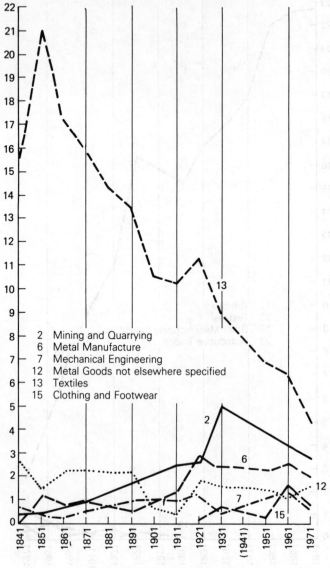

2   Mining and Quarrying
6   Metal Manufacture
7   Mechanical Engineering
12 Metal Goods not elsewhere specified
13 Textiles
15 Clothing and Footwear

(g) Yorkshire and Humberside

FIGURE 4.5 *Great Britain: Regional Employment in Selected Industrial Sectors, Percentage Points Deviation above the National Employment Share of each Sector, 1841–1971*

Sectors shown are those with a deviation of at least 1 per cent above the national share at any time during this period.

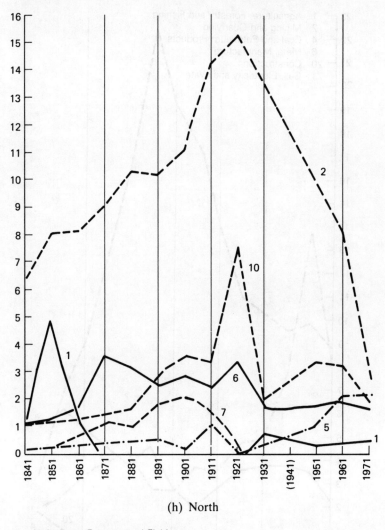

(h) North

1 Agriculture, Forestry and Fishing
2 Mining and Quarrying
5 Chemicals and Allied Industries
6 Metal Manufacture
7 Mechanical Engineering
10 Shipbuilding and Marine Engineering

120

FIGURE 4.5 *Great Britain: Regional Employment in Selected Industrial Sectors, Percentage Points Deviation above the National Employment Share of each Sector, 1841–1971*

Sectors shown are those with a deviation of at least 1 per cent above the national share at any time during this period.

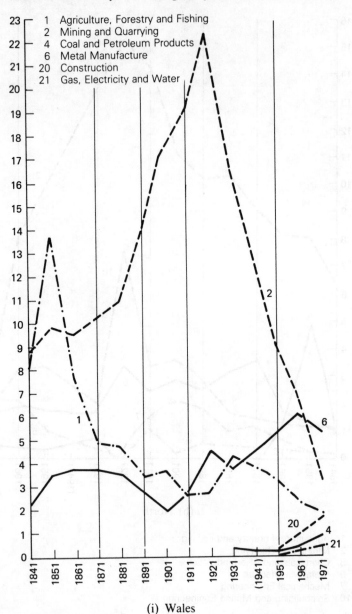

1	Agriculture, Forestry and Fishing
2	Mining and Quarrying
4	Coal and Petroleum Products
6	Metal Manufacture
20	Construction
21	Gas, Electricity and Water

(i) Wales

FIGURE 4.5 *Great Britain: Regional Employment in Selected Industrial Sectors, Percentage Points Deviation above the National Employment Share of each Sector, 1841–1971*

Sectors shown are those with a deviation of at least 1 per cent above the national share at any time during this period.

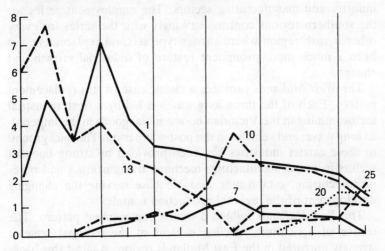

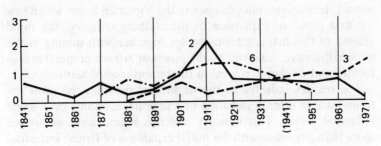

(j) Scotland

1 Agriculture, Forestry and Fishing
2 Mining and Quarrying
3 Food, Drink and Tobacco
6 Metal Manufacture
7 Mechanical Engineering
10 Shipbuilding and Marine Engineering
13 Textiles
20 Construction
25 Professional and Scientific Services

apex in the Victorian boom and the clothing and footwear sector in the interwar depression years.

The southern regions, then, have been historically dependent upon agricultural and service sectors which have remained relatively immune from the fluctuating fortunes evident in the heavy industry and manufacturing sectors. The employment series for the southern regions contrast strikingly with the series for every other British region where carrier-type sectoral replacement has been a much more prominent feature of industrial growth and change.

The *West Midlands* provides a classic case of this replacement pattern. Each of the three long waves is led by a fresh industrial sector: mining in the Victorian boom; metal goods in the imperialist long wave; and vehicles in the post-war period. The background to these carrier industries has been provided by strong buoyant sectors in metal manufacture, mechanical engineering and other manufacturing, establishing a stable base serving the changing development of the regional production complex.

The *East Midlands* follows a similar replacement pattern. The course of agricultural decline evident at the national scale is strongly mirrored in the East Midlands region. Against this background each long wave sees the expansion of fresh industrial sectors, textiles reaching its apex in the Victorian boom which saw the first phase of expansion of the clothing industry, the rapid growth of this manufacturing sector together with mining in the imperialist wave, followed by the post-war growth of metal manufacture and a relative revival in the importance of textiles.

The textiles industry of the *north-west* provides the most extreme case of utter domination of a regional economy by a single industrial sector. This industry and this region were associated more than any other with the initial expansion of British industrial capitalism in the Industrial Revolution of the 1790–1847 long wave. By the second wave of the Victorian boom the north-west textiles industry had reached the high-point of its relative growth, although textiles employment in the region continued to expand in absolute terms and maintained its dominance within the regional economy. It was not until the imperialist boom that employment in other manufacturing industries experienced levels of growth above the national average and not until the most recent expansionary wave that manufacturing industries, notably the distributive and vehicles sectors, have challenged the historical predominance of textiles.

Yorkshire and Humberside is another region where levels of growth in textiles during the Industrial Revolution were such that this industry continued to dominate the regional economy during the ensuing phases of the region's development. But, unlike the north-west, the relative decline of the textiles sector was accompanied by the expansion of a buoyant heavy industrial base in mining, metal manufacture, metal goods and mechanical engineering during the Victorian and imperialist booms. More recently the relative decline of heavy industry has coincided with the growth of light manufacturing in the clothing and footwear trades.

The *north* provides a classic picture of an industrial 'problem' region whose industrial employment patterns correspond to a carrier-type course, but which are largely carried by a single long wave. Unlike the industrial regions of the Midlands, there is no replacement of leading sectors over a succession of waves, but rather a synchronisation of the expansionary and contractive phases of development in the dominant industries. The agricultural employment rate quickly fell below the national average in the 1850s and 1860s which coincided with a rapid growth of mining, supplemented by shipbuilding and mechanical engineering in the imperialist long wave. The interwar depression witnessed the collapse of these sectors. Only the metal manufacturing industry maintained a relatively buoyant course. The post-war period has seen the expansion of a fresh carrier sector in the chemicals industry, laid on foundations established in the early twentieth century. But indicative of the decline of the traditional industries since the 1920s is the re-emergence of agriculture's share of the regional workforce at a level above the national average.

Wales and *Scotland* are spatially peripheral regions where large expanses of relatively under-developed agricultural production coexist with concentrated industrial centres. While agricultural employment has remained relatively buoyant, unlike the southern English agricultural regions Scotland and Wales have also experienced significant industrial development of the carrier type. In the case of Wales, industrial employment has been dominated until recently by mining. This expanded dramatically in the Victorian and imperialist booms until the interwar depression after which its collapse has been equally striking. The metal manufacturing industry has been more buoyant, growing in importance relative to mining during each of the three expansionary waves. Most recently the decline of these traditional sectors has been accompanied by the growth of a more diverse industrial base. Construction, coal and petroleum products, gas, electricity and water have all exhibited above national average growth rates.

Diversity has been a characteristic of the Scottish employment structure for much longer than that of Wales. For the major part of the nineteenth century the Scottish economy, like the Welsh, was dominated by its traditional industries of agriculture and textiles, although this dominance was much less so than for the Welsh agricultural and mining sectors. The Victorian boom witnessed the first expansionary phases of employment in mining and shipbuilding which, together with metal manufacture and mechanical engineering, grew rapidly during the imperialist wave. The decline of these sectors in the post-war period has been accompanied, like the Welsh experience, by the growth of a diverse range of sectors, including light manufacturing (food, drink and tobacco), construction, and a recent pronounced expansion of professional and scientific services.

III   The Patterns of Regional Employment Change as a Whole: Regional Employment Activity Rates, 1841–1971

The above examination of sectoral movements in employment at the regional level reveals an extremely complex process of industrial change with each long wave involving a combination of different sectors in various phases of expansion and decline. These series illustrate the uneven nature of the long waves in the wide variety of different regional and sectoral movements. But the aggregate impact of these sectoral patterns on regional employment movements as a whole reveals the striking unity of each long wave. Figure 4.6 shows regional employment activity rates between 1841 and 1971 calculated from Lee's Census data. These represent the ratio of employees in employment to population in each region.[6]

There are a number of problems inherent to the nineteenth-century Census data which affect the calculation of activity rates.[7] Until 1871 the retired population were treated as active and categorised by their previous employment. From 1881 onwards the retired were returned as non-active. From 1871 onwards all children under ten were classified as unoccupied and the size of this group thence varied with the school-leaving age. In the 1891 Census year, which Lee calls 'perhaps the most eccentric of censuses',[8] housewives were returned as employed in domestic service.

All these problems provide difficulties in the interpretation of long-term activity-rate series. 'The overall figures as well as those for individual industrial orders', Lee notes, 'must be treated with great caution.'[9] Specifically we should expect to find:

(i)   a break in the series between 1871 and 1881 with an exaggerated fall in activity rates;

(ii)   an inflated rise in female activity rates for 1891;

(iii)   a secular fall in activity rates over the series with the progressive exclusion of various categories of the population from the 'active' range.

Certainly it would be dangerous to approach the data 'blind' and seek to derive explanations from the statistical series alone. However, in the light of the long-wave hypothesis I believe that the statistical series provide useful insights on the phases of regional development in the British economy.

In the first long wave of the Victorian boom the highest activity rates were found in the textile regions of the north-west, East Midlands and Yorkshire & Humberside, reflecting the very high level of involvement of women in both cotton and wool production. The rise in regional activity rates during the imperialist boom was generally not as high as for the previous expansionary wave. While the textile regions maintained their positions, in the other industrial regions the nature of the boom in heavy industries with low female involvement accounts for this smaller rise. Until the 1911 data-year all the regional series synchronise closely in their movements. But during the interwar depression the division between north and south emerged strongly, the southern regions reaching the trough and expanding again before the northern regions. Surprisingly Scotland experienced rising activity rates during the depression, perhaps explained by out-migration tending to reduce both unemployment and the size of the dependent

FIGURE 4.6   *Great Britain: Regional Percentage Employment Activity Rates, 1841–1971*

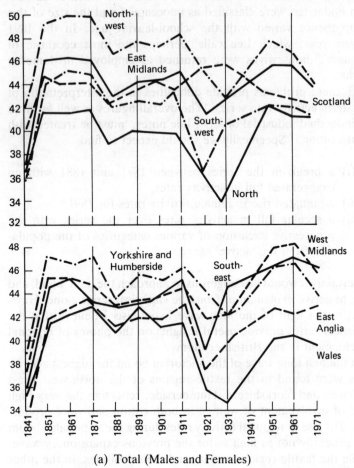

(a) Total (Males and Females)

population (families of the unemployed).[10] During the post-war boom the old textile regions were surpassed for the first time by the 'congested' regions of the West Midlands and south-east. Since 1961, activity rates have fallen for almost every region.

The breakdown of the activity rate for total employment into its male and female components indicates markedly different patterns. The male rate shows comparatively little variance between regions for the whole period with the exception of the interwar

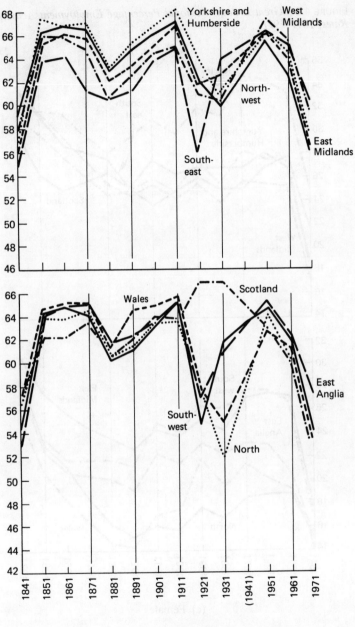

(b) Males

FIGURE 4.6 *Great Britain: Regional Percentage Employment Activity Rates, 1841–1971*

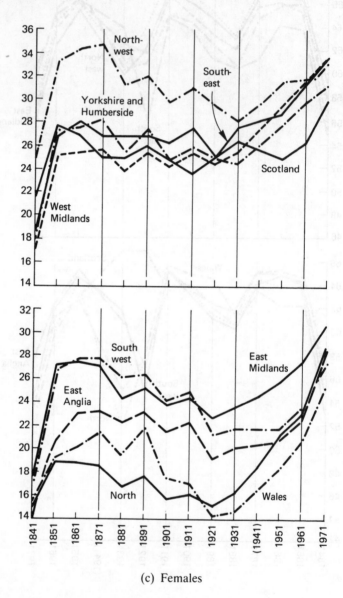

(c) Females

years when the north–south division is more pronounced than for the total series. The movements of all three long waves are very clearly illustrated by the male series, the imperialist boom showing a much more pronounced take-up of male employment than in the total series.

In contrast until the most recent period the female activity rates show a much higher interregional variation than the male. While the female rates are always lower than the male series they display a sharp rise in the Victorian boom followed by a period of fluctuating decline until the interwar depression with only a very minor representation of the imperialist upswing. The latter is partly explained by the eccentricities of the 1891 Census (noted above) and partly by the male employment-oriented nature of the heavy industries which led the imperialist boom. It is only during the post-war boom that female activity rates have risen to the levels achieved during the Victorian boom with an especially strong increase in the south-east and Midlands. These increases have been maintained in the most recent phase with no parallel of the sharp fall in activity rates suffered by the male series after 1961.

IV Employment Change and Regional Inequalities

Section III has shown that changes in each region's employment activity rates have moved in accordance with each long wave of economic development. This section examines the differences between the regional activity rates and the variation of these inequalities with the long waves.

Figure 4.7 shows two measures of regional disparities in the total, male and female employment activity-rate series presented above in Figure 4.6. The *standard deviation* provides a simple statistical measure of the degree of dispersion of the regional figures around the national average for each data year. *Williamson's 'index of regional inequality'*, which I have computed following Williamson's methodology, provides an aggregate figure for each region's deviation from the national activity rate weighted by each region's share of the national population.[11] Disparities between the two series reflect this difference in emphasis where the former statistic takes no account of each region's relative significance within the nation as a whole while the latter adjusts

FIGURE 4.7   *Great Britain: Measures of Regional Inequality in Employment Activity Rates, 1841–1971*

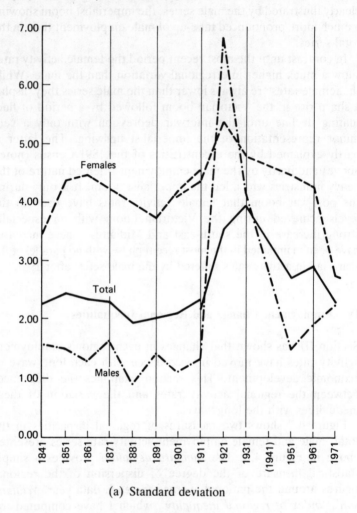

(a) Standard deviation

each regional figure's impact on the aggregate index in accordance with its relative significance measured by population size.

The series demonstrate a number of general points. First, there has been no secular tendency for regional inequalities to fall over the period shown. Interregional disparities in female activity rates have fallen considerably in the post-war period, but inequalities

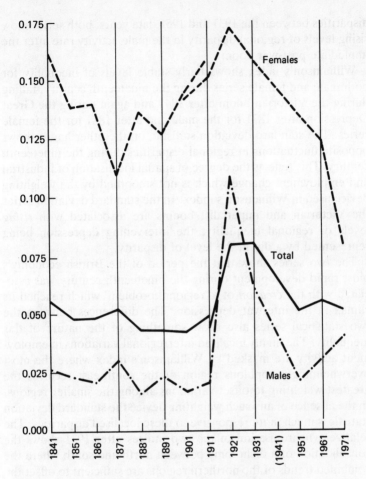

(b) Williamson's Index of Regional Inequality

for the male series were as high in 1971 as they had been during the nineteenth century.

Second, there is no necessary correspondence between falling regional inequalities and high rates of national economic growth. The literature of regional economics often associates 'regional problems' with falling rates of national economic activity, mostly drawn from the experience of the interwar depression which stands out in the two measures here as an unparalleled peak in regional inequalities. But while there was a marked fall in regional disparities between the 1931 and 1951 data years, both series show rising levels of regional disparity in the male activity rate after the immediate post-war boom.

Williamson's index shows fairly stable levels of inequality for both male and female series during the nineteenth century, falling during the Victorian boom after 1841 and again during the Great Depression after 1871 for the male and after 1881 for the female series. The standard deviation statistic, on the other hand, shows opposite fluctuations in regional disparities during the nineteenth century. This reflects the degree of spatial localisation of industrial and employment change which is not smoothed by the weighting device used in Williamson's index. In the standard deviation series the Victorian and imperialist booms are associated with *rising* levels of regional inequality, the intervening depression being represented by a dip in the level of disparity.

The two series show that the period of the British economy's most rapid development during the nineteenth century was associated with the *creation* of a 'regional problem' which reached its climax in the interwar depression. The differences between the two statistical series also show something of the nature of this inequality. The highly localised interregional variations in employment activity are masked by Williamson's index where the most overwhelmingly populous region of the south-east receives the greatest weighting to offset variations among the smaller regions. In the absence of any such weighting device the standard deviation statistic is much more responsive to these localised disparities. The relative synchronisation of the two indices after 1931 shows the consolidation of a dichotomy between north and south where the combined trends of the northern regions are sufficient to offset the influence of the southern regions in the Williamson's index series.

Intensive and extensive phases in the utilisation of the labour force
In a much more detailed and extensive survey of historical trends in regional inequalities in his native Italy, Bernardo Secchi calculated Williamson's index of regional inequality for a range of economic indicators.[12] Secchi found a correlation between rising inequalities and phases of upturn in the Italian business cycle and between falling inequalities and phases of national economic downturn. He called these movements phases of 'extensive' and 'intensive' utilisation of the labour force. The *extensive phases*

were associated with rising national employment but rising inequalities due to the spatial localisation of the leading industrial sectors during the boom. The *intensive phases* were characterised by falling national employment and a reduction in regional differentials with the relative decline of the leading sectors in the most prosperous northern regions, expelling workers from production and reducing indicators of economic activity closer to the levels of the most underdeveloped southern regions. Secchi believes that his results may be applicable beyond the Italian case:

> I think the Italian example could perhaps be adopted to some other countries, perhaps during particular phases of their economic development.
> I believe the Italian example may be characteristic of countries without important raw materials, in which a modern sector (technically advanced) with a labour force representing a sufficiently modest part of the total employed workforce . . . coexists with backward sectors employing, in contrast, a very large part of the labour force, and where the excess of supply over demand for any type of labour is large (that is, overpopulated countries). All three conditions seem to me to be important.[13]

The British experience during the nineteenth century by no means fits all Secchi's conditions. But it does seem to me to provide an illustration of the relationship, identified by Secchi, between rising spatial inequalities and the existence of highly regionalised advanced and backward sectors of production. This relationship is made more complex than the Italian case due to the division in Britain, not simply between an industrial north and agricultural south, but between quite different patterns of development between the industrial regions themselves. The spatial diversification of British industry after the interwar depression has broken this historical relationship while it remains as strong as ever in the Italian case where the north–south split continues to dominate the development of the national economy.

The applicability of Secchi's framework to the British case does not end with the empirical similarity between the Italian and nineteenth-century British experiences. The intensive and extensive phases in the utilisation of the British workforce indicate the fundamental importance of the capitalist labour process as the hub of the historical pattern of industrial transformation. The latter, I have repeatedly stressed, is not simply a process of technological and sectoral change in accordance with some predetermined logic of capital accumulation. It is a process of class restructuring involving the continual reconstitution of capitalist social relations at the points of production and *reproduction*.

The importance of the latter is borne out especially strongly in the employment activity-rate series for female labour. Accounts of Britain's industrial and regional development are nearly always couched in terms of male employment in industrial production. The evolving role of women's labour is usually confined to the attention of social historians as though this were somehow separate and distinct from the supposedly more immediate concern with male labour in industry. In this present work I cannot pretend to have set any alternative example. But it is poignant to note that in the employment activity-rate series, shown in Figure 4.6, the male pattern shows a generally lower level of regional disparity than the female pattern which displays the most marked regional inequalities and makes the major contribution to the overall levels of inequality in the series for total employment (see Figure 4.7).

Changes in the regional pattern of female employment activity rates provide as important an indication as the male series of the changes in the capitalist labour process which accompanied each long wave. During the Victorian boom it was the textile regions of the north-west, Yorkshire and the East Midlands which exhibited the highest activity rates. It was the north-west more than any other region which pioneered the machinofacture process of production, drawing all categories of male and female labour from domestic work into the formal wage-relation of subordination of wage labour to capital at the workplace. In the imperialist boom the universal fall in female activity rates was most extreme in Wales and the north. These regions lacked the textiles sector which partially protected female employment in Scotland while experiencing high growth rates in male-orientated heavy industry. Elements of these two phases in the utilisation of the labour force remain evident in the most recent period, while the generalised spread of women's employment in light manufacturing and services, particularly in the south-east and West Midlands, has led to a renewed rise in female activity rates and a reduction in the level of interregional disparity.

Conclusion

The long waves of industrial transformation are not strikingly apparent for employment change at the national level. While there is some evidence of what I have called carrier/replacement-type patterns among heavy industries and manufacturing sectors, these are swamped by the processes of structural change in agriculture and services and by the more buoyant patterns of some sectors which have a share in each long wave of development.

The association between changes in industrial structure and the long waves of economic activity is much stronger at the regional scale where the localised manifestations of industrial change in regional employment structures are reflected in quite distinct patterns of regional development. Some regions are as marked by their relative immunity from the fluctuations of the long waves as are others which have experienced dramatic swings in their industrial structures, corresponding with the ebb and flow of the historical waves.

The sectoral patterns of employment change reveal different relationships of different industries to the movements of the long waves. Some sectors exhibit what I refer to as a 'carrier pattern' where rapid growth in an upward wave is succeeded by equally sharp contraction in the downward movement. Other echo sectors continue to enjoy renewed, but progressively weaker, expansion in the long waves following their initial rise. Some sectors follow a buoyant pattern, possessing some share of growth during each wave of development. Others show patterns of structural expansion, involving secular growth which is temporarily halted in the downward waves, or of structural contraction where secular decline pauses briefly in the upward waves.

These patterns of sectoral employment change are unevenly represented in the British regions. The regions of southern England generally exhibit service and manufacturing sectors of a buoyant nature. The midland regions enjoy a succession of carrier sectors which replace each other as the leading regional industry across each long wave. Scotland, Wales and the northern regions of England suffer a historical pattern where the carrier-type growth of their leading sectors is confined to a single wave of development.

The aggregate regional employment activity rates show patterns of rise and fall which follow the movements of the long waves. There has been no secular tendency for regional inequalities in these activity rates to fall. Rather, regional disparities have fluctuated with the shifts in the direction of the long waves.

Part III
Nineteenth-century Long Waves of Regional Development

Part III
Nineteenth-century Long Waves of
Regional Development

5
From Industrial Revolution to Imperialist Workshop: Contrasting Regional Experiences

Introduction

Chapter 5 examines the major features of British capitalism's development during the nineteenth century from industrial pioneer to imperialist 'workshop of the world', focusing on the role played by regional economic and social differences within the national pattern. This chapter provides further evidence of the historical changes and turning-points which marked the development of the national economy. At the same time it is argued that the national pattern was not homogenously reflected in all industries in all parts of the country. There were important social and economic differences between the British regions which are indispensable to an understanding of the national process of development.

The great industrial and technological changes during this period can be more fundamentally analysed as processes of social restructuring. While factors such as entrepreneurship, the availability of capital and physical locational factors like the distribution of raw materials and ease of transportation played an important role in different regional experiences, such elements of industrialisation were brought into effect by underlying processes of social transformation. The rise of industrial manufacturing involved the creation of a wage-dependent working class and relative decline of agricultural labour. This did not occur spontaneously but was more easily achieved in some regions than others. The creation of an urban working class brought the new middle-class owners of capital into conflict, not only with the working class itself, but also with the older land-owning class of merchant capitalists and financiers. The division between provincial industry and metropolitan commercial and financial interests remains one of the most enduring characteristics of British capitalism. It has played a major part in shaping both the internal contrasts between the British regions' experiences of economic development and in the external relationship between British capitalism and the world economy.

I   The Industrial Revolution and the Rise of Manufacturing

Economic historians have hotly debated the question of why the Industrial Revolution occurred in Britain rather than elsewhere and in the late eighteenth and early nineteenth centuries rather than sooner or later. The issue of why (or indeed whether) this Revolution was largely led by one industry, cotton textiles, mainly located in one area of one region, north-east Lancashire in the north-west region, is similarly controversial.

1. *Lancashire Cotton and the Industrial Revolution*

Theses advanced to explain Britain's Industrial Revolution include the rise in population and consequent expanded demand, the scientific and technological advances of the period and the availability of investment funds. The population-rise thesis, following Gilboy's influential study, has often been proposed as at least part of the explanation.[1] But, as Hobsbawm notes, the rapid rise in population *coincided* with and did not precede the increasing pace of industrialisation, casting doubt on the causal significance of this factor.[2] Hobsbawm similarly argues that technical innovations such as steam power were widely applied only *after* the initial cotton take-off.[3] To this it can be added that nor did the early innovations in cotton textiles originate in Lancashire. Early technology was imported via London from Holland. In 1750 about 1500 of these 'Dutch engine looms' were concentrated in the Manchester area.[4] The early technical advances in cotton were not especially revolutionary, most being based on simple mechanical applications of existing technology. As late as 1838 one-quarter of British cotton production remained water-powered.[5] With regard to the capital investment thesis Ashton has argued:

If we seek – it would be wrong to do so – for a single reason why the pace of economic development quickened about the middle of the eighteenth century, it is to this we must look. The deep mines, solidly-built factories, well-constructed canals, and substantial houses of the industrial revolution were the products of relatively cheap capital.[6]

But the availability of investment funds, whether plentiful and cheap or otherwise, cannot account for the growth of the Industrial Revolution's leading industry. On the contrary, the role of cotton in the Industrial Revolution can be explained in part by its *low* capital requirements. Hobsbawm notes that cotton machinery:

> could be installed, if need be piecemeal, by small men who started off with a few borrowed pounds, for the men who controlled the great accumulation of eighteenth-century wealth were not greatly inclined to invest large amounts in industry.[7]

By the late eighteenth century Britain's merchants had overcome their rivalry with Holland for commercial dominance and consolidated their trading power through the North American and West Indian plantations and the slave trade. The domestic cotton industry linked up with the pre-existing trade network. By the 1820s and 1830s half the value of all British exports were cotton products and in the mid-1830s raw cotton constituted one-fifth of total net imports.[8]

But the early development of the domestic cotton industry was not fuelled by profits from colonial commerce. Nor did the initial textile development originate in Lancashire. The technique of printing fustians (coarse, diagonal-ribbed cloth) was copied from Indian craftsmen and imported to London before it migrated to the north-west and became the foundation of the Lancashire calico-printing industry. The original role of Lancashire was to weave fustian cloth for London manufacturers.[9] The future dominance of Lancashire lay not in its capital stock, its trade or its technology, but in its social structure – the rise of a distinctive relationship between capitalist and worker upon which the later developments were founded. As Chapman puts it, 'the Lancashire region saw the evolution of a capitalist class and an experienced work-force for nearly two centuries before the first water-powered mills were built in the area'.[10]

In mid-eighteenth-century Lancashire there existed an embryonic capitalist class of merchants in the towns buying up raw cotton from London and distributing it via local agents to a dispersed army of domestic spinners and weavers. These wage-earners frequently owned their own wheels and looms and were partly tied to small agricultural holdings. The textbook cases of Hargreaves's jenny, Arkwright's water-frame and Crompton's mule, which are usually cited as the technical innovations which precipitated the Industrial Revolution, were founded on a pre-existing social relationship in production. This relationship was essential to the transition from dispersed domestic production to concentrated factory manufacture through the real subordination to capitalist control of a labour force already familiar with the experience of formal dependence upon capital for wage-labour.

The decisive factor in Lancashire's predominance was not the character of capital but the conditions of labour. The engagement of women and children in domestic production paved the way for an enormous level of involvement of these sections of the labour force in the factory system. Indicative of this were the extremely high female activity rates in the north-west region which, as shown in Chapter 4, were maintained throughout the nineteenth century. Indeed, this seems to have been a feature, not just of north-west England, but of many textile regions where the initial industrial take-off relied on cheap sources of female and child labour.[11]

2. Rural Resistance and Urban Agitation

This new social relationship between wage-labour and capital did not arise spontaneously. The picture of displaced agricultural workers clamouring for work at factory gates in the rising industrial towns, often conjured up by statistics on the pace of early-nineteenth-century urbanisation and population growth, is a mistaken one. Arkwright turned families away when recruiting for his new Manchester mill in 1783, but elsewhere in the region employers were forced to recruit directly from agriculture and the workhouses.[12] Chapman relates that in Nottingham and Glasgow there was a similar contrast between the experiences of employers in the urban centres and the surrounding agricultural districts.[13] Given the hardships of factory life it is not difficult to see why agricultural workers were reluctant to subject themselves and their families to the new forms of productive organisation.

The resistance of rural labour to proletarianisation and subordination to capital took a variety of regional forms. In 1830–1, the 'Captain Swing' protests of agricultural labourers against low wages and rural unemployment erupted in hundreds of cases of machine-breaking and arson in the southern counties, the south-west and east Midlands. In Lancashire and the north-west there were, in contrast, only six cases of machine-breaking and no reports of incendiarism.[14] The traditional forms of rural protest, such as the East Anglian food riots of 1816, were superseded by these fresh forms of revolt. Old agrarian forms of protest were confined to a few localities, such as the riots against enclosure in Oxfordshire and the food riots in Cornwall. Elsewhere, rural revolt was orientated against the new symbol of class domination – the machine. Rural resistance to urban industrialisation was itself conditioned by the urban social form.

In his study of three nineteenth-century English towns, John Foster poses the question as to why labour militancy was so much more pronounced in the Lancashire town of Oldham than in Northampton and South Shields.[15] All three towns were dependent upon one main industrial sector, respectively cotton textiles, footwear manufacturing and shipbuilding. All three towns exhibited a similar pattern of social deprivation, Oldham perhaps less so than the others. But in Oldham, unlike Northampton and South Shields, working-class experience was pervaded by what Foster calls the 'language' of the factory labour process. This culture of working-class existence, linked with the spread of radical ideas, provided the basis for popular agitation for legal and constitutional change. The movements for franchise reform, the Anti-Corn-Law League and the People's Charter were articulated by the rising industrial middle classes, but backed by the working masses.

3. *Cotton Textiles' Industrial Leadership*

It was Lancashire which provided the locus of industrial, technical, social and political leadership of the Industrial Revolution. But in what sense can the focus of this social transformation, the cotton textiles industry, be called a leading or 'carrier' sector? Discussions of this question have attempted to analyse the impact of the cotton industry on the wider regional and national economy. Among economic historians the notion of key leading sectors propelling the economy into more widespread and prolonged phases of expansion was popularised by W. W. Rostow in his theory of *The Stages of Economic Growth*.[16] As described in Chapter 1, Rostow subsequently related these stages to a theory of long waves in economic development. He identified cotton as the leading industry in the British 'take-off' between 1783 and 1802, evidenced by the dramatic increase in raw cotton imports in the decades 1781–91 (319 per cent) and 1791–1801 (67 per cent).

In opposition to Rostow's interpretation, Deane and Cole calculated that cotton contributed only about 5 per cent of the British national income in 1801 by which time the iron industry provided an equal contribution.[17] On the basis of these estimates, Habakkuk and Deane have concluded that, while the cotton industry served a mass market and possessed the potential for rapid growth, it had a low level of linkage with other domestic industries.[18] Its raw material was imported and the multiplier effects of cotton investments could not have been great.

Chapman, on the other hand, has found flaws in Deane and Cole's estimates which suggest that cotton already contributed 7 per cent of the national income in 1797 at the outset of the take-off period, implying that it must have made a much larger contribution in later years.[19] He accepts that cotton expansion may not have had direct and immediate multiplier effects upon other industries, but argues that longer-term impacts are certainly evident. The cotton industry was the first to introduce standardised machinery in the 1830s. The first railway-line built for both passenger and freight traffic linked Manchester with Liverpool and the major expansion of rail investment owed much to Lancashire capital. Many of the ironfounding, engineering and chemicals firms in Lancashire, the West Riding of Yorkshire and the Glasgow and Nottingham areas were stimulated by demands from the cotton industry during the take-off period. The multi-storey, iron-framed and gas-lit cotton mills had a far-reaching influence on industrial architecture and construction, as did the early factory estates of working-class housing, provoking imitation elsewhere.[20] The growth of the cotton trade also stimulated shipbuilding, which in turn imparted an expansionary impetus to iron and coal.

But the rise of these latter industries belongs to a later period after 1850. Manufacturing industries in the towns, such as clothing, footwear and furniture, continued to rely on the traditional domestic or small workshop systems of production. Before 1850 the nuclei of the future heavy industries continued to apply simple mechanical techniques, including steam power, to small work-shops rather than factory units. Some of these complexes of interrelated workshops were urban in character, such as those of Sheffield and Birmingham, while others, such as the Black Coun-try villages, remained largely rural. Some were based on tra-ditional craft guilds, as in the Sheffield cutlery industry. Others were widely fragmented and engaged in barbaric work practices, such as those of the Dudley nail and chain workshops in the Black Country.[21]

Thus, while in popular historiography the period spanning the late eighteenth and early nineteenth centuries is labelled as Britain's Industrial 'Revolution', in fact the revolutionary transfor-mations were quite limited. In 1841 Britain remained a predomi-nantly rural society. Agriculture and the land accounted for 22 per cent of national employment. Of the British regions only the north-west had less than one-tenth of its workforce engaged on the land while over one-third of its employment was in textiles.[22] Elsewhere, Scotland, the East Midlands and Yorkshire & Hum-berside possessed significant proportions of textile employment while Wales had one-eighth of its labour force in mining. But the dominant pattern of employment distribution lay in the division between rural labour and various categories of service employ-ment in the towns.

A number of factors limited the potential of the cotton industry to lead the national economy into a phase of continuing rapid expansion in the second quarter of the nineteenth century. Among these were external factors connected with the dependence of cotton production upon foreign trade, such as the falling prices after the Napoleonic period, Continental emulation of British industrial performance, and the instigation of tariff barriers which limited the extent of overseas markets. In addition there were difficulties associated with the cotton production process itself. The high productivity of spinning processes relative to weaving led to problems of vertical integration and a consequent tendency towards periodic phases of overproduction. But the fundamental constraint lay in the lack of a mass domestic market and its associated wage-labour and consumption norms – the limitations characteristic of a 'regime of extensive accumulation'.

II From Victorian Boom to Great Depression

The second expansionary long wave in the British economy during the Victorian boom after 1850 owed as much to the changing structure of the world economy as to British capitalism's own internal development. From the 1830s and 1840s trade in commodities and raw materials with new colonial areas of Latin America and India grew in importance relative to the older British trading spheres in Europe, North America and the West Indies.[23]

1. *The Textiles Industry and the Changing Pattern of Overseas Trade*

Expanding world demand and rising prices after 1850 stimulated the expansion of investment and production in British domestic industry. Among economic historians there has been some debate over the relationship of rising prices to British industrial profitability. Some historians, drawing on Hamilton's thesis on the origins of the Industrial Revolution, have argued that wage costs tended to lag behind raw material prices, widening profit margins and leading to accelerated capital formation through the reinvestment of profits.[24] Others have suggested that, while wages lagged behind prices, raw material costs tended to rise faster than the prices of manufactured goods and hence depress, rather than expand, profit levels.[25]

The latter perspective is supported by the case of the cotton industry where material prices constituted a greater proportion of total costs than wages. This was the reverse of the more labour-intensive industries such as engineering, metal manufacture and shipbuilding. The squeeze on cotton profits propelled the industry into a phase of defensive restructuring and reorganisation of production. Lee has shown that before 1850 market uncertainty favoured vertical integration of cotton production in combined spinning and weaving mills.[26] But, thereafter, the growth of the new colonial markets led to greater security, favouring horizontal integration and specialisation.

In woollen textiles raw materials were of similar importance to total production costs as those of cotton. Domestic wool supplies were increasingly overwhelmed by imports. In 1830 wool imports were mainly drawn from Western Europe including 24.6 million pounds weight of wool from Germany and 1.6 million from Spain with Australia supplying only 1.9 million. But, by 1850, imports from Australia had risen to 38 million pounds while German imports had fallen to 9 million and those from Spain were negligible. By 1870 Australia supplied 175.1 million pounds of wool to the British industry, British South Africa provided 32.8 million and South America 12.7 million.[27]

Whereas cotton output was overwhelmingly re-exported, woollen manufacturing largely served the domestic market where it encountered the same problems of uncertainty as had been experienced by cotton in the earlier expansionary long wave. Consequently the reorganisation of the woollen textiles sector after 1850 followed an opposite trend to that of cotton with a decline in specialisation and growth in combined mills.

2. The Growth of Northern Heavy Industry

This relationship between imported raw material prices, final production prices and profitability did not hold for other industrial sectors, which relied on *domestic* sources of iron and coal. Here, the principal pattern of development was one of fluctuating over-capacity with changes in domestic demand, typical of heavy industries in phases of rapid growth. The most extreme amplitude of the industrial production cycle was found in the shipbuilding industry.[28] Until the mid-1860s both steam and sail production exhibited a similar pattern of fluctuation, steam subject to sharper swings than sail output as demand resorted to the older and cheaper sailing vessel during the downward phases of the cycle. But the sectoral patterns diverged after 1866 as steam output met and overtook sailing-ship production.

While the expansion of shipbuilding predates that of the railways by about a quarter-century it was the latter industry which experienced the most dramatic growth rates. The pattern of rail investment was characterised by sharp swings: the mini-mania of the late 1830s, the massive boom of 1845–7 and the smaller boom of 1863–4.[29]

The regional impact of these industrial fluctuations was to transform the pattern of industrial location in Great Britain. Between 1831 and 1871, male employment in shipbuilding tripled from under 20 000 to over 61 000.[30] During this period the centre of the industry shifted from the old wooden sailing shipyards of the south and east to the new steel steamship production sites of the north and west. In 1831 employment along the south coast, the Bristol Channel and the Thames accounted for nearly half the total. The north-eastern rivers from the Tyne to the Humber had nearly as much as the Thames total of 15 per cent but only 8 per cent of shipbuilding employment was located in the north-west, Mersey and Dee, while Scotland possessed 12 per cent of the national total. By 1841, however, the share of the north-eastern rivers surpassed that of the Thames. The former areas employed nearly one-quarter of the national shipbuilding workforce by 1871, compared with 22 per cent in the southern regions. In terms of individual rivers the Thames remained the largest site of ship-building employment until the 1860s when it was replaced by the Clyde, whose share of the national workforce grew from an insignificant 3 per cent in 1831 to 6 per cent in 1851 and 21 per cent by 1871. By that time the distribution of shipbuilding employment had been completely transformed with two-thirds of the total located in the northern regions: 26 per cent in Scotland, 24 per cent in the north-east and 13 per cent in the north-west.

The pattern of locational change in shipbuilding was closely related to that in iron production. In the 1820s the production of pig-iron was dominated by South Wales, Shropshire and the Black Country. But throughout the 1830s and 1840s the dominance of these regions was increasingly challenged by Scotland, which became the leading producer by 1852. Scotland was in turn surpassed in the late 1860s and early 1870s by the north-east and north-west respectively.[31]

The expansion of the railways had a profound effect on the coalfields. The railways provided a growing market for coal, both directly through the demands of railway production and operation themselves, and indirectly by making accessible new territorial markets for coal consumption. But this expansion was not entirely beneficial with respect to the pit-owners. Church notes that 'lower transport costs, brought about by the railways, destroyed those regional monopolies which until the late-1840s had dominated the coal trade and especially the supply of the huge London market'.[32] Taylor expresses this pithily:

> In the mid-nineteenth-century growth of the coal industry the railway had been the industry's essential handmaid. The railway

had been created by coalowners in the north-east to serve their own immediate needs. But, Frankenstein-like, it turned on its creators, first intensifying competition within the north-east itself and then depriving the coalfield of the monopoly it had hitherto enjoyed in supplying coal to the highly prized London market.[33]

The revolution in the means of transportation had the effect of reducing coal prices, opening up new inland coalfields and ending the monopoly of the coastal fields over the southern market. The impact of this locational shift was to accentuate the inter-regional division between the north and east as primary producers of raw materials and capital goods, and the south and west as agricultural producers, service centres and finishing and distribution-points for consumer goods.

3. *Deterrents to Industrialisation in London*

Gareth Stedman Jones has suggested that the effect of the Industrial Revolution on London was, paradoxically, to 'accentuate its pre-industrial characteristics'.[34] After 1850 the high-value/low-bulk commodity trades prospered in London while the low-value/high-bulk industries migrated to the outskirts of the city or to the provinces:

> Throughout the second half of the nineteenth century London remained first and foremost a finishing centre for consumption goods; indeed the decline of her capital goods and semi-finishing industries reinforced this characteristic. These were the industries most suited to London conditions, not only because of market factors, but also because they demanded relatively little space or fixed capital.[35]

Mellor has described the seeming anomaly of London's position: 'the world's largest city . . . capital of the first industrial nation, which was itself largely non-industrialised, and had at its heart the greatest pool of unemployed and underemployed, in that nation'.[36] London remained a complex of small workshops engaged in clothing, furniture, printing, engineering and manufacture of precision equipment. Industrial competition from the north led to the collapse of many of London's traditional industries (such as the Thames shipyards) and the proliferation of small sweatshops with low fixed costs, low wages and employing a high proportion of casual labour.[37] London, centre of the world's greatest empire, was the world's largest slum. Yet in spite of its industrial backwardness, the hegemonic role of London in the national and international economy remained secure. London maintained its position as the nation's first port, major distribution centre, major domestic market and centre of government, administration and financial control of international commerce and empire.

There was a striking contrast between the class structures of London and the northern industrial towns. In the industrial regions there was an obvious dichotomy between the new factory and pit-owners and a proletariat subjected to the structures of factory or colliery discipline. In London the old class of gentry, bankers and merchants remained untouched by, indeed disdainful of, industrial capital. The urban working class remained fragmented and impoverished. London saw no movement towards polarisation between industrial capital and labour so central to the social transformations taking place in the provincial regions.

The reasons for this cannot be found in the simple physical and locational characteristics of the London area. Mellor notes that, while London was remote from the coalfields, it had imported coal from the north-east for over 300 years.[38] Land for factory construction was expensive at the centre of London, but remained cheap at the fringes. London possessed a large consumer market and an extensive reserve of cheap labour together with the advantages of the world's major financial centre. But these latter factors, far from stimulating industrial investment, presented a *deterrent to industrialisation*. London financiers preferred the lucrative overseas markets to more precarious and immobile domestic fixed assets. The availability of a large, cheap labour pool deterred technical advance and labour-saving innovation. The transformation of the former agrarian interests of the landed gentry into financial and commercial concerns coincided with the relative stagnation of agriculture in the Home Counties. But, unlike their northern industrial counterparts, this fraction of the English ruling class offered no solution to the flood of immiserated rural labour to the London districts.

4. *Industrial Change and Economic Fluctuations*

The characteristic pattern of development in the expanding industrial sectors was a phase of manic boom in investment followed by crash. This was most evident in the rail and shipbuilding industries where the boom-crash cycle had feedback effects on the raw material industries of iron and coal. One influence was certainly the fluctuations in demand with the foreign wars in each decade. But these factors tended only to act as triggers upon an inherently unstable system. Industrial fluctuations followed a fairly regular cycle of expansion, over-accumulation and relative contraction, most marked in the heavy industries. One consequence of this instability was the intensified competition which led to the accelerated concentration of capital into fewer and larger enterprises. This feature was particularly prominent in the railways. The annual rail revenue of £19 million in the 1850s rose to £52 million by 1870–5 – double that of coal.[39] By 1875 the capital raised amounted to £630 million, equivalent to an annual rate of £12.5 million, dwarfing the rate of capital formation in cotton, coal, iron and steel. This enormous economic power of railway enterprise was concentrated into the hands of a small number of companies. The investment mania of 1845–7 left (by 1850) a total of 61 per cent of railway capital and 75 per cent of revenue in the hands of just 15 companies. These amounted to a mere 8 per cent of the 180 companies then involved in rail construction and operation. By 1870 the same fifteen companies accounted for only 3.5 per cent of the 430 rail enterprises controlling 80 per cent of total rail capital and 83 per cent of revenue.

Rail investment was significant not just for its size. The massive investment booms played a pronounced counter-cyclical role in the regulation of the national economy. This was indicative of the growing autonomy of banking and credit-capital from industrial capital fluctuations. Speculative investments as a source of release for crises of over-accumulation contributed to the relatively indecisive nature of downturns in the fluctuations of the 1850s. Intense competition and capital concentration reinforced the interregional pattern of industrial location. There were failures of several Midland iron manufacturers during the 1860s in the wake of rail-induced competition from the north-east. These included some notable bankruptcies such as the liquidation of the Derwent Iron

Company in 1864. Competition with the south eliminated the Tyne glass industry, formerly the nation's leading glass-making centre. By the mid-1860s the growth of the northern iron shipbuilding industry posed a serious threat to the southern shipyards. In the 1866 commercial crisis several Thames shipbuilders failed and the Thames industry fell into lasting depression. It was the crisis of 1866 which marked the end of the cyclical dynamism of the preceding expansionary long wave. Church observes:

> changes in the trend of prices, interest rates, net imports of manufactures and industrial productivity suggest that the mid-1860s mark an important economic watershed, the commercial crisis of 1866 ending the cyclical dynamism which was characteristic of mid-Victorian industrial capitalism and arguably essential to the unprecedented levels of economic growth.[40]

Coppock's measures of industrial output and productivity between successive cycles from 1847 onwards, shown in Figure 5.1, confirm this change in the pace of economic development.[41] After the mid-1870s there was no return to the previous levels of growth in production and productivity. For British industry as a whole this period marks the turning-point of cyclical development from an undertone of expansion to one of contraction. But when cotton is excluded from the estimates the downturn can be seen to originate in the earlier crisis of 1866. The evidence is far from clear and there has been some debate over the timing of this turning-point or, indeed, whether there was a swing from growth to depression at all. Coppock presented his evidence as a counter to the argument of Phelps Brown and Handfield-Jones that the Victorian 'climacteric' could be located in the 1890s.[42] In their view the check to expansion occurred at this later date due to the exhaustion of possibilities for further productivity advances in steel and steam technology. Coppock's research dates the climacteric in the mid-1870s with its roots stretching back a decade earlier.

More recently, however, Saul has challenged the whole notion of a late-nineteenth-century climacteric: 'The sooner the "Great Depression" is banished from the literature, the better.'[43] In Saul's view *The Myth of the Great Depression* has arisen from the over-emphasis placed by economic historians on a few exception-

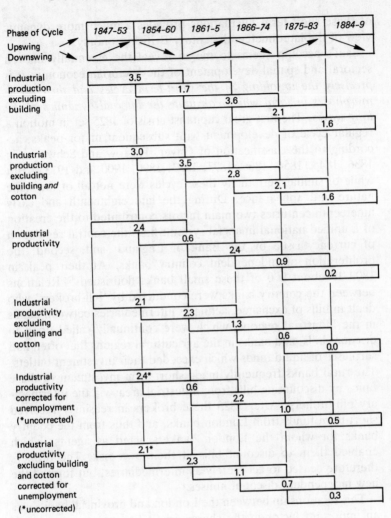

FIGURE 5.1 *Intercyclical Average Annual Growth Rates in British Industrial Production and Productivity, 1847/53–1884/89*

SOURCE Figures from Coppock, 1956, pp. 7–8.

ally high peaks in commodity prices, tending to underestimate the importance of cycles within these peaks which deny the alleged unity of the so-called Great Depression. For Saul an examination of these short-term fluctuations provides a much more dynamic view of the late-nineteenth-century British economy.

Saul's account seems to me to reveal the essentially uneven sectoral and spatial development of the Victorian economy. *It is precisely the unfolding of the short-term cycles and their metamorphoses in form which constitute the internal dynamics of the long waves.* The first great capitalist crisis of 1825 set in motion a regular cycle of development with subsequent major peaks, according to the classification of Gayer, Rostow and Schwartz, in 1836, 1845, 1854, 1866, 1873, 1883, 1890, 1900 and 1913.[44] But while of similar periodicity these cycles were not all of the same nature and appearance. During the late eighteenth and early nineteenth centuries two main factors contributed to the creation of a unified national financial system: first, the central regulation of currency issue by the Bank of England; and, second, the proliferation of independent country banks. At their peak in 1809–10 about 900 of these small banks flourished.[45] Relations between the country banks were conducted by 'bill-brokers' who dealt in bills of exchange, acting as intermediaries between banks in the industrial regions, which were continually called upon to discount bills, and banks in the agricultural regions that often had surpluses of liquid funds which exceeded their investment outlets. The rural banks frequently made short-term investment of these funds by discounting bills from industrial areas via the intermediary bill-brokers. After 1825 these brokers increasingly received short-term funds from London banks, and thus from the country banks for whom the London bankers acted as agents, which enabled them to discount bills at their own risk. The brokers therefore ceased to act merely as intermediaries, but formed the new independent discount houses.

This relationship between the London and provincial banks was an important factor in the characteristic boom–crash pattern of financial fluctuations from 1825 to 1866. In their rush to share in periodic speculative booms the bankers frequently expanded their discounting business beyond their call on liquid reserves. When conditions deteriorated any crisis and 'run' on the banks with a sudden rush to exchange issue notes for cash led to numerous banking failures among both the small banks and their London agents. The speculative mania which ended in the panic and crisis during the winter of 1825–6 was of precisely this nature, leading to the collapse of at least seventy London and country banks.[46] The pattern was repeated throughout the railway era of the Victorian boom with speculative peaks in 1845, 1854 and 1866. But thereafter the structure of each cycle changed. Even Church, who tends to side with Saul in the debate, notes that the 1866 crisis was the last of the manic speculative 'bubbles' which had characterised the previous forty years of development.[47] Moreover, Saul himself observes that before 1873 the British domestic cycle had tended to synchronise with that overseas, but thenceforth this synchronisation was broken.[48]

This seems to me to indicate a quite distinct break in the pattern of British capitalist development. Just as in the expansion of the 1850s and 1860s, when London financiers offered no industrial solution to the decline of agriculture, so in the contraction of the 1870s and 1880s the City provided no financial solution to the problems of heavy industry. They preferred the more lucrative short-term gains of capital investments *abroad* to the long-term, less immediately appreciable benefits of investment in the regeneration of domestic industry. As Cottrell argues:

> The crisis of 1866 not only rent the London money market but also dislocated the capital market. Investors found that the new limited companies, especially the banks and finance companies, had hidden dangers and risks through high share denominations and large uncalled capitals.[49]

The secular rise in the volume of capital exports before 1860 had been largely generated by the demands for foreign railway construction. But the crisis of 1866 precipitated the first of three more generalised upsurges in capital exports to overseas industry, to the colonial economies and to the USA after the Civil War. The first upsurge petered out in the generalised downturn of the industrial economies after 1873. But thereafter the pattern of capital exports exhibited a growing relative autonomy from industrial fluctuations through the unprecedented booms peaking in 1889–90 and 1913.

Among historians who recognise the existence of these 'long swings' in capital exports, there has been some debate over their origins. The 'Atlantic economy' thesis, popularised by Brinley Thomas, explains these swings through fluctuations in the rate of population migration from Europe to the USA.[50] Thomas argues that population movements were accompanied by capital exports to meet fresh investment demands, chiefly for house-building by the construction industry. This set up a counter-cyclical relationship between British creditor/migration-donor and US debtor/migration-receiver.

In an alternative explanation Habakkuk also sees fluctuations in house-building as a major indicator of long swings in international capital flows.[51] But, unlike Thomas, he does not account for these flows by the semi-spontaneous trends of international population migration. Rather he stresses the contribution of fluctuations in the British *domestic* economy, particularly the counter-cyclical relationship between construction and mortgage-lending. This is consistent with my argument that *the divergence of industrial and financial fluctuations can be explained by the changing relationship between their respective capitals.* The relative independence of financial interests from domestic industry meant that, during periods of downturn in the domestic industrial cycle, financial investment could be switched to more profitable outlets, both at home and overseas. The important point here is that the pattern of investment did not originate in some spontaneous swing in demand for funds. It was ultimately conditioned by and responsive to the instability of industrial production.

From a Marxist viewpoint, David Harvey has similarly attempted to explain the long swings (which he confusingly refers to as 'long waves') in urban development as a response on the part of capital to crises of overproduction in the circuit of industrial capital.[52] In what he calls 'switching crises', capitalists periodically redirect surpluses of capital accumulated in industrial production to alternative profitable outlets. While Harvey sees this as a more or less permanent feature of the capital accumulation process, I would argue that its form depends upon a *particular* historical relationship between banking, industry and property. Specifically, it depends upon the fusion of capitals into centralised financial blocs, the phenomenon which Marxists identify with the monopoly capitalist epoch of imperialism.

III   The Imperialist Boom

1. *The Relative Decline of Traditional Industry*

After the depression years of the 1880s production in the staple industries picked up and entered a phase of renewed expansion. Between 1880 and 1900 the value of British exports of iron, steel, coal and machinery doubled to reach £95 million.[53] During the same period, while through sheer size cotton remained as important as these sectors together, its significance in the British export trade declined. The value of cotton exports fell from £105 to £97 million between 1880 and 1890. Yet after this decade, investment in cotton experienced a further marked boom, capital equipment in this industry growing from 44.5 million to 59.3 million spindles and from 616 to 805 thousand power looms between 1890 and 1914.[54] By 1907 coal, textiles, iron and steel together contributed 46 per cent of net industrial output, employed 25 per cent of the working population and accounted for 70 per cent of exports.[55]

But this boom in the traditional industries was largely based upon investment in *old* technology. This period of their greatest expansion coincided with the beginnings of their decline. Iron-ore production, which had fallen dramatically after the mid-1870s, picked up and expanded in the 1890s. But the significance of imported iron and steel products and iron-ore grew rapidly during the boom.[56] In terms of their size the British sectors of heavy industry continued to lead their international competitors. But in terms of technical advance and productivity they fell behind their foreign counterparts, particularly in Germany and the USA.[57]

Explanations for the failure of British industry to modernise during the imperialist boom frequently draw attention to the over-specialisation of the regions in particular industries, the lack of flexibility in both capital and labour deployment and the lack of innovative dynamism among the oldest-established national class of entrepreneurs.[58] But the problem was one of investment and more essentially of profitability, both actual and expected. As Hobsbawm argues, in the face of growing competition from European and North American producers, British investment tended to flow into new colonial territories rather than face competition head-on in existing markets.[59] During the Victorian depression and the subsequent imperialist boom the British economy retreated from industry to its commercial and financial interests where British services in fact aided foreign competitors but made lucrative short-term profits.

2. British Capitalism's Changing International Role

It is perhaps surprising to note that during the whole of the nineteenth century, for most of which British capitalism was the undisputed world industrial leader, at no time did exports of commodities and materials actually exceed imports.[60] Britain's trade deficit, which had been rising slowly since the 1850s, expanded during the Victorian boom, fell gradually during the Great Depression, and expanded again during the imperialist upswing. As the trading deficit rose, income from services and from interests and dividends rose with it. Investment income surpassed service income in the 1890s with the onset of the imperialist boom in capital exports. In the quarter-century from 1890 to 1914 the total credit accumulated abroad equalled that accumulated during the previous century, while in the climactic boom of 1911–13 investment abroad was double that in the domestic economy.[61]

These figures indicate a major shift in the international role of the British economy from mercantile commodity-exporter to capital-exporter and imperialist power. As noted above, this period marked the beginnings of decline in the old export industries and the growth of new consumer sectors, electrical power and engineering. The latter industry was already well-established in the old centres of northern England and Scotland. In the early years of the twentieth century these older engineering centres continued to prosper, serving the heavy industrial and textile sectors. But the further development of heavy engineering was very much dependent upon the demands of the traditional industries. In terms of its later multiplier effects on new industrial sectors, leadership belonged not to the heavy engineering centres of the north, but to the light engineering and metal-based industries of the West Midlands which lay at the heart of the imperialist 'workshop of the world'.

3. *The Rise of West Midlands Industry*

In the northern regions the development of engineering served the wider regional industrial complexes. In the West Midlands, in contrast, these roles were reversed where the wider regional economy was orientated towards the industrial demands of the central city.[62] The growth of Birmingham led to the decline of the crude metal-working trades in the Black Country where production became directed towards the demands of Birmingham manufacturers for raw materials and semi-finished products. As well as being the industrial nucleus of the region, Birmingham provided its financial and commercial focus. During the 1840s and 1850s much of the capital invested in Black Country coal-mining and iron-smelting was provided by Birmingham ironmongers. The boom in railway investment led to the formation of the Birmingham stock exchange and consolidated the city's function as a distribution centre through its geographical position at the heart of the rail network.

However, industrial production in Birmingham remained dominated by a jungle of small trades and workshops. It was not until the 1870s that the factory system became firmly established and skilled labour subordinated to capital in production.[63] Consequently the Birmingham economy remained much more flexible and responsive to the pressures of depression and increasing competition from the economies of the northern industrial regions. The local economy suffered during the depression with the decline of many old-established manufacturing industries such as the wrought-iron, button, nail and glass trades.[64] By the end of the century foreign competition led to the contraction of several other sectors such as tinplate wares, metal bedsteads, saddlery and harness. But many of the old trades were consolidated into new and expanding sectors, notably cycles, electrical engineering and machine tools, which by 1914 had stimulated the growth of further new industries, most importantly motor-vehicles. The rise of these new industries went hand-in-hand with the growth of factory production and the beginnings of Fordist production methods. The new gas engines required a smaller initial outlay than the steam engines for which they were substituted, proving attractive to the small factory owner. This new energy and fixed capital technology facilitated mechanisation and the standardisation of new products and processes in larger productive units.

4. *Regional Industry and Imperialist Finance*

The increasing concentration and centralisation of capital were major features of the imperialist boom. In the banking sphere this process tended to break down interregional divisions in monetary circulation. Between 1891 and 1902 there were 114 amalgamations and the total number of independent banks fell from 168 in 1891 to 66 by 1914.[65] Of these, twenty had more than 100 branches while the Midland, Lloyds and Barclays each had over 500. This concentration of banking capital mostly involved the entry of provincial banks into the London market. One of the two major Birmingham banks, Lloyds (established in 1765), took over two London banks in 1884 and eventually transferred its head office there in 1910. The Midland (established as a joint-stock bank in 1836) moved from Birmingham to London in 1891. But there were also some movements of London-based banks into the provinces, notably the formation of Barclays in 1896.

This centralisation of banking capital accentuated the split between the overseas investments of banking capital and the needs of domestic industry. Industrial capitalists in the provinces became increasingly peripheral to the centralised stock of investment funds and were forced to draw on their own resources. A number of studies have chronicled the evolution of distinct regional capitalist classes in the old industrialised regions.[66] In addition to the growth of the capital controlled by the largest units, leading industrial capitals branched out into new, closely linked activities. In their study of the north-eastern coal combines, Carney, Lewis and Hudson list gas, electricity and water, insurance, investment trusts and banking, wholesaling and retailing, housing trusts, electrical engineering and chemicals, as well as the old coal, iron, steel and shipbuilding sectors, as activities centralised in regional capitalists' hands.[67] This centralisation involved complex chains of overlapping directorships, shareholdings, loans, debentures, rents and royalties, pricing, output and quota arrangements.

Largely indigenous regional capital was the source of even the most advanced new sectors in the most newly-prominent region of the West Midlands. Saul notes that, with one or two exceptions, the rise of the Midlands car industry before 1914 can be traced to the evolution of small capitalist concerns and their predecessors through small family metal-working businesses dating back to the mid-nineteenth century and beyond.[68]

Conclusion

The development of British capitalism from industrial pioneer to imperialist power was punctuated by fluctuating fortunes represented as alternate long waves of expansion and relative stagnation. Within these long waves the dominant direction of development in the national economy was by no means universally the norm in all of the nation's economic, social and spatial components. The rise of some industrial sectors, regional economies and social classes was accompanied by the relative decline of others. Indeed, the processes of development and underdevelopment went hand-in-hand, the one an inevitable concomitant of the other.

The historical process of regional development in nineteenth-century Britain can be divided into three fairly distinct phases corresponding to three long waves of expansion followed by decline. Each of these three phases involved a fresh form of spatial organisation of the British economy in two senses: first, in the sense of the *actual regionalised map* of the accumulation process; and, second, in the *process* of regional development shaping that spatial map.

The clearest manifestation of these phases of regional development is the changing hierarchy of regional production complexes during the course of the century. The first long wave of the Industrial Revolution was heavily associated with the cotton textiles industry of the north-west. The development of this region was mirrored by less spectacular textiles developments elsewhere in Scotland, Yorkshire and the East Midlands, involving the steady growth of urban manufacturing centres and decline of agricultural employment in the surrounding regions. The second wave of the Victorian boom and Great Depression was led by a more diverse combination of heavy industries located around the coalfields of northern England, central Scotland and South Wales. The development of these regional production complexes frequently involved the decline of others, particularly the collapse of some industries such as shipbuilding in the south. This resulted in an enhanced spatial division of production between capital equipment and raw material sectors in the north and the southern service sectors and consumer-goods manufacturing, finishing and distribution industries. In the third wave of the imperialist boom leadership passed to the light engineering, manufacturing and metal trades of the West Midlands and was accompanied by the beginnings of the decline of the northern heavy industries.

This changing hierarchy of leading regional centres of industrial production was closely associated with the evolving role of British capital in the world economy. In the Industrial Revolution the leading sector of the cotton industry linked into the pre-existing overseas trading network established during the era of mercantile capitalism. With the advent of industrial capitalism the new leading sectors played a more independent role in the establishment of a fresh network of trade in industrially produced commodities. The relative stagnation of these sectors during the imperialist period was connected with the outflow of investment funds from the UK in favour of colonial territories to the detriment of domestic industry.

This division between finance and industrial capital was a constant carrier of economic instability throughout the nineteenth century and also entailed a particular regional dimension. The first generalised economic downturn in 1825, after the expansionary wave of the Industrial Revolution, initiated a fairly regular industrial cycle of growth and retrenchment marked by flows of funds between rural capital exporters and industrial capital importers. The inter-regional chains of debt were such that from the late-1840s the economic cycle of boom-crisis became one of speculative mania followed by crash. Until the commercial crisis of 1866 the industrial and financial cycles followed a synchronised pattern of development. Thereafter the centralisation of finance capital in the City of London, and the increasing export of capital overseas, led to a growing autonomy of the financial cycle from domestic industrial fluctuations. The destruction of industrial capital during the downward phase of the cycle no longer precipitated a semi-automatic crash in the banking sphere. The relative independence of finance capital from domestic industry was an important factor in the gradual stagnation of traditional industries during and after the Great Depression. Unlike Britain's chief international competitors there was no large-scale wave of investment in modern industrial technology during the imperialist boom which, paradoxically, was the moment at which British capital was enjoying its heyday as imperial workshop of the world.

This chapter has described the changing hierarchy of leading regions during the nineteenth century long waves of development in the British economy. But simply identifying this changing hierarchy does not suffice to *explain* these changes. It does not explain *why* the Lancashire area led the initial phase of expansion in cotton textiles; why the northern region, South Wales and central Scotland were favoured in the Victorian boom; why industrial leadership passed to the West Midlands during the imperialist upturn; and why London, the commercial and financial centre of the national and international economy, never experienced industrial expansion to match its other economic roles. I have suggested that the solution to these questions cannot be found in any simple combination of physical, geographical or technical factors. The key to the changing process of regional development lay in the social relationships of capitalist production derived from the particular class structure of British society. This feature is examined more closely in Chapter 6.

6
Region, Class and Nation: The Uniqueness of the British Experience

Introduction

The last chapter showed how the development of industrial capitalism in nineteenth-century Britain involved very different patterns of development at the regional scale. It has been suggested that the process of industrialisation was fundamentally a process of social recomposition which entailed the transformation of the social structure and modes of social existence centring upon the formation of a wage-dependent industrial working class. Different economic interests and social traditions, among the ruling class groupings as well as the subordinate classes, played an important part in determining the uneven pattern of regional industrialisation.

This chapter goes on to show how the articulation of economic and social forces of change at a regional scale exerted an important influence upon national political life. Just as different industries in different regions led the process of national economic development through each long wave, so the leading regions formed the base of political movements which contested the lines of national as well as regional development.

In examining the nineteenth-century British experience it should always be borne in mind that we are dealing with a particular capitalist economy which was the leading international industrial and imperialist power throughout the period covered here. The issues confronted by political movements in the regions extended far beyond parochial problems or even national questions. They were sharply focused upon the international role of British capitalism in the world economy. By examining these regional movements we are able to better understand, not only the internal divisions within the British economy, but also the factors which distinguished the British experience from that of other countries and which played a key part in the rise of the world's first industrial nation.

I The Role of the English Aristocracy in British Capitalism's 'Take-off'

1. *Industry and Agriculture*

A prerequisite for urban industrialisation is the appropriation of an ever-larger agricultural surplus, over and above that required for the consumption of the agricultural population itself, so that increasing numbers of workers can be freed from the land and engaged in the production of durable goods, equipment and materials. As Hobsbawm observes of the Industrial Revolution in Britain:

> For every village which specialised in manufacture, every rural area which became an industrial village area (like the Black Country, the mining regions, and most of the textile regions) implied some other zone which specialised in selling it the food it no longer produced.[1]

This exploitation of a rural/agricultural periphery is not unique to industrial capitalism, but was just as important to the economies of ancient city states and empires as well as to medieval feudalism. However, the capitalist mode of production is distinguished from preceding modes in that accumulation and its social relationships centre upon the production, consumption and exchange of *commodities*. These are defined as products or goods which embody not only a use-value, but also an exchange value. In ancient economies agricultural foodstuffs and materials, as well as labour, were directly appropriated via war, plunder and enslavement. In feudal societies the produce of an ostensibly 'free' peasant class was directly appropriated in kind by the landed nobility and clergy through levies and tithes backed by an ever-present threat of military repression. In the capitalist mode, on the other hand, the products of industry and agriculture are exchanged for their monetary equivalents as commodities. The distinctive characteristic of commodities, as opposed to other goods or products, is that they are produced, not for their direct usefulness or use value, but for the exchange value which they command at the market-place where they are converted into a universal currency. In capitalism agricultural products are not directly appropriated in kind but bought and sold in free exchange. Moreover, labour power in capitalism is itself commodified and bought by the owners of capital in exchange for wages.

The commodification of agricultural production has a number of contradictory implications for the development of capitalist industry. On the one hand, industrial capitalism has a vested interest in securing the subordination of agriculture in rural areas to industrial production in the towns and cities. In Britain the dependence of agricultural producers in rural hinterlands upon central urban markets was reinforced by a variety of organisational and institutional procedures. The most important of these was the existence of a layer of middlemen, under contract from merchants, who were the forerunners of the later factory overseers, supervisors and foremen. The semi-agricultural workforce was channelled into contractual obligation with merchant capitalists via middlemen. In this way capitalist commerce secured monopolistic access to rural producers.

However, the maintenance of this relationship, manifested in the physical, economic and social division between town and country, acted as a *barrier* to the further development of industrial capitalism and the factory system of production. It presented an obstacle to the development of a mass-consumption market and the spread of wage-labour essential to the growth of capitalist industry. So long as agriculture provided at least a partial means of subsistence, the rural labour force were loath to surrender their relatively autonomous control over day-to-day production, free from the hardships of factory discipline and routine. As described in the last chapter there were violent campaigns against attempts to capitalise agriculture while factory recruitment met with passive refusal in many rural areas during the late eighteenth and early nineteenth centuries. Resistance to industrial capital on the part of the rural workforce was matched by that of the landed gentry who steadfastly defended rents and agricultural prices through the protectionist Corn Laws which prevented imports of cheaper foreign grain.

2. *Capitalist Trade and Commerce*

This conflict between industry and agriculture explains in part why it was the Lancashire cotton industry which took the lead in British industrial expansion. The industry had tenuous direct links with the domestic economy and grew up in a region where centralised workshops were already strongly developed and which had access to abundant supplies of cheap labour, both at home and from across the Irish Sea. The Lancashire cotton industry took advantage of Britain's unique position as the first emergent capitalist economy by leapfrogging domestic barriers to expansion by penetrating pre-industrial markets and raw-material sources overseas. It was only later, in the post-Napoleonic period of the 1820s and 1830s, when industrial capitalism suffered its first generalised slow-down in growth, that the latent class tensions between industrial capital and landed gentry ascended to the forefront of social and political life.

The British state was – and still is – a peculiar amalgam of modern capitalist and anachronistic aristocratic and monarchistic elements. The nature of this class amalgam has been hotly debated among Marxist historians. The most influential position is that of Perry Anderson, who argues that the success of the seventeenth-century English bourgeoise revolution lay in that it transformed the roles of the ruling class without displacing its personnel.[2] The Parliamentarian forces secured their victory in the Civil War by the symbolic execution of the reigning monarch, but they did not end his line. Nor did they eliminate, either physically or politically, the opposing aristocratic forces. The post-revolutionary period of the seventeenth and eighteenth centuries was marked by two key processes: first, the increasing *capitalisation of agriculture at home*; and, second, the *spread of mercantile capitalism abroad* through the consolidation of colonial rule in North America, the West Indies, India and West Africa.[3] But both these processes were pursued *not* by an industrial bourgeoisie, but by the old landowning aristocracy itself. For Anderson the primacy of Britain's industrial take-off was determined by the fact that the new industries, especially cotton, were able to permeate a pre-existing mercantile network established by an ancient aristocratic class. Moreover, in so doing, the industrial bourgeoisie posed no challenge to the class interests of the gentry and merchant aristocrats. There was no revolutionary confrontation in England *between* industrial capitalist and agricultural aristocratic classes. The English Revolution was essentially a struggle *within* the old ruling class against the parasitic, literally cavalier Stuart monarchy which threatened the growth of agrarian and commercial capitalism that had been proceeding since the Tudor era. The victory of the progressive section of the aristocracy, Anderson argues, was a sufficient condition for the later development of industrial capitalism:

> The colossal industrial concatenation which followed inevitably produced its own, new bourgeoisie – the manufacturing middle class of Manchester and the North. Yet the condition of its appearance in England was the prior existence of a class which was also capitalist in its mode of exploitation. There was thus from the start no fundamental, antagonistic contradiction between the old aristocracy and the new bourgeoisie. English capitalism embraced and included both. The most important single key to modern English history lies in this fact.[4]

It was this peculiarly British mode of class articulation which conditioned the mode of regional industrial development throughout the nineteenth century and the first half of the twentieth. The emergence of industrial capital as a distinctive class layer in the northern regions did not counterpose itself to the southern landed and commercial interests since the reproduction of these twin classes depended upon one and the same process – the maintenance and extension of Britain's hegemonic role in the world economy. As Anderson's close theoretical ally Tom Nairn puts it, 'the temporality of England's new capitalist social system was in symbiosis with the country's maritime and conquering adventures'.[5]

II   Independent Movements of the Industrial Middle Class

The 1825 crisis and the ensuing downward long wave of relative capitalist stagnation undercut the factors which united the rising industrial capitalist class and the older landed gentry, exposing the latent antagonisms between these classes. The landed gentry presented a number of limits to the growth of industrial capital. In so far as the land remained in the hands of aristocratic magnates it imposed a direct cost of production on industry in the form of rents and royalties. This was true of some factory production sites, but was most severe in the case of mining. In the early expansion of the coal-mining industry, mines were largely developed by the landowners under whose property the seams ran. But most landowners subsequently sold the mining rights to entrepreneurs and by 1830 landowners constituted a minority of colliery owners. However, their power outweighed their number. Mining in Cumberland, Lancashire, Yorkshire, the Black Country and particularly County Durham was dominated by one or two landed families in each area.[6] As well as these direct costs the conditions of landownership and agricultural production imposed indirect costs on industry by setting employment levels and food prices, both of which entered into the determination of the wage-price of labour power.[7]

1. *The Manchester Free-Trade Movement*

These antagonisms between industry and the landed interests were crystallised into two political movements: first, the struggle of the industrial middle class for political representation through an extension of the franchise which culminated in the Reform Act of 1832; and, second, the struggle for the repeal of the protectionist Corn Laws. Mobilisation of the exploited classes in the 1820s and 1830s was universal, although varying in form and intensity from the protests of agricultural labourers and the less-articulate violence of the London masses to the organised political expression of the north-west. Middle-class articulation of working-class revolt was most advanced in the leading industrial region of Manchester and the north-west through the catalyst of Chartism. Asa Briggs describes how deepening depression propelled Manchester industrialists towards political leadership of their class with the foundation of the Anti-Corn-Law League in Manchester in 1839.[8] The 'progressive' symbol of 'Manchester Man' focused the movement of the industrial classes against the aristocratic 'parasites' expressed through the counter-symbol of London.

The opposing class ideologies and cultures were very much associated with these alternate spatial poles. This was not confined merely to the conflict between northern industrialists and southern gentry. It penetrated and divided the industrial middle class movement itself. Addressing a London meeting of the League, John Bright told the assembled Londoners that:

> they were the centre of a great empire, the fate of which was trembling in the balance. . . . The provinces without which they could not exist, and from which they drew all their wealth . . . had done that which was the duty of the people of London.[9]

Another Mancunian leader complained of the low intensity of feeling in London which he described as 'something like descending into an ice-box compared with Manchester'. 'My hopes of agitation are anchored on Manchester', he commented, 'we can do more there with a sovereign than a mixed committee in London would do with two.'[10] For the Londoners' part, W. J. Fox wrote after the tactical removal of the League headquarters to London in 1842 that conditions in the office had become 'worse than living in a factory' since the influx of 'Goths and Vandals' from Manchester.[11]

The movement revolved around not only objective class interests, but also more subjective class ideologies in which regionalism was a striking feature. What had begun as a pragmatic movement of northern industrialists to reduce corn prices and thereby depress wages became a moral crusade against the 'evils' of feudalism and the old order through which industrial capital could crystallise the discontent of the working class, some sections of the gentry and even rural labour. As an ideological vehicle the movement propagated the virtues of industrialism, mechanisation, the factory system and the Protestant work ethic. Caught up in the momentum of his own campaign Cobden wanted to extend the aims of the movement towards the abolition of primogeniture, the bastion of hereditary landownership and the basis of the self-reproducing perpetuation of a property-owning class. But, having achieved its first aim with the repeal of the Corn Laws in 1846, the movement evaporated. Anderson describes this sectional conflict as 'the last moment at which the industrial middle class played an independent role in British history'.[12] Henceforth industrial capital was assimilated into the nucleus of the old ruling class. This was achieved not by horizontal integration of property ownership, but through vertical integration, inter-marriage and ascendancy. The public schools, universities and Civil Service all played their part in the creation of a unified ruling strata with a common class core.[13] A generation after the repeal of the Corn Laws, the economic difficulties of the Great Depression led some industrialists to withdraw altogether from their businesses and assimilate themselves entirely into the gentry.[14]

III Contrasting National Experiences

The victory of industrial capital with the repeal of the Corn Laws in 1846 marked the political watershed which precipitated the second long wave of the Victorian boom during the 1850s and 1860s. Indeed, Andrew Gamble has suggested that 'the move to free trade proved one of the decisive events of modern British history, perhaps *the* decisive event'.[15] In Britain the process of regional industrialisation and national economic development during the historical period of competitive capitalism can be divided into two phases or long waves. The first wave of the Industrial Revolution was led by cotton textiles centring on the north-west which linked into the commercial network established by Britain's mercantile role in the world economy. The second wave of the Victorian boom and ensuing depression generated a more dispersed pattern of regional industrialisation involving a variety of specialised regional production complexes chiefly centring on the coalfields. The railway boom after 1850 played an important part in the process of dispersion by breaking down interregional economic divisions and creating a comparatively unified national economy.[16]

The second expansionary long wave in Britain began the process of *economic* unification of industrial capitalism on the basis of the *political* unification of the two main class fractions of capital – industry and commerce/finance – achieved during the preceding years of conflict and change. Elsewhere, the nineteenth-century pattern of regional industrialisation and national capitalist development was quite different to the British experience. The spatial development of capitalist production in Continental Europe did *not* follow the same two-phase pattern as the British case. In large part this was precisely because the European emulation of the British example proceeded only *after* British capital had already established supremacy in world markets. In Continental Europe the two phases in the spread of commodity production and trade through national unification and international expansion, which characterised the British case, tended to be merged into a *single* expansionary phase of economic development.

While British capital was achieving world market hegemony, German and Italian capital had still to achieve domination within their respective nation-states. Although formal political unification of Italy was attained in 1861 the process of economic and social unification remained markedly underdeveloped. This was especially striking in the contrast between industrialising northern regions and the semi-feudal agricultural regions of the south. Even between the relatively advanced northern regions there were enormous disparities in the level and pace of capitalist development. The core of emergent Italian capital remained firmly stationed in the north-western region of Piedmont which at the time of political unification contained 850 kilometres of railway linking the major urban centres of Genoa, Turin, Alessandria and Milan, while the neighbouring regions of Tuscany and Lombardy contained only 300 and 200 kilometres of railway respectively.[17]

In Germany, as in Italy, capitalist development was dominated by the single region of Prussia, but the latter did not suffer like Piedmont from a shortage of capital for expansion. In 1850, while Italy had a total of only 400 kilometres of railway, Germany as a whole had 6000 (a total which Italy only achieved twenty years later) and Prussia possessed a rail network equivalent in size to that of the whole of France.[18] Long before the unification settlement of 1871, German capital had succeeded in securing internal economic expansion such that by 1860 output of coal and lignite exceeded that of France and Belgium, while in the 1860s iron production expanded even more rapidly. Moreover, while in Britain there remained a spatial separation between provincial industrial capital and banking capital concentrated in the City of London, in Germany there was an unparalleled fusion of financial capital in the Prussian Bank. The latter was a joint stock organisation of private capital holdings under state direction and control which became the Imperial Bank of Germany following unification in 1871.

The examples of Britain and Germany thus stand at opposite extremes in the pace of their urban-industrialisation. As the first industrial capitalist nation the British economy went through every distinct phase along the historical continuum of transition from petty commodity production to a fully-fledged industrial capitalist economy and hegemonic imperialist power. These different phases were spread over at least a century of economic and social transformation. In the German case, in contrast, the processes of consolidation of commodity production and exchange within the national territory, the expansion of German capital into foreign markets and the monopolistic development of finance capital were inseparably concentrated into the comparatively short period of perhaps only three decades.

The key variant between these two contrasting examples of capitalist development is the *uneven transformation of their social relationships*. The world's first bourgeois revolution in the English Civil War and its consolidation in the settlement of 1688 established the political prerequisites for the unbroken chain of social transformations which preceded the emergence of the first industrial nation. Progressive elements of the landed gentry directly instigated the capitalisation of agriculture during the eighteenth and early nineteenth centuries and provided the nucleus of the rising urban-industrial bourgeoisie. No pure form of feudal economic relation between landed nobility and peasant farmer had existed in England since the Middle Ages, bypassing the 'land question' which dominated nineteenth-century social and political life throughout central and eastern Europe.

The most extreme contrast to the progressive contribution of the gentry to English 'gradualness' is afforded by the case of France where the nobility of the eighteenth century frittered away their accumulated wealth in conspicuous luxury consumption, undermining any economic basis for their reproduction or transformation as a class and preparing the conditions for their physical liquidation in the Revolution of 1789. The lack of any demonstrably unified bourgeois state apparatus capable of consolidating French capitalism meant that the revolutionary upheaval gave way to the long decades of the 'Terror' and foreign war until 1815, civil strife and uncertainty following the bourgeois thermidor of the June Revolution in 1848, and the precarious reign of Louis Bonaparte described by Marx in *The Eighteenth Brumaire*. The century of indecisive class war between bourgeoisie, peasantry and rising urban proletariat was only brought to a close with the crushing of the Paris Commune in 1871, providing the constitutional foundations for the construction of a unified bourgeois nation-state.

In France the political vacuum within which the French bourgeoisie was compelled to assert its emergent economic power may account at least partly for the long-drawn-out process of consolidation of capitalist social relations in that country. In Germany, on the other hand, the *durability* of southern feudal relations into the third quarter of the nineteenth century may explain why the rapid explosion of northern industrial capital and its penetration of southern pre-capitalist territories could only occur under the direction of an autocratic, centralised Prussian state closely related to the fusion of industrial and banking capital represented by the state-controlled Imperial Bank.

The fundamental point to be drawn from these divergent patterns of uneven capitalist development is that there is no simple internal economic rationale for the emergence and consolidation of capitalist social relations. A prerequisite for the dramatic growth of capitalism's productive forces, represented by the sustained industrial take-off in Britain after 1790 and elsewhere about a half-century later, was a decisive transformation of the social relationships of production made possible through the formation of a system of unified bourgeois nation-states within which surviving feudal modes of economic and social organisation could be subordinated to capitalist commodity relations. In the embryonic European nations this process of social transformation assumed particular regional dimensions because the very raw material of the capitalist space-economy – the land – constituted the material focus of entrenched feudal interests. In Britain the emergence of industrial capitalism occurred in provincial regions notable for their geographical and social distance from the merchant and banking interests of the capital city. In Italy, Germany and France, on the other hand, emergent capitalist interests were very much associated with merchant and banking capital in the leading regions of their respective nations, Piedmont, Prussia and the Parisian metropolis. These regions can be thought of as the territorial bases from which European capitals launched their assault upon pre-capitalist regional societies.

However, the very weakness of the nation-state as the political power base of the capitalist class in France and Italy meant that the process of consolidation of capitalist commodity relations within their respective national markets was cut short. Having achieved some degree of national unification after 1848, Italy and France could not follow the same pattern of spatial dispersion of urban-industrialisation set by Britain, due to the simple fact that British capital had already achieved this level of development and was proceeding to establish its domination of international trade. The need to counter the British trading monopoly through the establishment of their own overseas colonial markets left large expanses of southern Italy and central, eastern and southern France unpenetrated by capitalist commodity production and exchange – territories where remnants of semi-feudal social and economic organisation survive to the present day.

European theorists are well aware of the responsibility borne by English capital in determining the trajectories of economic development in their own nations. It is a measure of the pervasive influence of the British experience in urban theory that the processes of urbanisation and industrialisation are so often equated together and referred to interchangeably. But this interpretation often makes little sense outside the British context. As Enzo Mingione argues, in England urbanisation and industrialisation went hand-in-hand because of that nation's unique and unrepeatable role as the *first* industrial capitalist economy. Elsewhere, and particularly in his native Italy, Mingione shows that urbanisation owed more to its relationship with agriculture than to industry.[19] But Mingione does not extend this argument to explain the European experience of uneven development between cities and regions as in major part a *consequence* of the British priority. This step has been taken by Claudia von Braunmühl in her analysis of the capitalist nation-state and its role in the world market:

> in every metropolitan country which underwent primitive accumulation and an industrial revolution in the wake of England, class relations and the relation of the state apparatus to society bear in a specific manner the imprint of that country's position on the world market.[20]

After 1870 the leading impetus of the imperialist long wave shifted from Britain to Germany and the USA. The experience of the latter country differs markedly from that of any European nation due to the centrality of what Aglietta calls the 'frontier principle' in its industrial and spatial development.[21] The pattern of capitalist development in the USA was not directed towards the subordination of pre-existing social relations to the capitalist mode of production, since in vast areas of the country no such relations existed. The problem was rather one of imprinting capitalist social relations upon virgin territory.[22] The existence of a massive spatial reserve devoted to the production of an agricultural surplus provided the stimulus to industrial development along the north-east seaboard. But it also presented an obstacle to capitalist expansion. The immunity of vast areas from penetration by capitalist commodity production and consumption limited the possibilities for transition to a 'regime of intensive accumulation' on the basis of these structural forms of social relationship. By the 1860s the USA was composed of three quite distinct, semi-independent regional agglomerates: the centres of developed industrial capital in the north-east; the western homesteads engaged in cereal production and ranching with tenuous trade in manufactures from the east; and the southern slave-based cotton economy, constituted on a social relation in production antithetical to the free exchange of wage-labour and remaining locked in the social structures established under British colonial rule. The success of the northern industrialists in the Civil War of 1861–5 secured the unity of the chief fractions of American capital, completed the advances of the bourgeois revolution in the anti-colonial War of Independence and began the process of consolidation of the US capitalist economy.[23]

IV Industrial Stagnation and Midlands Social Imperialism

In the late nineteenth century British industry increasingly lost ground to its German and US rivals. Moreover it did so not only in quantitative terms of its share in world economic activity, but also in qualitative terms of technological and social advancement. While the British industrial structure became relatively archaic, American industry in particular was revolutionised through the spread of the regime of intensive accumulation based on scientific management and the beginnings of Fordism. As described in Chapter 5, British capital became increasingly defensive in the face of intense inter-imperialist competition, drawing on its exclu-

sive colonial sphere and avoiding direct aggressive market competition with foreign capitals.

Just as in the 1830s and 1840s when the new class of industrial
capitalists challenged the old ruling strata over the future of
Britain's international role upon which the development of the
former depended, so in the late nineteenth and early twentieth
centuries a section of industrial capital formed a new movement
against the complacency of the established order. As in the earlier
period of upheaval the new movement was drawn along regional
lines. Whereas earlier it was the Lancashire mill-owners who
undertook the assault on London's financial and commercial oli-
garchy, at the turn of the century that role passed to Midland
manufacturers.

However, while the Manchester free-traders fought for an aggressive policy of overseas development, the Birmingham 'preference'
or 'social' imperialists campaigned for a defensive policy of tariff
barriers to protect the British economy and its empire from foreign
import penetration.[24] The social imperialist vision of a global
union of Anglo-Saxon settler states centring upon the British
motherland and isolated from antagonistic foreign blocs by a
military and tariff wall had implications which contested many
economic and ideological tenets on which Britain's former growth
had been founded. It challenged the ideological hold of Smithian
capitalism in which 'the firm' was the basic economic unit. The
proposition of *nations* as economic units in mutual competition
was still a relatively new one.

However, social imperialism entailed more than a simple reaction to the external economic threat from Europe and the USA. It
also expressed an overt political strategy for containment of the
domestic working class. Its objective was pithily expressed in 1895
by Cecil Rhodes whom Lenin called an 'honest social-chauvinist':[25]

> My cherished idea is a solution for the social problem, i.e., in
> order to save the 40,000,000 inhabitants of the United Kingdom
> from a bloody civil war, we colonial statesmen must acquire new
> lands to settle the surplus population, to provide new markets
> for the goods produced in the factories and the mines. The
> Empire, as I have always said, is a bread and butter question. If
> you want to avoid civil war, you must become imperialists.[26]

The strategy of buying-off working-class discontent with imperialist profits had been tried and tested in the municipal administration, public works, social infrastructure and architectural projects of Birmingham's 'Civic Gospel'.[27] The same social factors which made Birmingham the centre of the new light engineering and manufacturing industries during the imperialist boom provided fertile ground for nationalist ideologies of imperialism. The relative affluence of Birmingham's skilled craftsmen, the diversity of occupations and the persistence of small workshop production militated against the development of a collective labour consciousness and formed the basis of support for bourgeois 'radicalism'. The foundation of the Birmingham Political Union by Thomas Attwood in 1829, designed to cement an alliance of industrial capital and working class in 'harmonious co-operation', predates the Anti-Corn-Law League in Manchester.[28] Cobden himself wrote that 'the state of society' was 'more healthy and natural in a moral and political sense' in Birmingham than in his own Manchester base: 'There is a freer intercourse between all classes than in the Lancashire town where a great and impassable gulf separates the workman from his employer.'[29]

The Birmingham alliance partnered the Manchester radicals in the struggles for extension of the franchise achieved in the 1832 and 1867 Reform Acts. But it was not until later in the century that Birmingham gained national prominence when Joseph Chamberlain used his Unionist base as a vehicle to transplant the imperialist 'ethic' from municipal government to national economic and political strategy in Westminster. The most obvious difference between the significance of social imperialism and the free-trade movement is that, in their immediate aim of tariff reform, the imperialists failed to achieve any strategic change in British policy. But in its less immediately tangible aim of domestic social reorientation the movement was an undoubted success. As Anderson puts it:

> the primary impact of imperialism on the working class – as throughout English society – was at the level of consciousness. The British working class was not in any profound sense mobilized *for* imperialism; to this extent, the options of many of its leaders were ineffective and insignificant. But it was, unde-

niably, deflected *from* undistracted confrontation with the class exploiting it. This was the real – negative – achievement of social-imperialism.[30]

Conclusion

The theory of long waves is usually presented in terms of very broad changes in global economic development. One of the prime purposes of this work is to show that processes of change in smaller localities can play an important part in these wider international transformations. The process of development at the regional and national scales is not simply an outcome of global mechanisms. The processes of change in nations and their regional components form a *part* of the long waves and, in some cases, may have results which extend far beyond their spatial boundaries.

This chapter has suggested that the economic, social and political forces underlying nineteenth-century industrial development in the British regions were of such a character. In economic life the growth of different regional industrial sectors was strongly associated with the alternate long waves of accumulation. In social life the existence of different regional class structures was crucial to the growth of successive leading industries through the advance and extension of the capitalist labour process. In political life the leading regions of each wave formed the social base of political movements which contested the lines of national development. The ensemble of regional economic, social and political forces combined to direct, not only the internal development of British capitalism, but also the external relationship of British capital to the emerging world economy.

It was the existence of a large pool of cheap labour, already drawn into the wage relationship of subordination to capital, which selected the north-west as the site of the first great expansion of mechanised manufacturing. The initial expansion of the north-west cotton textiles industry during the Industrial Revolution was based on imported raw materials, imported technology, imported entrepreneurial initiative and served a large export market. It was the *lack* of integration of the leading industry with the rest of the national economy which favoured cotton's initial take-off. The development of the cotton industry complimented the prevailing role of Britain in the international economy created by the long-established class of merchant capitalists and financiers.

It was not until the economic downturn of the 1830s and early 1840s that the latent conflicts between industrial capital and domestic landed interests came to the surface. The decisive victory of the northern industrialists over the old landed gentry through the repeal of the Corn Laws in 1846 created the conditions for the second expansionary wave which ushered in a period of generalised industrialisation in northern England and the Celtic fringes.

In London and the south the same factors which promoted industrial advance in the north acted as obstacles to industrialisation. The availability of large reserves of cheap labour proved a disincentive to technological progress and mechanisation. London's role as the hub of an international commercial and financial empire promoted the flow of capital investment overseas at the expense of the national economy in general and the London region in particular. In the upturn of the 1850s London's merchants and financiers were loath to commit capital to the industrial development of their own region, preferring speculative ventures elsewhere. In the upturn of the 1890s they were more prone to invest abroad than in the modernisation of the northern heavy industries.

In this context it was the very backwardness of production in the Midlands, the prevalence of small craft-based workshop trades, which made this region most flexible and responsive to the new competitive pressures on the domestic economy. It was the West Midlands which took the lead in the growth of light engineering and metal-based trades serving the new consumer goods manufacturing industries. For these reasons, it was this region which succeeded the North West in leading the renewed political onslaught of industrial capital against the London financiers in the protectionist movement of social imperialism.

In each long wave the different patterns of regional development in the domestic economy were circumscribed by, and contributed to, the particular class character of British society and the unique role of British capitalism in the world economy. In other European countries the patterns of national and regional development were dependent upon the outcomes of class confrontations that had been met in Britain a century or more earlier. Britain remained immune from the violent revolutionary conflicts which swept Europe in 1848. In Britain there was no necessity for the national unification movements found in many leading European countries during the 1860s and 1870s. The British experience was not marked by the dramatic upheavals which punctuated the turning-points of each long wave in the development of the European economies. In Britain the qualitative changes which marked each quantitative change in the pace and direction of economic development were of a much more gradual and transitional nature. This was because the *political* prerequisites for capitalist *economic* development had already been achieved in the bourgeois revolution of the seventeenth century. It was the violence of a preceding phase which made possible the subsequent course of British 'gradualism'.[31]

British industrialisation did not *fundamentally* challenge the interests of the prevailing ruling strata. Nor did it necessitate any fresh round of *fundamental* change in the nature of state power and the state apparatus. On the contrary British industrial capitalism reinforced the economic basis of the nobility's class rule by integrating itself with the pre-existing trade network established by the nobility themselves to serve their own mercantile aspirations. British industrial capitalism avoided the internal class confrontations which divided its rivals. The decisive conflicts between industrial capital and gentry were fought, not over domestic divisions, but over the external orientation of British capitalism towards the international economy through the state's tariff and trading policies. It was this unique nature of British capitalist development which conditioned, and was conditioned by, the different patterns of regional development that appeared across the nineteenth-century long waves.

Part IV
Twentieth-century Long Waves of Regional Development

Part IV
Twentieth-century Long Waves of Regional Development

7
Economic Fluctuations and the 'Regional Problem'

Introduction

The last two chapters examined the role of uneven regional development in the nineteenth-century rise of British industrial capitalism. It has been shown that the dominant direction of industrial development and change in the national economy was by no means mirrored in the pattern of development in all the nation's component regions. Interregional differences were an important determinant of the overall national pattern and, because of the British economy's dominant global position at that time, these regional differences sometimes had impacts of an international significance. Chapter 7 now goes on to examine the regional dimension to twentieth-century fluctuations in British economic development. It is suggested that the 'regional problem', which was itself in no small part a product of the nineteenth-century patterns of development, was reflected in spatially uneven cyclical fluctuations of the British economy.

I The Imperialist Legacy: The Interwar Depression and the Regional Problem

The problems of British economic development which had begun to emerge during the imperialist boom of the 1890s and early 1900s became fully apparent after the First World War. The deepening trade deficit, the lack of industrial modernisation and the growth of capital exports relative to domestic investment combined to undermine the basis of British capitalism's former prosperity.

It is now a commonplace to relate the contemporary British

economic decline to the fact of that nation's earlier predominance in the world economy and to the inflexibility of its economic organisation and industrial structure.[1] Britain's imperialist past had been built upon the staple industries of coal, iron, shipbuilding and textiles. These owed their rapid growth from the 1850s to the nation's relationship with the world economy through the policy of free trade. By 1918 that relationship, which had been under pressure for a quarter-century, reached its apogee. The world economic crisis of 1921, the crash of 1929 and the depression of the 1930s led to a contraction of world trade in which British exports suffered particularly acutely. The determination of the international financial community to cling to the gold standard of currency exchange led to the over-valuation of sterling which further undermined the price-competitiveness of British exports and accelerated the decline of the traditional, export-based industries.

The social results of this decline, in terms of widening interregional inequalities, are well known. Unemployment averaged less than 9 per cent in the south-east between 1929 and 1938 compared with 19 per cent in the north-east and 29 per cent in Wales. At the local scale unemployment differences between cities in the depressed and relatively prosperous regions were vastly wider.[2] Most standard texts ascribe the origins of this 'regional problem' to the legacy of Britain's imperialist past. As Gavin McCrone puts it:

> It is really to the collapse of this policy [of free trade] that the regional problem, at any rate in the industrial areas, owes its origins. The over-valuation of the pound in the 1920s, the emergence of economic blocs in the 'thirties, changes in technology and competition from lower wage countries, all combined to produce a secular decline in the traditional export industries. When the cyclical effects of the great depression were added to these long-run trends, the result was acute economic distress and unemployment in the areas where these industries were concentrated.[3]

The formation of the British regional problem in the interwar depression coincided with particularly severe slumps in the national economic cycle. This revealed the profound structural problems of traditional industries which had formerly fuelled

British economic development during the nineteenth and early twentieth centuries. The business cycle experienced a marked structural metamorphosis after the Second World War. The fairly regular boom–slump cycle which had predominated, certainly since the 1830s and perhaps since the late eighteenth century, was replaced by a growth cycle of development without the sharp slumps of the previous century and a half.[4] But this national pattern of development concealed quite pronounced differences between economic fluctuations in individual regions. In unemployment rates at least, which have generally been accepted as the chief statistical indicator of regional inequalities in the UK, there were distinctive, although interrelated, regional cycles which varied in both timing and amplitude.

II Employment Fluctuations and Regional Inequalities

The tendency for regional unemployment rates to fluctuate with the national business cycle is well known. In addition studies in the mid-1960s identified the tendency for regional *inequalities* in these unemployment rates to vary with the movements of the national cycle. Using the standard deviation as a statistical measure of the dispersion of regional unemployment rates around the national average Thirlwall observed the tendency for regional unemployment differences during the 1950s and early 1960s to expand when the national rate rose and contract when the national figure fell.[5] I have updated Thirlwall's series in Figure 7.1 to show that this relationship held true for the later 1960s and 1970s.

These series illustrate a number of features of inequality between the UK regions. First, *there has been no long-term tendency for regional unemployment differentials to disappear*. The phases of decline in regional unemployment differences (falling standard deviation) during the booms in the national business cycle (falling unemployment rate) have been generally offset by the rise in regional inequalities during the national recessions. Smoothing the year-to-year changes by calculating a five-year moving average of the standard deviations reveals a fairly stable level of inequality over the three decades.

Second, the statistical series show the *striking variations in amplitude of the fluctuations in regional inequalities*: the dramatic

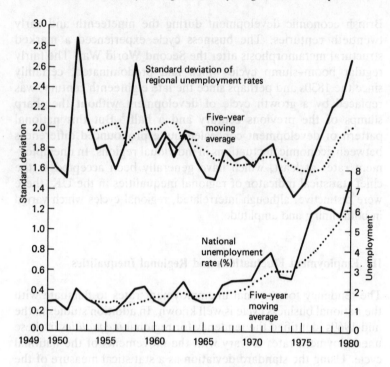

FIGURE 7.1   *UK: National Unemployment Rate and Standard Deviation of Regional Unemployment Rates, 1949–80*

SOURCES   1949–64 – Thirlwall, 1966, p. 43.
1960–80 – Data from Central Statistical Office.

swings of the 1950s, the relatively smooth fluctuations of the 1960s and the renewed sharp swings from the early 1970s. While the level of inequality has changed little *between* successive cycles (peak–peak/trough–trough) the *intra*cyclical changes (peak–trough/trough–peak) shown in Table 7.1 have varied quite markedly. The hierarchy of regional unemployment rates in the UK has scarcely changed since 1960, as illustrated in Figure 7.2. The low and high unemployment regions have maintained their respective positions or, to put it crudely, there is almost no crossing of lines on the graph. But it is the high-unemployment regions which have exhibited the greatest amplitude of fluctuations, experiencing the greatest relative increase in unemployment during the national recessions (rising UK unemployment) and, until the late 1970s, the

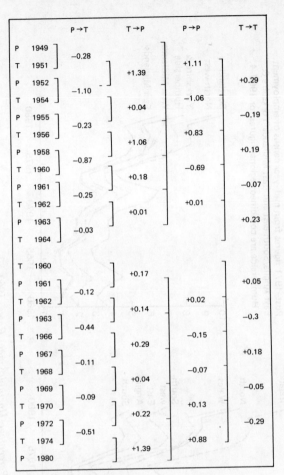

P = Peak in Standard Deviation
T = Trough in Standard Deviation

TABLE 7.1 *Inter- and Intra-cyclical Changes in Standard Deviation of UK Regional Unemployment Rates, 1949–80*

SOURCE See Figure 7.1.

greatest proportional reduction of their unemployment rates during the national booms (falling UK unemployment). This pattern is clear from Figure 7.2 and is described in detail in Table 7.2.

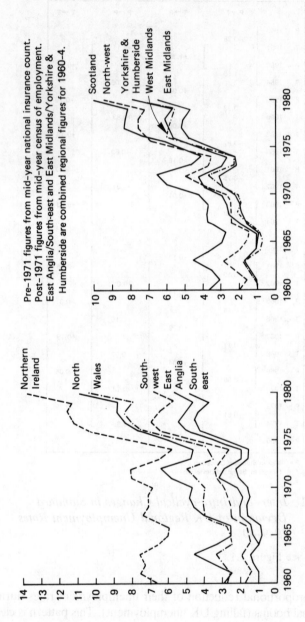

FIGURE 7.2   *UK Regional Percentage Unemployment Rates, 1960–80*

SOURCE   Data from Central Statistical Office.

	P→ 1961	T→ 1961	P→ 1963	T→ 1966	P→ 1972	P→ 1977	T→ 1979	1980
United Kingdom	−0.1		−0.9		−1.3	−0.5		
		+0.8		+2.0			+3.6	+1.7
North	−0.4		−2.1		−1.8	+0.3		
		+2.1		+3.9			+3.8	†2.2
Yorkshire and Humberside	+0.1		−0.6		−1.6	−0.1		
		+0.6		+3.1			+3.2	+2.1
East Midlands	+0.1		−0.6		−0.9	−0.5		
		+0.6		+2.1			+2.9	+1.8
East Anglia	0.0		0.0		−1.0	−0.9		
		+0.4		+1.5			+3.5	+1.2
South-east	0.0		−0.5		−0.7	−0.8		
		+0.4		+1.3			+3.0	+1.1
South-west	−0.3		−0.4		−0.8	−1.2		
		+0.5		+1.9			+4.3	+1.0
West Midlands	+0.1		−0.9		−1.4	−0.3		
		+0.6		+2.8			+3.6	+2.3
North-west	−0.3		−1.5		−1.4	−0.4		
		+1.3		+3.5			+4.0	+2.2
Wales	−0.1		−0.6		−1.2	−0.2		
		+0.8		+2.1			+4.4	+2.4
Scotland	−0.5		−1.8		−2.5	−0.3		
		+1.4		+3.8			+4.3	+2.0
Northern Ireland	+0.8		−1.7		−2.4	+0.1		
		+0.1		+2.2			+5.5	+7.4

P = Peak in UK National Unemployment Rate
T = Trough in UK National Unemployment Rate

TABLE 7.2   *Intra-cyclical Changes in UK Regional Unemployment Rates, 1960–80*

SOURCE   See Figure 7.2.

III   The Uneven Timing of Regional Employment Fluctuations

The factors which influence unemployment rates clearly vary between regions. Frank Brechling sought to break down regional unemployment rates between 1952 and 1963 into three causal components:[6]

(i) 'Aggregative cyclical components' which reflect the general level of economic activity in the nation as a whole.

(ii) 'Structural components' which are unique to each region and remain stable or exhibit a smooth, secular trend over successive cycles. These reflect the regional industrial structure, skill mix of the labour force, migration patterns and the size of the regional income multiplier.

(iii) 'Regional cyclical components' which are also unique to each region but vary cyclically. These reflect cyclical fluctuations in a region's dominant industries which may differ from industrial fluctuations in the nation as a whole.

Brechling's calculations of the timing of the *aggregative cyclical component* showed that fluctuations of unemployment rates in London, in the south and east and in the Midlands tended to *lead* the national movements while those in the Yorkshire Ridings, north Midlands, north west, north and Scotland tended to *lag* behind the national fluctuations. The remaining four regions tended to synchronise with the timing of the national movements.

According to Brechling's estimates, then, during the 1950s and early 1960s it was the most prosperous, low-unemployment regions which led the national economy into the cyclical troughs and peaks while the 'problem', high-unemployment regions lagged behind. Moreover, there was a significant variation in the size of the regional movements as well as their timing. A given movement of the national unemployment rate was followed by a greater absolute change and smaller relative change in the problem regions than in the more prosperous, 'leader' regions. This describes the sharper swings and greater amplitudes of cycles in the high-unemployment regions than in the low-unemployment regions discussed above.

Going on to examine the *structural component* Brechling found that, contrary to conventional wisdom, there was no tendency towards 'structural convergence' among the British regions for the period covered. This factor differed substantially from unity (i.e. no contribution) in most regions. Moreover, in some regions the time series revealed an *increasing* deviation from unity, i.e. an

increasing structural contribution to the determination of regional
unemployment rates. There was no simple division between high-
and low-unemployment regions in either the size or trend of this
factor.

However, in his effort to focus on the unity of the 1952–63
period (the changes between beginning and end of the data series),
Brechling tends to overlook the different phases *within* the structural component patterns. While defined as factors subject to
smooth, non-cyclical movement the structural components do *not*,
for the most part, exhibit a unidirectional pattern throughout the
sample period. Significantly it was the Midlands, north Midlands
and north-west, the regions with the strongest concentrations of
export-based manufacturing industries, which exhibited the only
secular reduction in their structural components. Their leading
industries, such as motor-vehicles and engineering, were most
strongly associated with national economic growth rather than
'autonomous' regional conditions. In the south-west, the south
and east the structural components of employment change tended
to decrease in importance (draw nearer unity) during the phase of
most rapid national economic expansion in the boom years of the
1950s and make an increased contribution to unemployment in
these regions as the phase of rapid growth gave way to one of
relatively slow development in the early 1960s. London, on the
other hand, exhibited the reverse pattern, the structural component increasing during the 1950s and stabilising thereafter. In the
high-unemployment regions the north's structural component de-
creased during the boom years and increased rapidly in the subsequent slow-down. Wales exhibited the reverse pattern. Only the
Yorkshire Ridings showed a stable pattern, while Scotland experienced a secular rise in its structural component.

The 'structural component' is an umbrella-term which covers a
variety of actual industrial structural configurations. In regions like
the south-east a diversified manufacturing and service base may
account for the increasing importance of the structural element
and the regions's relatively low-unemployment rates. In Scotland
and the north, on the other hand, an increasing structural component may more likely be a symptom of their continued dependence
upon traditional declining industries which make the major contribution to the regions' poor employment performances.

There is clearly no necessary relationship between a declining structural component and an improving regional unemployment record or vice versa. The most that can be read from looking at the structural trend *in isolation* from other components is that the 1952–63 period was one of quite rapid change in most of the British regions. An assessment of the *nature* of this change can only be made in the light of information from the cyclical component series.

Having isolated the 'aggregative cyclical' and 'structural' components of regional unemployment rates Brechling assumed that the remaining residual factor could be accounted for by the '*regional cyclical*' component. The time series for this component were much clearer than for the structural element:

> When the residual cycles were plotted and inspected, two distinct cyclical patterns could be distinguished. London, the South and East, Wales, the South West, the North Midlands, and the Midlands conformed to the first pattern; their residuals were low in 1954–5 and again in 1959–60 and high in 1957–8 and again in 1961–2. The second cyclical pattern is represented mainly by the Ridings, the North West, the North and Scotland; they have high residuals in 1954–5 and again in 1959–60 and low residuals in 1957–8 and again in 1961–2.[7]

A comparison of Brechling's estimates with changes in the *national* unemployment rate for his four periods, shown in Table 7.3, reveals that the cyclical component was low for the first regional group during the national booms (when unemployment fell) and high during the recessions (when unemployment rose). Conversely, for the second group, the cyclical element was high during the national booms and low during the recessions. In other words, when the aggregate economy was expanding and national unemployment falling, the cyclical element was most significant in the regions of relatively high unemployment. During the phases of relative national economic contraction (rising unemployment), the cyclical component was most important in the low-unemployment regions.

Contrary to the assumptions inherent to Brechling's methodology the aggregative cyclical, structural and regional cyclical components of regional unemployment changes were *not* mutually exclusive or autonomous factors. Seen together they provide a dynamic view of a changing spatial employment pattern moving

TABLE 7.3 *Great Britain: Brechling's Estimates of 'Cyclical' Contributions to Regional Unemployment Levels Compared with Changes in the National Unemployment Rate, 1954–62*

Regional group	'Cyclical' component of regional unemployment change			
	1954–5	*1957–8*	*1959–60*	*1961–2*
London, south, east, Wales, south-west, north Midlands, Midlands	LOW	HIGH	LOW	HIGH
Yorkshire Ridings, north-west, north, Scotland	HIGH	LOW	HIGH	LOW
Change in GB total unemployment as percentage of year earlier	−18.5	+46.4	−24.2	+36.0

SOURCES Brechling, 1967, p. 17; GB unemployment figures from Mitchell and Jones, 1971, p. 43.

with the cyclical fluctuations of national economic development. The low-unemployment regions of the south and Midlands were the most dynamic regions, tending to *lead* the national economy through successive cycles of development, exhibiting the greatest proportional change in their unemployment rates between turning-points of the cycle. The high-unemployment areas of the northern regions, in contrast, tended to *lag behind* the fluctuations in national employment, experiencing the smallest proportional change (although the highest absolute change) in their unemployment rates between the peaks and troughs of the national cycle.

The national cycle of development, of course, does not have any independent origin, but is an aggregate reflection of fluctuations in the nation's regional components. It is significant, then, that when this aggregate cyclical component, together with the structural factor, had been accounted for, the remaining regional cyclical residuals were highest for the southern regions during the phases of national boom and highest for the northern regions during the phases of recession. This indicates that *it was economic development in the southern regions which was most strongly related to the phases of national expansion* (when their regional residuals were low), *while the northern regions exerted more influence on the national pattern during the depressive phases of the cycle.* Taking the regional cyclical residual as an indicator of the degree of insulation of each regional group from the national fluctuations it can be seen that the southern regions were relatively immune from the phases of national economic contraction during which the northern regions suffered most acutely. Conversely, the northern regions took a smaller part of each national boom while the southern regions played the leading role.

IV   From Desynchronised to Synchronised Regional Fluctuations

National economic fluctuations during the long boom from the end of the Second World War to the mid-1960s were unevenly represented at the regional scale. Employment fluctuations in what were conventionally referred to as the 'problem' regions were generally stronger than in the more prosperous parts of the country. Moreover, the regional fluctuations were uneven in timing, employment movements in the relatively depressed areas tending to lag behind those of the more prosperous areas. However, from the mid-1960s onwards it is possible to detect a quite abrupt change in this desynchronised pattern of regional fluctuations as employment changes in the regions tended to synchronise with the national cycle.

The uneven timing of regional employment fluctuations identified in Brechling's study of the 1954–62 period ceased to be apparent from the mid-1960s. Frost and Spence have attempted to update Brechling's findings by searching for regional leads and lags in response-timing to changes in the national unemployment rate between 1963 and 1976.[8] But, contrary to expectations, they found no continuation of desynchronised regional responses during this later period, forcing them to conclude that: 'although response-timing differences may have once existed between different regions of the country, no interpretable effects of this can be found in the series between June, 1963 and February, 1976'.[9]

Turning their attention to employment changes in Britain's major cities, Frost and Spence discovered that the disappearance of leads and lags in the regional fluctuations coincided with the appearance of uneven response-timing on an *urban* scale. For the period between 1963 and 1969 changes in male employment levels in Leeds, London, Bristol, Cardiff, Nottingham and Manchester all lagged behind employment changes for the national economy as a whole while employment changes in Birmingham and Glasgow remained synchronised with the national movements. These urban lags were confined to the 1963–9 period and were not present in the statistical series for the subsequent period from 1970 to 1976.

In an important recent study two other researchers have similarly detected a significant shift in the pattern of unequal spatial growth from the mid-1960s which they summarise in the phrase 'urban decline and rural resurgence'.[10] Fothergill and Gudgin have used the technique of shift-share analysis to measure three components in manufacturing employment changes for the UK regions between 1952 and 1979:[11]

   (i) The *national component* measures the change that would have occurred if a region's total manufacturing employment had grown at the same rate as total manufacturing employment for the UK as a whole.

  (ii) The *structural component* (sometimes called the 'proportionality shift') measures the regional manufacturing employment change, relative to that of the UK as a whole, that can be attributed to the particular mix of sectors within the region. This is given as the national component subtracted from the change which would have occurred if each sector in a region had grown or contracted at the national rate for that sector.

 (iii) The *differential shift* is the difference between the expected change (the sum of the national and structural components) and the actual manufacturing employment change in a region.

Fothergill and Gudgin's estimates of the structural and differential shift components in regional manufacturing employment changes between 1952 and 1979 show a striking shift in the nature of regional manufacturing employment change around the year 1966. Until that year employment growth in the south-east and the Midlands, coupled with employment losses in the northern regions, could be mainly attributed to structural factors, i.e. the particular mix of industries in each region which tended to expand or contract in accordance with the aggregate trend of these industries nationally. But after 1966 the importance of this structural factor stabilised. Henceforth, employment growth in some regions, accompanied by losses in the West Midlands and south-east, was mainly accounted for by the differential shift, i.e. residual factors which cannot be attributed simply to trends in the national economy.

The greatest positive contribution of the structural component to employment growth was in the south-east and West Midlands. The largest negative contribution was found in the old textile regions Yorkshire and Humberside, the north-west and Northern Ireland. Elsewhere the structural contribution to manufacturing employment change was more marginal. Until the mid-1960s the importance of the structural component was generally increasing, i.e. diverging from zero. After 1966 there was a significant fall in the rate of change in this component for almost every UK region.

This fall in the structural component was synchronised with an equally abrupt rise in the differential shift for employment change. In the historically depressed industrial regions of Scotland and the north-west, there was a steady fall of their structural components and a stable differential shift throughout the period from the early 1950s. The most marked changes in the differential shift were represented by the manufacturing employment losses in the West Midlands and south-east and by the employment gains in East Anglia, the south-west and East Midlands.

In Fothergill and Gudgin's view these patterns represent a massive flight of manufacturing employment and investment from the urban conurbations towards formerly under-industrialised suburban areas and rural regions. They have broken down the differential shifts by manufacturing sectors to show that it was the fastest-growing industries, most characteristic of the preceding post-war boom, which led this flight from the metropolitan cities.

The electrical engineering sector accounted for over one-quarter of the south-east's negative differential shift while it provided an important source of job gain in Scotland, Wales, Northern Ireland, the north, south-west and East Midlands. Similarly the contraction of employment in the West Midlands motor industry was largely responsible for this region's negative differential shift while the growth of new branch plants in Merseyside and central Scotland contributed to the positive differential shift in these areas.[12]

Fothergill and Gudgin interpret this transformation in the pattern of manufacturing employment as the outcome of four main factors: first, the decline of regional differences in 'industrial structure' which they consider to have become 'more-or-less irrelevant' from the mid-1960s onwards; second, the 'urban structure' of the big conurbations which they consider to be the newly dominant factor in employment change, tending to push manufacturing firms out of the inner-city areas due to physical constraints on expansion and other diseconomies inherent to the congested fabric of the large cities; third, the 'size structure' of factories in the metropolitan areas where large, old-established companies tend to force out new, small firms in the more modern and innovative sectors upon which the long-term vitality of a region's manufacturing employment base may depend; finally, the impact of regional policy as a response to these causes of slow growth through inducements to manufacturers in the congested cities to move out to the financially assisted areas.[13]

All these factors may have had some influence on the new spatial pattern of manufacturing employment which developed after 1966. But the mere identification of these factors does not suffice to explain why they suddenly became so crucial in the mid-1960s. In my view, Fothergill and Gudgin, like Brechling before them, are trapped by the strict 'scientific' definitions of the statistical categories around which they have built their analysis. The differential shift 'by definition' represents regionally autonomous factors which cannot be attributed directly to macroeconomic variables at the national or international scales. Following this reasoning an expansion of the differential shift component of manufacturing employment change in a region must be the outcome of local peculiarities rather than of national and international conjunctures of forces. Hence, Fothergill and Gudgin are forced to resort to factors like the physical fabric of urban areas and the characteristics of local inter-firm competition to explain these autonomous shifts.

In my view these local variations were *not* fully autonomous of national and international structural forces. It is only through the movements of the latter that internally contained regional forces exert their relative autonomy. Shortages of land for expansion in the urban areas and the unequal competition between big business and small firms date back a century or more. While there was certainly a marked rise in the intensity of regional policies after 1963, as Fothergill and Gudgin themselves concede, this represented a *response* to the new industrial problems rather than a cause of them. Moreover if the differential shift represents autonomous factors within each region it is rather strange that these forces should have been simultaneously elevated in importance in nearly every region during the mid-1960s. I believe that these factors became prominent after 1966 due to a marked transformation in the underlying cyclical process of economic development in the national economy and its component regions. By now it will not surprise the reader that I characterise this threshold as the turning-point from an expansionary long wave to one of relative stagnation.

Conclusion

Why were regional employment and unemployment fluctuations desynchronised with the national cycle during the long boom following the Second World War; and why was there such an abrupt synchronisation of the regional cycles in the mid-1960s? A major part of the answer to these questions lies in the regional distribution of industries in the post-war period which corresponded to the spatial structure laid down during the latter half of the nineteenth century. This was primarily a spatial division between regions specialising in consumer-good manufacturing and regions concentrating upon the older-established raw material and capital-equipment sectors. The desynchronised regional employment fluctuations reflected the uneven development of these industrial sectors during the course of economic fluctuations in demand for their respective outputs.

As described in Chapter 1, a number of theorists such as Forrester and Mandel have shown how consumer-good manufacturing sectors tend to be most responsive to changes in demand for their products. Capital-goods and materials producers are more prone to overshoot demand given the scale of investment required for their expansion combined with the relatively long time periods needed for investment in these industries to respond to demand by augmenting capacity.

The post-war regional problem was symptomatic of the spatial-industrial structure inherited from Britain's imperialist heyday and reproduced by post-war cyclical fluctuations. During the late nineteenth century the traditional heavy industries of shipbuilding, steel and mining, centring on the coalfields of central Scotland, South Wales and northern England, maintained British capitalism's continuing position as dominant imperialist power. While light engineering and manufacturing industries had been gradually developing in the Midlands and south-east during the late-nineteenth-century and interwar depression, their most rapid expansion occurred with the release of pent-up demands after the Second World War. But just as the interwar depression exposed the underlying problems of British heavy industry, so the slow-down of world growth from the mid-1960s revealed the structural weaknesses of British manufacturing. Moreover, in the same way that the interwar depression gave rise to the pattern of regional inequalities which endured throughout the post-war boom, the latest Kondratieff downturn has witnessed the emergence of new spatial divisions. This new pattern of imbalanced development is examined in Chapter 8.

8
Industrial Restructuring and the New Spatial Division of Labour

Introduction

The last chapter drew upon a variety of statistical studies to show how post-war growth cycles in the British economy hid diverse patterns of fluctuation at a regional scale. In general terms the désynchronised regional cycles reflected the uneven development of traditional heavy industries and modern manufacturing sectors and hence of the different regions within which these industrial branches were concentrated. From the mid-1960s, however, the former pattern of désynchronised regional fluctuations changed into one of synchronised regional cycles. Uneven fluctuations thenceforth were manifested on a subregional scale, reflecting the newly prominent process of urban economic decay. Chapter 8 now goes on to examine the causes of this shift in the pattern of spatial development, relating it to fundamental changes in the character of national and international economic development which marked the arrival of the fourth Kondratieff downturn. It is suggested that this latest extended crisis of the British economy has provoked a fresh phase of industrial change and social recomposition, giving rise to the beginnings of a new spatial division of labour.

I The Fourth Kondratieff Downturn

1. *The Underlying Weakness of Post-war Prosperity*

Several observers have characterised the difficulties experienced by all industrial capitalist economies over the past fifteen years or so as the crisis of a Fordist mode of accumulation.[1] But, as Dunford, Geddes and Perrons have pointed out, the British crisis has been particularly acute partly because of the *absence*, rather than presence, of sufficiently strong Fordist norms of production.[2] Some new capital equipment industries with modern labour processes were established in Britain during the 1920s and 1930s, often employing imported American techniques. But they did not develop the characteristically large-scale standardised production processes necessary to strengthen their international competitiveness. This was due to rigidities in the labour supply and the lack of a sufficiently large and stable domestic market.[3]

After the Second World War the British trade-union movement remained organised along sectional lines and did not adopt the wider political perspectives of labour movements in other countries. They successfully defended their members' living standards and resisted any far-reaching technical change in the labour process. The continuing dominance of financial and banking interests within British capital maintained the sterling exchange-rate at higher levels than were desirable to expand markets for manufactured goods in other industrialised countries. The pattern of British overseas trade remained heavily geared to neo-colonial preferential relationships with the Commonwealth. Unlike other countries, particularly West Germany, France and Japan, public resources were largely devoted to welfare and armaments rather than to planned investment in manufacturing industry. The combination of these factors meant that during the 1950s and 1960s British industry suffered relatively low rates of investment, a falling share of world trade in manufactured goods, declining rates of profit and a relatively high share of wage costs in the value of manufacturing output.

2. *The Synchronisation of National Conjunctures*

During the late nineteenth century British industry enjoyed the advantage of being based within the dominant imperialist power whose performance and policies to a large extent set the parameters within which subordinate national economies determined their own paths to industrialisation and overseas expansion. By the 1960s British capitalism had long since lost that position and became, in turn, subordinate to an international pattern of trade and monetary circulation centring upon the dominance of the USA. Just as desynchronised regional fluctuations (discussed in Chapter 7) underlay the overall national economic cycle in the UK, so the relative stability of post-war growth cycles in the Western capitalist bloc rested on desynchronised *national* fluctuations. Michel Aglietta has shown how the post-war international economic order consisted of a number of what he refers to as 'virtuous circuits' formed by each national economic territory.[4] So long as the dollar currency unit continued to function as the dominant medium for international finance and commodity flows, it was quite possible for countries with low or high rates of growth, low or high rates of inflation and surpluses or deficits of their balance-of-payments current accounts to develop in mutual complimentarity. For as long as the USA maintained a healthy underlying surplus in its trade of manufactured goods, and enjoyed a low level of inflation, any short-term balance-of-payments deficit could be rectified at the expense of overseas competitors through dollar exports which adjusted exchange rates to the benefit of US manufacturers and detriment of foreign producers. Since the flow of dollar exports tended to fluctuate according to the rhythm of the US economic cycle, a cyclical downturn in the USA had a delayed effect on the US's chief competitors in reinforcing obstacles to their growth. A downturn in the USA tended to open up or widen the trading deficits of high-growth countries, forcing them to take internal stabilisation measures designed to strengthen their competitiveness. The first result of these measures was generally a temporary economic downturn sufficient to reverse their currency slide.[5]

However, Aglietta argues, the combination of several factors destroyed this post-war order in the late 1960s and early 1970s:[6]

(i) *The inflationary expansion in the USA* undermined the functions of the dollar: first, as a limitation on the supply of international funds that prevented the synchronisation of expansion in the Western countries; second, as a reserve currency whose inflation rate lay below that of its chief international competitors; and third, as the hub of an international finance market providing sufficiently attractive long-term yields on investment to keep international liquidity above the level required for financing international trade.

(ii) *The convergence of national industrial structures* led to the loss of American technological supremacy and the international synchronisation of accumulation cycles in manufacturing sectors.

(iii) *The Japanese economy* was able to become a global power through exports of manufactures without laying open its own market to foreign import penetration. This further undermined the stability of international trade.

(iv) *The international debt economy became relatively immune from regulation by any one nation-state* due to the collapse of the dollar's functions. This led to currency rivalries and a destabilisation of the international banking system which had formerly secured complementary modes of national economic growth.

(v) *The shock to the system brought on by the OPEC oil price rises* raised production costs simultaneously in all major Western economies. This accelerated the trend towards synchronisation of national cycles *already* pending due to the combination of the other factors listed above.

During the 1960s and early 1970s, the UK was the first major industrial economy to feel the symptoms of this approaching collapse of the post-war economic order. The balance of payments, which Michael Stewart called 'the King Charles's head of any discussion on the British economy',[7] ran into increasing difficulties and was met by the stop–go cycle of deflation–reflation by Conservative governments up to 1964. The Labour government's devaluation of the pound in late 1967, as a response to the fourth sterling crisis since 1964, was intended to improve the competitiveness of British manufacturing exports, but succeeded only in removing Britain from the Western European virtuous circuit, the immediate sign of which was the French veto on British entry of the EEC.[8]

3. *From 'Regional Problem' to 'National Problem': The Crisis of British Manufacturing Industry*

The desynchronisation of the British crisis with the recessions in other Western economies, which were both later and less severe, had a far-reaching impact upon the pattern of industrial change and regional development. Henceforth the regional problem was subsumed within the national problem of ailing industrial competitiveness which affected, not only the traditional industries of the 'problem' regions, but also the manufacturing sectors of the formerly prosperous West Midlands and south-east which had fuelled Britain's part in the post-war boom. It was in this context that the 'new' spatial problems, involving the flight of manufacturing capital from the older urban areas, began to assert themselves.[9]

The economic decline and social decay in the UK over the past decade and a half have frequently been compared with the depression years of the 1930s. In some senses, most notably the return of mass unemployment, such comparisons appear strikingly valid. But in other ways the similarities between the interwar depression and the latest contractive long wave are relatively superficial.[10] The geography of unemployment in the present period of stagnation is quite different to that during the 1930s. While some regions during the interwar period suffered unprecedented – and unrepeated – unemployment levels, others remained relatively immune from industrial decline and job loss. The rough division between north and south remains a marked characteristic of the contemporary geography of employment and unemployment. But the differences between comparatively high- and low-unemployment regions are not as great today as they were in the 1930s.

This is because the *process* of industrial decline and job loss today is itself markedly different to that during the last depression. Industrial decline during the interwar years was predominantly concentrated into traditional heavy industrial sectors while the more modern manufacturing sectors were growing in the south-east and West Midlands (excluding the Black Country). But the contemporary industrial decline is notable, not only for the continuing contraction of the surviving traditional sectors, but also for the spread of this decline to the very manufacturing industries and areas which led British economic growth during the post-war period. With the slow-down of national economic growth in the mid-1960s, the manufacturing heartland of the UK in the West Midlands lost the cyclical dynamism which had characterised its industrial performance during the previous two decades. During the cyclical fluctuations of employment in the 1950s the West Midlands was first into and first out of each trough, tending to lead the rest of the country through each alternate upturn and downturn. But during the late 1960s the West Midlands lagged behind the national movements and then synchronised with the national fluctuations of the early 1970s.

Several observers have drawn attention to the marked change that occurred in the performance of British manufacturing industry from the mid-1960s. During the economic fluctuations of the 1950s and early 1960s problems of excess capacity were generally resolved with the revival of demand during the succeeding upturns. But from 1966 onwards over-capacity became a semipermanent or chronic problem which endured across the fluctuations. As one commentator observed in 1972:

the capital stock in manufacturing generally does not seem to have been used at full stretch since the second quarter of 1966. So far as one can judge from the available evidence, nothing like this has happened since the war. The earlier recessions may have been as severe in terms of capital under-utilisation, but they were much shorter.[11]

The decline of UK manufacturing has accelerated with each successive recession since 1966. Figure 8.1 compares manufacturing output, employment and productivity levels over the four national economic cycles since 1964. Levels of manufacturing output and employment have grown progressively worse with each successive cycle. The earlier improvement in productivity (measured as output per employee) during the uncompleted 1979–81 cycle is only a reflection of the fact that manufacturing employment has fallen even faster than output during the most recent recession. The full extent of Britain's decline as a manufacturing economy was revealed in early 1983 when the national economy suffered a deficit in its trade in manufactured goods for the first time in its 200-year industrial history.[12]

II Industrial Restructuring and Spatial Inequalities

Statistics like those presented in Figure 8.1 conjure up an image of practically unbroken collapse of the British economy's manufacturing base. But a closer inspection of this decline reveals complex processes of change within the manufacturing sector. The quanti-

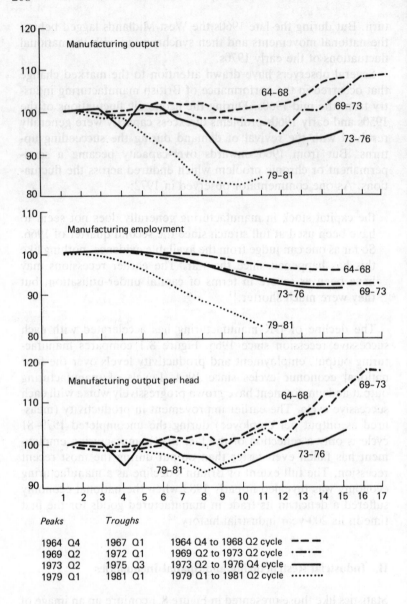

Peaks	Troughs

1964 Q4	1967 Q1	1964 Q4 to 1968 Q2 cycle — — —
1969 Q2	1972 Q1	1969 Q2 to 1973 Q2 cycle ·—·—·
1973 Q2	1975 Q3	1973 Q2 to 1976 Q4 cycle ———
1979 Q1	1981 Q1	1979 Q1 to 1981 Q2 cycle ·········

FIGURE 8.1 *Changes in UK Manufacturing Output, Employment and Productivity over Successive Cycles, 1964–81*

SOURCE HM Treasury, Jan 1982, p. 3.

tative decline of manufacturing in terms of employment, output, productivity and so forth, has been accompanied by qualitative changes in ownership and control, technical organisation and spatial distribution. For these reasons many observers prefer to characterise the recent changes in the manufacturing sector as a process, not simply of contraction or decline, but of industrial restructuring.

1. *Industrial Restructuring*

Like the term 'deindustrialisation', which is another label commonly used to describe recent changes in the manufacturing sector, the term 'restructuring' seems to have several meanings.[13] At minimum the term refers to changes in the ownership and control over capital in response to competitive pressures.[14] At maximum, 'restructuring' has been used to denote the broad ensemble of economic, technical, social and political changes necessary to reintroduce stability into the capitalist economy as a whole during a period of relative instability or crisis.[15] In this section I use the term in its more minimal sense, but later show the reorganisation of industry has far wider implications for the restructuring of capitalist societies, not least in the realm of regional economic and social structures.

The economic difficulties experienced by most industrialised countries since the slow-down of growth in the mid-1960s prompted intensive international competition and a phase of far-reaching international restructuring. During the post-war boom, US capital had been steadily flowing into the UK economy. Between 1943 and 1950 US investments in the UK rose from $519 million to $847 million while they fell for Europe as a whole from $2025 million to $1720 million in the same period.[16] By 1966 US companies owned 7.2 per cent of the net capital stock in Britain, accounting for over one-tenth of total manufacturing sales.[17]

While US capital was consolidating its base in the UK, British multinationals tended to defer domestic investment in favour of decentralisation abroad. Direct UK investment overseas (setting up or buying extra capacity) rose from annual averages of around £220 million per year in 1959–63 and £280 million in 1964–7 to £410 million in 1968 and £531 million in 1969.[18]

These international movements of capital were associated with a

phase of accelerated restructuring in the network of capital ownership and control in the late 1960s through what one contemporary
observer called 'an unprecedented wave of mergers' in British
industry.[19] Over £5000 million was spent on the acquisition of sub-
sidiaries by industrial and commercial companies between 1967 and
1970.[20] Comparing this with the total book-value of net company
assets of £24 000 million at the end of 1968 it can be deduced that
ownership of almost one-fifth of all UK industrial and commercial
assets may have changed hands in the space of just four years
before 1970.[21]

2. Spatial Consequences of Restructuring

All these characteristics of the accelerated phase of international
restructuring which marked the close of the post-war boom had
important consequences for industry and employment in the British cities and regions. The influx of multinational companies meant
that incoming manufacturers were less dependent upon regional
industrial linkages than their indigenous counterparts. The
enhanced ability of incoming multinational companies to shift
investment from one region or country to another increased the
vulnerability of host areas to job losses accompanying any subsequent company rationalisation. The outflow of British investment
from the 'home' regions has had direct effects in terms of employment losses in many older industrial areas. Likewise, mergers and
take-overs have frequently been accompanied by rationalisations
involving plant closures, contractions and redundancies in dated
plants located in the older industrial areas.

The 'external control' of regional development   A number of
studies have drawn attention to the problems of regional industrial
development based on multinational branch plants.[22] Drawing on
investment from outside the receptor region, branch plants are
often poorly integrated into the local economic network of inter-
company linkages. They frequently import materials and components from external sources, serve external markets for their
output and are subject to decision-making and control from externally based managements. McDermott's study of the Scottish
electronics industry in the mid-1970s, for example, revealed that
the North American multinationals were 'the least integrated into

the Scottish economy and the least dependent upon the market provided by local manufacturers'.[23]

During the 1950s and 1960s US investment in the UK was concentrated into three industries: chemicals and petroleum, mechanical engineering and motor-vehicles.[24] The arrival of US companies in the UK 'problem' regions was almost invariably welcomed for the employment it brought to the depressed areas. With hindsight more recent research suggests that incoming multinationals tended to hasten the collapse of smaller, indigenous firms less able to compete and were apt to 'poach' workers with appropriate skills from other firms rather than recruit from the dole queues. It has been estimated, for example, that only 2 per cent of recruits at Ford's Halewood plant on Merseyside were previously unemployed.[25]

However, the more damaging aspect of multinational investment in the regions has been the added instability which they introduce into the local industrial and employment base. While often referred to as a problem of 'external control', in one sense the label is confusing. From the point of view of the workforce the control of production is always external, lying in the hands of managers and owners. Previous chapters have shown how the history of the capitalist labour process has been the history of capital's attempts to cement and extend that control and of labour's attempts to resist it. From this perspective it would seem to make little difference to a Glasgow workforce whether boardroom decisions are taken by managers and directors sitting around a table in Glasgow, London or New York. It is not the control of development from external *spatial* sources which is so significant as the expanded strategic options over which that managerial control can be exercised. In the case of indigenous regional capital the impacts of a firm's management decisions on the wider local and regional economy may be of no small consequence to the local enterprise, having some effect on the future economic environment within which the firm will continue to operate. Even a medium-sized or large business with plants in several regions may have some commitment to the wider prosperity of its plants' localities. Austin Rover in the West Midlands, for example, may prefer to maintain its long-standing links with component manufacturers in the region through a policy of local component sourcing in order to maintain complementary relationships between the materials, equipment, components and assembly subsectors even though considerations of short-term cost-cutting might suggest a policy of cheaper, overseas component sourcing. A giant multinational corporation, on the other hand, may be constrained by no such commitment. The recent controversy over the government-assisted establishment of the Nissan motor plant in the north-east, for example, revolved around fears that the Japanese company intends to use its Sunderland plant as a springboard to penetrate the domestic and European markets, while the plant may be little more than a kit assembly site for imported parts, undermining the indigenous British motor and component industries.[26]

This lack of commitment to and integration with the receptor region means that any gains from attracting inward industrial investment may be comparatively short-term and lead to further problems in any subsequent round of company rationalisation or corporate restructuring. As one study of Merseyside's industrial collapse, has argued, industrial expansion based on imported multinational capital 'was always a fragile development':

> The ease with which these multinationals can come and go has become all too clear recently. Their plans are short term with no commitment beyond their profitability. As we enter the 1980s these very multinationals which promised to be the saviours of the 'depressed' areas are turning their sights to cheaper Third World labour markets.[27]

The merger boom and the inner cities   One of the most striking features of the economic slow-down of the late 1960s was the effect of industrial restructuring upon Britain's older urban areas. Chapter 7 has shown how the synchronisation of *regional* employment fluctuations at that time coincided with the appearance of leads and lags in cyclical turning-points on an *urban* scale.[28] Recent studies, most notably that of Fothergill and Gudgin, have demonstrated that the mid-1960s turning-point was accompanied by a loss of manufacturing employment in the older industrial cities of quite abrupt timing and on a massive scale.[29] Other studies have attempted to uncover the mechanisms behind this employment decentralisation and have discovered that a large proportion of job losses in the urban areas were associated with corporate reorganisation through mergers and takeovers. Massey and Meegan's study of *Industrial Restructuring versus the Cities* examined the process of restructuring in twenty-five electrical engineering companies accounting for almost one-fifth of total employment in that industrial sector.[30] Between 1966 and 1972 restructuring in these firms resulted in a total net loss of 36 000 jobs equivalent to a decline of 16 per cent. The manufacturing heartlands of the south-east, West Midlands and north-west regions accounted for 94 per cent of this overall employment loss. But disaggregation of the data revealed that 89 per cent of the losses in these regions were concentrated into the four major cities of Greater London, Birmingham, Liverpool and Manchester.

Such academic studies were supplemented in the mid-1970s by the graphic accounts of urban–industrial decay provided by the Home Office-sponsored Community Development Projects. Local and national studies showed how the mergers, take-overs and rationalisations which gave rise to such industrial giants as British Leyland, Unilever, Tate & Lyle, Courtaulds, GEC, Vickers and Swan Hunter played a large part in the decline of older urban areas like Saltley in Birmingham, Canning Town in London's East End, Batley in West Yorkshire, Benwell in Newcastle upon Tyne and North Shields on Tyneside.[31] Set up partly to examine the so-called 'inner city problem' in terms of social and economic inadequacies stemming from the fabric of the localities themselves, several of the local Projects rejected their Home Office briefs in showing how the decline of their areas could only be understood in the context of a far wider national and international process of economic restructuring.[32]

Regional decline and the flight of multinational capital   During the late 1960s and early 1970s the new gographical inequalities in employment levels and social conditions were frequently referred to as an 'inner-city problem' in much the same way as the 'regional problem' was equated with spatial inequalities during the 1930s.[33] The relative levelling of inter-regional economic performance and social indicators contrasted with the widening inequalities between smaller localities at a subregional scale. As Doreen Massey put it: 'In terms of the changing *geographical* basis of "spatial problems", it is of course the combination of regional "convergence" with the new prominence of inner city areas which is the dominant aspect of change'.[34]

But, as Massey is careful to emphasise, while economic and social deterioration may *appear* in particular spatial localities, the *causes* of geographically concentrated decline need not necessarily – and rarely do – lie within the same spatial boundaries. The so-called 'urban problem', like the regional problem, is symptomatic of a broader national *industrial* problem whose causes extend in space far beyond the inner-city areas and can be traced back in time much further than the 1960s and 1970s. During the mid-1970s several studies drew attention to the phenomenon of interregional convergence of industrial structures.[35] For some observers the emergence of an inner-city problem and the declining importance of the older regional problem were not unconnected. Fothergill, and Gudgin, for example, argue that the relative levelling of structural inequalities between the UK regions was for the most part a product of the decentralisation of manufacturing industry from the inner urban core.[36]

However, with the onset of the generalised industrial recession in 1974–5, and particularly since the last recession, beginning in 1979, it has become clear that the growth of an inner-city problem during the late 1960s and early 1970s did not signal the end of the regional problem, but was rather the advance guard of a new phase of widening regional inequality. The badly affected inner urban areas were the first localities to feel the effects of the approaching period of national industrial contraction which has witnessed the extension of regional inequalities on a fresh scale.

Nowhere has this been more strikingly apparent than the West Midlands. This region, perhaps more than any other, has felt the effects of the national and international restructuring which char-acterises the present industrial slump. By the end of the post-war boom the jungle of small trades and independent manufacturers, which was such a prominent feature of Birmingham's industrial structure during the nineteenth century, had long since ceased to exist. Between 1959 and 1973 there was a 41 per cent fall in the number of smaller-sized Birmingham manufacturing plants em-ploying more than ten but less than a hundred workers.[37] By 1976 some 43 per cent of total manufacturing employment in Birming-ham was accounted for by just ten companies with no less than 39 per cent of the city's total workforce concentrated into thirty plants.[38] The West Midlands economy is dominated by a dozen giant multinational companies. These are almost all 'traditional'

West Midlands firms with roots stretching back to nineteenth-century family businesses. But since the mid-1970s, and especially since 1979, they have been increasingly deserting their home base in favour of cheap labour markets in the Third World.[39] The ten major West Midlands companies (excluding British Leyland) in 1978 were GEC, Dunlop, GKN, Cadbury, Lucas, Tube Investments, IMI, Delta, Glynwed and BSR which employed a total of 687 000 workers worldwide of whom 513 000 were employed in the UK.[40] By 1982 their global workforce had fallen by 23 per cent to 530 000. This fall was accounted for wholly by cutbacks in the UK where total employment in these multinationals fell by 31 per cent to 354 000 between 1978 and 1982 while their combined overseas workforce actually rose by 2 per cent from 173 000 to 177 000. Precise figures on job cuts in the West Midlands region are unavailable. But the fact that the West Midlands Metropolitan County accounted for an estimated 27 per cent of these companies' combined UK workforce in 1978, coupled with readily observable evidence of major local plant closures and contractions, provides an indication of the heavy responsibility borne by these and other multinationals for the estimated loss of one-third of West Midlands manufacturing jobs that occurred between 1979 and 1983.[41] The West Midlands' unemployment rate now bears more resemblance to those of the historically depressed areas of Scotland, Wales and the north than to the south-east with which the West Midlands once shared the status of most stable and prosperous area of the UK.

The making of another depressed industrial region is indicative of the profound process of international restructuring which has undermined the UK industrial and employment base over the past decade or so. The old north-south divide between the British regions remains as sharp as ever and has become increasingly polarised in spatial terms. For those who like to conceive of spatial inequalities in centre–periphery terms it is apparent that the geographical centre has shrunk relative to the periphery as the once-flourishing West Midlands has joined the depressed ranks of peripheral regions. The industrial division between north and south can perhaps now be more accurately defined as a division between the south-east and the rest of the country.

III   The New Spatial Division of Labour

1. *Different Processes of Employment Decline*

The decline of the UK manufacturing base over the past two decades has undermined, perhaps even destroyed, the former economic prosperity enjoyed by many older urban areas and some wider regional industrial complexes. But the processes of industrial restructuring associated with that decline have been more than simply destructive in nature. The destruction of old-established forms of industrial and spatial organisation has been accompanied by the construction of new ones.

On an international scale employment losses in the developed capitalist economies have been related to the growth of manufacturing employment in the underdeveloped countries as multinational manufacturers have decentralised their activities to the Third World labour markets. Third World countries which formerly exported raw materials and imported manufactured goods are now becoming major manufacturing exporters and, for the first time, are competing with the developed economies for manufacturing markets. This spatial shift of manufacturing production and employment has been commonly referred to as the 'new international division of labour'.[42]

However, overall job losses in the manufacturing sector of world production have been accompanied by similarly far-reaching spatial shifts in industrial organisation *within* the developed capitalist economies themselves. Manufacturing job loss is not a homogenous process. It can take different forms motivated by different pressures on the enterprise. In their recent study of employment decline in the UK manufacturing sector since the mid-1960s Massey and Meegan distinguish between three forms of job loss.[43] These are:

   (i) technical change, where new investment in labour-saving capital equipment displaces labour in production;

  (ii) rationalisation, involving disinvestment and cutbacks in productive capacity;

 (iii) intensification, where changing work practices reduce labour requirements within the prevailing technical framework of production.

Employment decline in manufacturing during the 1960s was primarily associated with the 'white heat' of technological change. The relative slow-down of growth, and the pressure on UK markets and profitability, meant that new investment in manufacturing was primarily directed towards filling the productivity gap between UK manufacturers and their chief international competitors. The drive to modernise British industry led to what Massey and Meegan call 'jobless growth'.[44]

Since the recession of 1974–5, and particularly since 1979, the *relative* employment decline associated with technical change has given way to *absolute* job losses due to rationalisation. Plant closures and contractions, involving cuts in output and capacity, have led to widespread job losses with successive rounds of redundancies in most major manufacturing sectors. Cutbacks due to rationalisation have been accompanied by attempts to increase productivity, not through technical change, but via intensification of the production process which in turn creates pressure for job loss in a climate of declining output and capacity. The processes of rationalisation and intensification are interrelated. Actual or potential employment contractions put pressure on those who remain in work to accept changes in working practices or risk redundancy in a labour market where the chances of securing alternative employment have, to put it mildly, deteriorated considerably. The threat of unemployment, itself a product of widespread rationalisation, creates the potential for further job cuts through the intensification of production processes performed by the remaining workforce in employment. Massey and Meegan cite the recent speedups and reorganisation of shift work in the motor industry, together with disputes over 'flexible rostering' on the railways and over 'washing-up time' at British Leyland, as examples of this process.[45]

2. *Industrial Restructuring as Class Restructuring*

The overall effect of industrial restructuring and these processes of employment decline has been to transform several important features which formerly characterised British urban and regional economic geography. Spatial inequalities are no longer to be found simply in the *quantity* of job opportunities available. There are now important spatial distinctions between the *quality* of working conditions. Interregional inequalities during the interwar depression and the post-war boom were overwhelmingly manifested in different regional unemployment rates. Since the generalised slow-down in national industrial growth which began in the mid-1960s, there has been a relative convergence of regional unemployment rates as unemployment in the formerly prosperous manufacturing areas has grown to resemble that in the traditionally depressed regions. But the decentralisation of manufacturing employment away from older industrial centres towards more recently industrialising suburban or rural areas has generated new inequalities in the kinds of jobs available in different areas. Job losses in the old industrial areas have often led to the decline of employment opportunities for traditional skilled, unionised male manual labour. Conversely, industrial growth in new areas has created job opportunities for unskilled, poorly unionised female workers, many of whom have been drawn into paid employment for the first time.

The destruction of old spatial divisions has been paralleled by the construction of new ones. The process of industrial restructuring has involved a process of *social* recomposition or class restructuring. New spatial divisions have been built upon the foundations laid by former phases of industrial development, reshaping social structures and employment patterns. The decline of traditional industries and the decentralisation of new manufacturing sectors have together involved the break-up of old working-class communities, the destruction of old class divisions and the formation of new social relationships and forms of social conflict centring on new labour processes in production.

Doreen Massey has recently conducted a study of the contrasting impacts of industrial change since the 1960s on female wage-labour in the old industrialised mining regions of South Wales and the north and in the relatively under-industrialised area of Cornwall in the south-west.[46] She shows how the same processes of industrial transformation have had what amount to opposite effects on the social structures and forms of social conflict in the two types of region.

In Wales and the north the decline of the mining industry has been associated with a displacement of the old-established and well-organised traditional working class, the decline of the indigenous regional capitalist class and the exploitation of formerly under-utilised reserves of female labour in the new manufacturing sectors. This has established fresh antagonisms both within and between the capitalist and working classes. Not least of these is the social and cultural crisis of working-class family life brought on by an increasing number of women obtaining work in communities where the male head of household has traditionally been the sole wage-earner, posing a challenge to the patriarchal family and masculine image of working in the pits. The old power-base of unionised labour and the distinctive regional network of inter-capitalist ties (the latter more prominent in the north than in South Wales) have been replaced by new sections of manual labour together with new strata of white-collar workers and middle management. The result has been a blurring of the historical dichotomy between male manual labour and local capital, the establishment of new class strata drawn into the wage-relation and the emergence of fresh dimensions to working-class organisation and resistance to Fordist control.

While South Wales and the north have been traditionally dominated by the social distance between manual labour and large capital, Cornwall has been a stronghold of the gentry and middle class.[47] The impact of industrial change here has been to replace this middle-class dominance with a fresh form of the capital-labour dichotomy which previously characterised the old-industrialised regions. In Cornwall the influx of external industrial capital has eroded the power of small capital while drawing displaced agricultural labour and reserves of female labour into factory work. In contrast to the experience of the old Welsh and northern mining areas industrial change in Cornwall has led to the establishment of a new working class and a new social layer of large capital, often resident in the locality due to the attractive physical and social environment. The latter has undermined the scope of the old-established intermediary class strata.

3. *The New Spatial Hierarchy of Economic Activity*

The twin processes of industrial restructuring and class restructuring described in this chapter have led to the beginnings of a quite different spatial hierarchy of economic activity to that which predominated during the post-war boom. Some authors, notably Massey, have referred to this fresh system of spatial organisation as a 'new spatial division of labour'.[48] Regional differences during the interwar depression and post-war boom were dominated by the dichotomy between traditional heavy industries in the north, Wales and Scotland and the more modern manufacturing sectors of the south and Midlands. This 'regional problem' essentially rested on an *inter*-sectoral split between areas specialising in raw materials and capital equipment production, on the one hand, and areas specialising in manufacturing for the emerging mass consumer market on the other. Since the mid-1960s a new spatial division has begun to emerge centring upon more complex *intra*-sectoral distinctions between different territories specialising in different stages or processes of accumulation within the same industrial sectors. Broadly speaking it is possible to discern a threefold spatial division of labour between regions.

First, the mass-production and assembly-line stages of production are increasingly located in areas of semi-skilled, low-waged and relatively poorly organised labour. These are typically, but by no means exclusively, areas formerly dominated by declining basic industries such as mining where there are reserves of displaced workers and formerly non-active female labour. This stage of accumulation is frequently based upon flows of commodity inputs from and to external regional sources. This contrasts with the high degree of internal linkage which characterised the heavy industrial complexes of the older spatial pattern.

The second stage of accumulation, based on processes not yet significantly automated, reduced to assembly-line work or producing standardised products, is still largely located in the old nineteenth-century industrial towns and cities which continue to function as centres of skilled labour. However, the decreasing quantitative importance of this stage means that industrial development is becoming increasingly freed from the locational ties of such skilled labour concentrations, leading to a relative disinvestment from the older centres associated with industrial decline in the conurbations.

Finally the central metropoles have become typified by the concentration of higher management, research and development and other control functions, specialising as financial and professional service centres. These areas are characterised by a distinctive presence of managerial and technical class strata relative to the older-established manual classes of labour.[49]

An important example of this new spatial hierarchy, with major implications for the future of British industrial geography, is provided by the growth of the microelectronics industry. Two areas of the UK have experienced particularly rapid growth in this sector during recent years – the 'Silicon Glen' area of central Scotland and the M4 motorway corridor of southern England to the west of London.[50] The Scottish industry has grown predominantly due the influx of foreign multinationals, particularly from the US. Between the beginning of 1980 and mid-1984 over £590 million was invested in the Scottish semiconductor industry associated with about 10 000 jobs.[51] The role of the Scottish branch plants is mainly one of final assembly of imported components and is largely orientated towards export markets. The workforce has been disproportionately recruited from reserves of unskilled female labour, union membership is low and the multinationals have frequently insisted upon 'no strike' agreements as a major condition of recruitment.

The microelectronics sector in central Scotland contrasts sharply with that in the M4 corridor, which is strongly orientated towards research-and-development-based activity and manufacture of specialised components and equipment rather than the standardised assembly work of the Scottish plants.[52] Employment in the M4 corridor is strongly characterised by the presence of highly skilled male scientific and technical staff, while the industry is more heavily represented by indigenous British companies. The latter was reflected in a survey of UK microelectronics companies' investment intentions for 1984 where firms intending to set up new establishments in the coming year showed an overwhelming preference for locations in the south-east.[53] The researchers concluded that 'there is a great danger of a North-South divide, where the South will receive the majority of the investment and the North, at best, will display only pockets of electronic activity'.

Conclusion

Regional economic differences during the post-war boom centred predominantly around the industrial divisions laid down during the nineteenth century between northern heavy industry and manufacturing sectors in the West Midlands and south-east. The slow-down of international growth from the mid-1960s dramatically undermined the former prosperity of the manufacturing centres. During the late 1960s and early 1970s the decline of British manufacturing was most strongly evidenced, in spatial terms, by the flight of capital from the older urban areas. However, the subsequent recessions of 1974–5 and 1979–81 have affected far wider spatial areas, creating a whole new depressed region in the former manufacturing heartland of the West Midlands.

The decline of British manufacturing over the past two decades has been associated with a process of industrial restructuring involving not only job loss, but also job reorganisation. The initial phase of the crisis during the late 1960s provoked a greatly accelerated period of capital concentration into giant corporations. During the most recent phase these corporations have decentralised their productive activities on both international and national scales. At the national level this process of decentralisation has begun to generate a new spatial division of labour embodying a fresh spatial hierarchy between social groups and economic sectors, marking the beginnings of a new phase of uneven regional development.

The extent of spatial socio-economic inequalities in Great Britain has changed little over the past two centuries of industrial development. But the *nature* of those inequalities and *perceptions* of them have changed markedly. With regard to national government economic policies and political programmes, regional differences during the nineteenth century played a prominent role in shaping the course of national economic development. But from the First World War onwards 'regionalism' as a political force became subsumed within an all-embracing concept of national identity. The glaring regional inequalities of the inter-war depression had to be rediscovered and awarded their own discrete sphere of public concern – the 'regional problem'.

This chapter has described how public interest in the 'regional problem' during the post-war boom gave way to concern over the 'inner-city problem' from the late 1960s to the mid-1970s which has in turn been superseded by the 'national problem' of accelerating unemployment and industrial contraction so far this decade. These different types and scales of economic and social decline have certainly exhibited different levels of prominence during particular phases within the past two decades. But they are, of course, all part of the *same* 'problem', namely the fundamental processes of socio-economic restructuring, in the widest sense, affecting all industrialised nations, the costs of which have been compounded in Britain by the national economy's acute crisis of competitiveness as an industrial manufacturing power.

It is this national and international crisis which forms the overriding background to the presently intensifying urban and regional problems. Does this mean, then, that the economic and social regeneration of Britain's cities and regions will, at least for the time being, be dependent upon a solution to the national crisis of the British economy? Will the 'regionalism' which has been such an enduring feature of past phases of change and development in the British economy become of only minor significance in future periods of socio-economic upheaval? These and other issues concerning the future of regional development in Britain are considered in the concluding chapter.

Conclusion

Long Waves, Regional Development and the fifth Kondratieff upturn

Long Waves of Capitalist Development

In essence the theory of long waves asserts that there have been successive long-term phases of relative expansion and contraction in the scale and pace of capitalist development since the Industrial Revolution, each phase lasting between twenty and thirty years. But these waves have been the subject of a very disparate range of alternative theories, drawing upon different sources of empirical evidence and proposing different explanations for the phenomena. As described in the Introduction, my initial intention upon embarking on this study had been to take the long-wave perspective and examine its potential insights for an analysis of uneven regional development in industrial capitalist societies. However, I quickly came to the conclusion that, of all the available theories of long waves, none was immediately suited to my purposes.

The commodity price-cycle approach originated by Kondratieff remains an essentially descriptive account. Attempts to explain the long waves in terms of the price movements themselves, notably that of Rostow, have proved highly unsatisfactory. The Schumpeterian theory of cyclical patterns in technical innovation over-emphasises the role of technological change in economic development while neglecting the wider social context within which technical change occurs and which ultimately shapes the nature and purposes of technological advance. The capital over-accumulation theories proposed, in somewhat different forms, by Forrester and by Mandel see technical change as a major component of the long waves, but relate this factor to more fundamental tendencies towards imbalanced industrial development.

Given my own interest in imbalanced *spatial* development the over-accumulation perspective seemed to be the most fruitful approach to analysing the long waves. But both Forrester's and Mandel's approaches suffer from being over-schematic and deterministic. These problems are supremely represented in Forrester's account of the long waves which is constructed from computer simulations. Mandel's interpretation of the long waves as historical periods of capitalist development is seductively attractive in its aim of uniting 'objective' economic mechanisms with 'subjective' social and political forces. The strongest feature of Mandel's theory is its attempt to show that while economic fluctuations in themselves are an inevitable and inherent characteristic of the capitalist framework, the precise course of these fluctuations is not predetermined, but is the outcome of social and political conflicts.

Closer inspection of Mandel's account, however, shows that the so-called objective and subjective factors are far from united in his approach. On the contrary, they occupy quite distinct and independent places in Mandel's theory. The internal pattern and rhythm of the long waves are explained by abstract 'laws of motion' at work in the capitalist economic system. Social and political factors are selectively introduced into Mandel's account solely to explain the specific lower turning-points which mark the conjunction between the contractive and expansionary waves. Indeed, Mandel deliberately excludes the influence of social and political factors in his account of the processes occurring within the timespan of each wave. He does so to demonstrate the inevitability of periodic crises arising from the internal logic of capitalist economies, regardless of the impact of so-called exogenous influences. Be that as it may, this approach provides an inadequate guide to analysing concrete historical situations where social and political forces interact closely with economic processes to shape the actual course of development.

In my view the distinction Mandel draws between 'internal' economic mechanisms and 'external' influences is a false and misleading one. Social and political structures and processes are just as internal to the capitalist system as the economic. The process of capitalist production is founded upon exploitative social relationships which adopt certain structures and generate latent or actual conflicts that are just as inherent and unavoidable within

capitalist societies as economic structures and their crisis tendencies.

In response to these difficulties I have adopted an unashamedly
eclectic approach to analysing the long waves. The term 'eclectic'
is sometimes used disparagingly, especially in the Marxist literature, to describe certain theoretical stances – and rightly so where
competing theories are simultaneously drawn on for convenience
with no attempt to identify and overcome the points of incompati-
bility between them.[1] In my view, however, a major strength of
the long-wave thesis is its capacity to merge a range of perspectives
which focus upon particular isolated elements of capitalist development, such as technical change and the labour process or crisis
tendencies and business cycles, to show how they impinge upon
one another and present them within a unified historical framework.

One central consequence of this approach is that I do not
believe it is possible to develop a complete theoretical explanation
of the long waves which, by their nature, defy any such totalising
perspective. The most that can be accomplished is to identify the
basic structures and processes of capitalist economies which generate the potential for long-term fluctuations. Every long wave of
capitalist development has entailed certain invariant factors which
are present in every historical phase. For example, they all involve
short-term fluctuations, crisis tendencies and qualitative technological advances. Such invariant factors give the long waves their
continuity as periods of ebb and flow in an ongoing historical
process. But the *nature and form* of these factors varies markedly
between each historical phase. There is no single panhistorical
theory of long waves capable of explaining the qualitative changes
in their historical form. The most such a theory can accomplish is
to show the inevitability of instability within the capitalist economic framework. There will always be certain critical areas of
indeterminacy and relative spontaneity which defy predictive theory
and give rise to what Stanley Aronowitz calls the 'jagged side' of
historical development.[2]

Long Waves of Regional Development

The problem of establishing the degree of interdependence and
independence of related structures and processes which are labelled
'economic', 'social' or 'political' is not confined to theories of long

waves. It has been a recurrent concern, not only in Marxist economics, but in all fields of social inquiry. Marxist regional analysis has not remained aloof from this problem. As described in the Introduction to this study, most Marxist theoretical frameworks for analysing uneven regional development have in one way or another tended to reduce regional processes to the operation of abstract or global economic forces, neglecting the specifically 'regional' inputs to those forces. One important purpose of this work has been to rehabilitate the concept of regional processes of development, not as a functional variable within some deterministic schema, but as a historically variable feature taking different forms in different times and places. At the same time I have sought to provide a historical analysis which goes beyond mere documentary description. The fact that historical experiences of development vary between different regions in different periods does not mean that these varying experiences cannot be analysed within a coherent framework.

The historical processes of industrial change and development in the British regions since the Industrial Revolution have not been simply microcosms of these processes at a national scale. The long waves of economic development in the national economy have involved a variety of quite distinctive patterns of development among the British regions. Some regions, notably the West Midlands until the most recent downturn, exhibit what the Schumpeterian perspective might refer to as a classic pattern of development marked by a historical succession of leading industrial sectors across the course of the long waves. But the British regions have not, for the most part, exhibited such a stylised pattern of sectoral growth cycles. Most industrial regions, including Wales, the north and the north-west, have been dominated by one or two industries whose development has been confined to a single wave. Other regions, especially the south-east, have experienced a more complex pattern of development involving relatively buoyant, largely population-related industries such as consumer-good manufacturing, construction and service sectors. These industries have taken some share of each successive long wave and do not display the classical two-phase growth-cycle pattern of expansion followed by stagnation within a single wave.

The long waves of industrial development have been associated with a changing spatial hierarchy of leading industrial regions, beginning with cotton textiles in the north-west during the Industrial

Revolution, followed by the development after 1850 of heavy industries like coal, steel and shipbuilding in Wales, Scotland and the north and succeeded after the interwar depression by manufacturing sectors in the West Midlands and south-east. This evolving regional hierarchy has entailed more than simply industrial structural changes. It has centred upon historical transformations in the social division of labour and the evolution of the capitalist labour process. The process of industrialisation in the first half of the nineteenth century revolved around a social and spatial division between town and country which circumscribed the transition from fragmented semi-domestic and workshop production to the centralised manufacturing system. This form of spatial organisation was superseded from the mid-nineteenth century to the interwar depression by the growth of an *inter*-sectoral spatial division between different regional production complexes specialising in particular branches of extensively mechanised industry. The more recent development of a new *intra*-sectoral spatial division between regions specialising in different subsectors within the same industry, such as research and development, component manufacture and final assembly, had its origins in the post-war period and has become increasingly prominent during the latest phase of Fordist industrial restructuring.

These evolving patterns of uneven regional development are not simply reflections or outcomes of the long waves in the national economy. They *are* the process of national economic change and development. At different times, and in different ways, the spatial divisions in economic organisation have played a role in the national patterns of short-term fluctuations characteristic of the successive historical periods. The succession of leading industrial regions have provided the basis for regional social and political movements which have, at critical moments, contested and to varying degrees determined the ensuing course of national and sometimes international economic development. The key factor in the overall course of British economic development has been the particular, even unique, class character of British capitalism in the division between industrial and finance capital which has itself entailed a spatial division between the industrial provinces and the metropolitan hub of finance and commerce. In my view the industrialised capitalist economies are once again reaching a critical point in their development whose course hinges upon social and political contests which will once again involve important spatial dimensions.

Regional Development and the fifth Kondratieff upturn

The latest revival of the theory of long waves has been strongly associated with renewed interest in the role of technological change in economic development, particularly the potential for advances in microelectronics and related fields to lift the Western economies out of their present industrial stagnation.[3] As described in the Introduction, a number of authors concerned with the future of economic development on a regional scale have applied the Schumpeterian perspective of the long waves to examinations of the spatial dimension to technical change and innovation.[4] In its most extreme form this approach sees the spatial distribution of innovative activity as the key factor which selects those regions where industrial growth or revival will take place and, equally important, where it will not occur. In his speculation on the geography of the coming fifth Kondratieff cycle, Peter Hall has argued that there is little, if any, prospect of an industrial revival in the depressed UK regions and that unemployment in these areas can only be brought down by employment-induced migration of workers and their families from old industrial areas to those selected areas where new industries are presently emerging out of spatial concentrations of innovative activity:

> what Britain needs now is someone to say . . . that tomorrow's industries are not going to be born in yesterday's regions, and that the aim of government should be to start planning for a massive move of people from the old areas and cities to the new. Britain's future, if it has one, is in that broad belt that runs from Oxford and Winchester through the Thames Valley and Milton Keynes to Cambridge.[5]

In Hall's view British governments should abandon their attempts to regenerate the economies of the old industrialised regions and concentrate resources on the generation of new, technologically advanced industries in the newly industrialising areas. For observers with an interest in reducing present levels of interregional social and economic inequality, as well as preventing their expansion in the future, the implications of this long-wave perspective must seem at best pessimistic and at worst outright reactionary. Hall's approach resurrects the idea, prevalent in the 1930s, that rather than taking measures to revitalise employment in the depressed regions or take 'work to the workers', unemployment in the depressed areas can best be tackled by moving 'workers to the work'.[6] This notion is embodied in the present Conservative Government's approach to regional policy and spatial disparities in employment opportunities.[7] Indeed, in another context Hall's views have allegedly inspired the government's Enterprise Zone programme which aims to regenerate industrial growth in depressed areas by market regulated industrial movement.[8] Above all, Hall's approach reinforces the notion that the social, economic and spatial effects of technological advance are predetermined and inevitable.

A recurrent theme of this work has been that technological change is only one force underlying the long waves and must be considered in interaction with a range of other factors which determine the course of social and economic development. I have focused upon a number of factors in particular:

  (i)   crisis tendencies and short-term fluctuations of capitalist development, particularly the tendency towards periodic phases of industrial over-accumulation;
  (ii) the capitalist labour process, representing the conjunction of the technical forces of production and the social relationships which circumscribe them;
  (iii) the uneven development of different industrial sectors and their labour processes;
  (iv) the uneven spatial development of all these factors;
  (v)   the social and political processes through which all these factors are brought into effect in different ways at different times and in different places.

If there is to be a fifth Kondratieff long wave in the UK economy, which is still far from guaranteed, it will be represented in all these areas and others besides. In my view it is necessary to examine the interrelationships between all these factors in order to assess the potential for a future Kondratieff upturn, the limitations of that potential and the forms an upturn might take.

Often implicit in recent writings on the economic potential of the 'microelectronics revolution' is the idea that industries in this field will be somehow immune from all the inner crisis tendencies that have beset other leading industries in previous long waves of economic development. While microelectronics will undoubtedly be a key future growth sector the spectacle of its development should not be allowed to obscure the fundamental instabilities which will remain in the capitalist economic framework. It has been suggested that one basic cause of long-term economic fluctuations is the uneven development of fixed capital and consumption sectors, particularly the tendency for the capital equipment sector to expand rapidly in the boom periods and overshoot demand from the consumer-good industries. Long waves of economic development in the past have tended to alternate every half-century or so, partly due to the timespan needed to assimilate previous technological revolutions and to saturate demand for new products and process technologies. But in my view there is no automatic reason why structural crises of over-accumulation should only occur at 50- or 60-year intervals. The rapidity with which new products and processes emerging from the latest technological revolution could potentially be assimilated in the economy may lead to an earlier shift in the pace and direction of a future fifth Kondratieff wave.

In the present climate of recessionary effects and uncertain demand the international semiconductor industry has already experienced several temporary crises of overproduction while the computer industry has engaged in regular price wars over market shares.[9] Like the motor industry during the post-war boom, the microelectronics industry is in a highly competitive phase of its development where intense price-cutting competition demands high-volume production in order to yield returns from low-unit profits. The world market for microelectronic 'hardware' can only support a limited number of such volume producers. For this reason the microelectronics industry, like the motor industry before it, can be expected to enter a phase of mergers and buyouts.[10] It will be the established giants, above all the US and Japanese multinationals, which will be best equipped to survive this process rather than the small and young entrants to the field among whom can be numbered most of the British competitors.

The growth and development of microelectronics will be very much dependent upon demand for electronic devices, not only in new industries, but also from old-established sectors. It has been suggested that the single largest industrial consumer of micro-electronic components for the rest of the century will not be a 'fifth wave' industry, like automated office-equipment manufacturing, but the 'fourth wave' automobile industry.[11] There is enormous potential for assimilation of microelectronic devices in this sector, not only in the motor-car itself through control systems and other components, but also in design and production process technologies like Computer-Aided Design and Manufacture (CADCAM), robotics and Computer Numerically Controlled (CNC) machine tools.

The distinction often drawn between older, declining 'sunset' industries and new, expanding 'sunrise' sectors is in many cases a false one. Many long-established manufacturing industries are not simply experiencing a process of decline or contraction. Old industries are undergoing a phase of adaptation and restructuring through which they are being made new. Evidence presented in this study has shown that the classical S-shaped product cycle of expansion, stagnation and decline has been, at least in employment terms, historically much rarer than the Schumpeterian theory would suggest. Several industrial sectors in the British economy and its regions have experienced more complex patterns of buoyancy and renewal of their development across the historical long waves.

While the microelectronics revolution offers great potential for a profound structural regeneration of economic development, like previous technological revolutions that potential can only be realised through equally far-reaching transformations in the social relationships surrounding the labour processes in which the new technology is deployed. Manufacturing and assembly sectors that have already been subjected to automation and flow-line processes are experiencing an intensification of this subordination of labour-to-machine regulation through technologies like robotics and CNC.[12] Moreover, some sectors which have hitherto remained relatively immune from machine regulation, such as retailing, financial services and office administration, are now experiencing the kinds of intensive labour processes formerly largely confined to the manufacturing sector. Numerous studies have pointed to the potential labour-shedding consequences of technologies like Electronic

Fund Transfer (EFT) in banking or at the retail point-of-sale (EFTPOS) and analysed the implications of technologies involved in office automation (such as word processors and data-base computer filing) for intensifying direct managerial control over the labour process, deskilling and routinising formerly relatively unstructured white-collar work.[13] In particular it has been pointed out how such technical changes reinforce the disadvantages of women employees with respect to pay, status and conditions in work as well as the opportunities for entering paid employment.[14]

A growing body of research and analysis has explored the new workplace inequalities likely to accompany the introduction of new technologies into factories and offices. Less attention has been devoted to the emergence of new *spatial* inequalities in terms of types and levels of income and employment opportunities which are accompanying the process of industrial and technological change. The last chapter of this study described how the process of industrial restructuring since the late 1960s has begun to give rise to a fresh spatial hierarchy of economic activity. The high-technology sectors have been in the forefront of this process of spatial change. The spatial distribution of the UK semiconductor industry is marked by the decentralisation of deskilled manual assembly work to peripheral industrial regions, contrasting with the concentration of a highly skilled technical élite in newly industrialising areas outside the old industrial centres.[15]

The geographical organisation of the developing high-technology industries is more complex than Peter Hall would have it. Since the example of 'Silicon Valley' in the Santa Clara area of California is frequently cited by proponents of innovation-sponsored regional economic growth, it is worth while noting the results of a recent evaluation of this area's experience.[16] The spectacular growth of the microelectronics industry in this area, through links between new firms, local universities and graduate entrepreneurs, has not led to a balanced expansion of industry and employment in Santa Clara. On the contrary it has been accompanied by a disproportionate influx of scientific and technical professionals with a relative shortage of employment opportunities for unskilled or semi-skilled manual workers. The multiplicity of small firms launched by graduates from the Californian universities have either been swallowed up by larger corporations or have become large corporations themselves. The growth of the California-based companies has involved the decentralisation of microelectronic hardware production to old industrial areas elsewhere in the USA or abroad while the economic structure of Santa Clara is distorted towards research and scientific functions.

It is important to note that the processes of technological and industrial change, as well as their workplace and spatial dimensions, are presently emerging in the UK only in very embryonic forms. Moreover these features are not developing naturally or spontaneously. Their emergence depends upon major social and political changes, frequently involving conflicts and confrontations. This process of social restructuring is presently being spearheaded in the UK by the Conservative government. While this is not the place to enter into a detailed assessment of the Conservative's economic and political programme the prevailing period of 'Thatcherism' clearly marks an important turning-point in the state's orientation towards the economy, contrasting sharply with the so-called 'Keynesian consensus' which predominated until the mid-1970s when it began to disintegrate under the 1974–9 Labour government.[17] The Conservative's economic programme can be distinguished from its predecessors by a number of main features:

(i) the prioritisation of anti-inflationary measures through monetary restraint, ending the preoccupation with 'full employment' which was the hallmark of past Keynesian policies;[18]

(ii) the emphasis awarded to permanently restraining the growth of public spending, contrasting with the preceding period of cyclical demand-regulation through public expenditure-led reflation/deflation;

(iii) the enforced 'slim-down and shake-out' of manufacturing employment and capacity in an effort to boost competitiveness, contrasting with past efforts to bolster or subsidise ailing sectors or intervene directly to assist industrial reorganisation;[19]

(iv) efforts to open up new outlets for private investment (while simultaneously reducing public spending and enforcing the industrial shake-out) through privatisation of state holdings;

(v) efforts to create a 'new worker' through direct legislative regulation of union activity as well as through special employment measures, such as the Youth Training Scheme, which accustom a future generation to lower wage levels and fewer employment rights, both of which are enforced through the 'new realism' generated by the climate of mass unemployment.[20]

Most of these areas have direct or indirect regional implications. As well as reducing public expenditure the two rounds of cuts in regional industrial aid in 1979 and 1984 have contributed to the shake-out of manufacturing industry by reducing the buffer of public grants and subsidies. This was reflected in a July 1979 editorial of the *Financial Times* which proclaimed the reductions in regional spending as 'a way to help the regions'.[21] The explanation for this at first sight contradictory statement was that wage rates in the Assisted Areas failed to reflect the relatively poor performance of other economic indicators. Reduced state aid would force manufacturers to achieve competitiveness by shedding surplus labour and capacity while holding down wage costs. In addition to such negative measures, Cooke, Morgan and Jackson have shown how positive steps to support the growth of new, predominantly microelectronics-based industries have entailed a hidden regional policy.[22] This is cementing the new spatial contrast between an unskilled, poorly organised mass workforce in areas like central Scotland and a technical-scientific élite along the M4 corridor of southern England.

The processes of structural change in the British economy and its spatial organisation are giving rise to social and political contests, some of which are reactions *against* those changes and some of which are products *of* the changes themselves. Again these conflicts are unevenly represented at the regional and local scales. Efforts to shed labour and capacity while holding down wage costs in traditional industries of some of the oldest industrial regions have generated bitter struggles like the 1979–80 steel strike and the 1984–5 coal dispute. The latter, in particular, was much more than a struggle over redundancies and pit closures in the coal industry. It presented a microcosm of the social and industrial restructuring taking place in contemporary Britain, the role of the state in overseeing that restructuring and the reaction of local communities whose survival is threatened by these processes.[23]

As well as these intense forms of protest in traditional industrial sectors and old-established working communities, social and economic change is generating the potential for workplace conflict in industries and areas hitherto regarded as relatively free from such unrest. The overall decline of manufacturing employment in the UK as a whole masks important changes in its spatial distribution and composition. The dispersal of manufacturing away from the old-established urban industrial centres towards newly industrialising areas (the so-called urban–rural shift) is drawing new sections of the population into potentially conflict-laden working situations. In particular the processes of deskilling and the search for relatively poorly organised and low-paid labour, which partly underlie the processes of industrial and spatial restructuring, are drawing increasing numbers of women into unskilled, manual work. The 'feminisation' of traditionally male-dominated industrial trade unions has been an important characteristic of changing patterns of trade-union membership over the past decade.[24] Indeed, some of the hardest fought labour movement *causes célèbre* so far this decade have centred around the struggles of predominantly women workforces.[25]

The dispersal of manufacturing industry has been accompanied by a growth and decentralisation of services which similarly hold out the possibility for workplace conflicts in new sections of the economy. The prospect of jobless (or even job loss) growth accompanying the introduction of new technology into areas like banking and financial services has given a new prominence to white-collar trade unions in these fields.[26] Pressure on public expenditure and staffing levels in state welfare and the civil service has stimulated memorable protests such as hospital occupations and strikes in social security offices – again, frequently involving a largely female workforce.[27] Indeed, the prominence of public-sector services as an arena and focus for labour-movement campaigns has been one of the most significant developments in labour politics over the past decade.[28]

Experiences like these have stimulated a shift of labour-movement activity and thinking away from traditional preoccupations with narrow issues, such as pay, and negative responses against job losses or changing working conditions towards broader, more positive movements for the development of alternatives to unemployment, economic decay and declining public services.[29] Disputes in the public sector have frequently been fought over the level and quality of service provision as much as the immediate interests of the workforce themselves. In industry, experiences like the Lucas Aerospace workers' alternative corporate plan for

retaining jobs by converting socially destructive armaments production to design and production for socially useful purposes stand
as isolated but influential examples of what has been suggested
may be 'a new trade unionism in the making'.[30]

In recent years one of the most important forums for developing
and initiating alternatives to economic decline has been the sphere
of local government. The intensifying socio-economic problems of
the metropolitan areas, coupled with the lack of any major national initiative to combat mounting unemployment, set in the
context of a decade of successive government attempts to constrain spending on local services, all of which were brought sharply
into focus by the inner-city disturbances in the summer of 1981
which followed the English local elections, stimulated many local
authorities to embark on wide-ranging programmes for regenerat-
ing their local and regional economies. Several Labour-controlled
authorities, most notably the Greater London Council, West
Midlands County Council and Sheffield City Council, although
there are many less well-known examples, have launched initiatives and set up new agencies for direct investment in local industry
while seeking to introduce new modes of planning and public
accountability into the process of local economic development.[31]

These experiences are not only posing alternatives to economic
decline and restructuring, or to the policies of the present government, but are also challenging traditional socialist approaches to
economic planning and conceptions of the role of urban and
regional development within a national economic programme.
They are demonstrating that state intervention in the economy
need not necessarily be equated with the centralised national
planning pursued by past Labour governments or with the monolithic and bureaucratic deformations of the Eastern bloc.[32] Local
councils are showing that economic initiatives and popular involvement at a local and regional scale are an essential ingredient
of any national programme for economic regeneration which must
accommodate and respond to a diversity of local problems and
uneven opportunities for resolving them.

Some influential recent studies of the British regions' future
economic prospects have suggested that a solution to the problems
of the depressed industrial regions and inner-city areas will be
dependent upon macroeconomic policies of reflation backed by
import controls and regulation of the terms of international trade

to resolve the problems of British manufacturing industry. Moore and Rhodes of the Cambridge Economic Policy Group have argued that:

> The fact is that there is no solution to double figure unemployment rates in the regions unless a solution is found at the national level. . . . The CEPG strategy is the most likely, of those available, to bring us nearer to rather than further away from a national solution.[33]

Along similar lines, Fothergill and Gudgin conclude in their influential study that:

> Britain's industrial base is shrinking so rapidly that any reduction in unemployment which urban and regional policies might achieve in depressed areas is far less than the reduction which a reversal of national trends could produce. The first priority for those in Scotland, South Wales, the North East and elsewhere who are desperately worried by rising unemployment must therefore be to secure a change in *national* economic policy, to halt the destruction of British industry. We believe that the appropriate strategy should be based on reflation backed by the regulation of imports.[34]

The assumption behind such arguments seems to be that stimulation of national economic growth will automatically bring benefits to the depressed regions; that 'regional problems' are a symptom of national economic stagnation and that regional prosperity inevitably follows from an upturn in national economic prospects. In opposition to this view the evidence presented in this work suggests that past waves of prolonged national economic expansion have been associated with the *formation* of spatial inequalities involving successive forms of uneven regional development. A sustained national economic revival in the 1980s would involve a process of industrial restructuring which would create new spatial hierarchies of economic activity.[35]

Recent practical examples of local economic intervention have suggested that policies for urban and regional economic regeneration must necessarily be aimed directly at the restructuring process itself rather than confined to arm's-length regulation of the macroeconomic context within which restructuring is taking place. Some local authorities have attempted to redirect the restructuring process in ways which contribute to, rather than damage, the local economic base, employment prospects and community life, counterposing unhindered 'restructuring for capital' with interventionist programmes aimed at what Ken Livingstone of the GLC has called 'restructuring for labour'.[36]

Recent local experiences have stimulated wide support for a new regionalism which acknowledges a key role for the development and implementation of initiatives generated from within the regions themselves. In the past few years support for the devolution of power to regional assemblies and development agencies has grown, not only within the labour movement, but also among academics and professionals.[37]

While the recent resurgence of regional and local political movements is often referred to as a 'new' phenomenon, many participants and outside observers regard these innovative measures as a reconstruction of the historic tradition of municipal enterprise and civic works pursued by nineteenth-century urban administrations.[38] However, any analogy between the contemporary local socialist initiatives and the nineteenth-century civic administrations should not be taken too far. The important point to be drawn from such comparisons is not any direct similarity between the civic works and administration pursued by the Victorian 'city fathers' and the modern municipal socialist initiatives. Rather the similarity lies in the way that these locally based movements can be seen to emerge at historic turning-points in the direction and nature of British social, economic and political development and have the capacity to assert their independence in influencing the ensuing course of that development.

It would, of course, be foolish to suggest that local initiatives can in themselves solve the deepening social and economic crises of Britain's cities and regions. The actual or potential impacts of these local movements should not be over-estimated, but nor should they be under-estimated. The significance of regional movements like the Manchester free-traders and the Birmingham social imperialists in the last century lay as much, if not more, in the sphere of political consciousness and ideology as in their objective achievements. In this respect the local and regional movements of the 1980s may yet yield similarly significant results extending beyond their immediate spatial and temporal confines. As over the past 150 years of industrial change and restructuring the British cities and regions will continue to provide a focus for contests over the future of British economic and social development.

Notes and References

Introduction

1. Searjeant, 1983.
2. See respectively Forrester, 1976; Freeman, Clark and Soete, 1982.
3. See respectively Organisation for Economic Co-operation and Development, 1979; the report by Shearlock, 1981; Institute of Measurement and Control, 1981.
4. See for example Rothwell and Zegveld, 1979; Benson and Lloyd, 1983.
5. Freeman (ed.), 1981.
6. Kondratieff, 1935.
7. Warren, 1982.
8. Beckman, 1983.
9. See Lorenz, 1982; Shearlock, 1981.
10. Reported in *Politics and Profit*, 1982.
11. See in particular Mandel, 1975 (first published in German in 1972); Arrighi, 1978 (first published in Italian in 1972); Glyn and Sutcliffe, 1972.
12. Mandel, 1975.
13. See Bell and Kristol (eds), 1981.
14. Eversley, 1975.
15. For example in his standard introductory text on regional planning, Glasson, 1980, p. 417, relates the cuts in regional assistance announced in July 1979 simply to the Conservative's 'clear mandate to restrain public spending'.
16. Lebas, 1977, p. 82, original emphasis.
17. I am conscious of the parallel here with my interest in regional development and the theory of long waves.
18. These perspectives variously label different categories of region as central/peripheral, dominant/dominated, developed/underdeveloped or advanced/backward. I have arbitrarily chosen to use the centre/periphery terminology here, but this is not intended to imply that I accept it or understand it to have any precise meaning.
19. E.g. see Martinelli, 1974; Lipietz, 1980.
20. See Carney, Hudson, Ive and Lewis, 1976; Hechter, 1975.
21. See Massey's review, 1978.

22. Lipietz, 1980.
23. Dunford, 1977, p. 37.
24. Marxist regional analysis was undoubtedly influenced by previous work in the field of urban studies, particularly Castells's celebrated critique of 'urban sociology' as an ideological and unscientific construction. See Castells, 1976 (first published in France in 1969).
25. Mingione, 1981, pp. 63–4.
26. Massey and Meegan, 1978.
27. Morgan, 1980, p. 1.
28. Pickvance, 1981, p. 241.
29. Damette and Poncet, 1980, p. 93.
30. Perrons, 1981; Dunford and Perrons, 1983.
31. E.g. Massey, 1983, p. 75, argues that 'the fact that the effect of a process will vary according to the conditions in which it operates means that it is fruitless to examine the real world for some empirically-generalised outcome in order to substantiate the operation of that process'.
32. On this see Asheim, 1979.
33. E.g. Hanappe and Savy, 1981.
34. Hall, 1981.
35. Rothwell, 1982.
36. Freudenberger and Mensch, 1981. Mensch's research on the clustering of technical innovations has been an important spur to the wider revival of interest in the Schumpeterian theory of long waves, see Mensch, 1979.
37. Freudenberger and Mensch, 1981, p. 201.
38. Marglin, 1974.
39. See particularly Steedman, 1977; Elson, 1979; Wright, 1979.
40. See particularly Braverman, 1974; Palloix, 1976; Aronowitz, 1978; Elger, 1979.
41. Dunford and Perrons, 1983.
42. See Holland, 1975, pp. 113–17, and the collection of articles in Carney, Hudson and Lewis (eds), 1980.

Chapter 1   Theories of Long Waves: From Kondratieff to Mandel

1. These are the most influential theories of long waves. For a more comprehensive survey see Van Duijn, 1983, part II.
2. Cleary and Hobbs, 1983, p. 167.
3. See Tinbergen, 1983; Van Duijn, 1983, pp. 59–63.
4. Biographical details of Kondratieff's life and work presented here draw on Garvy, 1943.
5. See his 1925 paper, Kondratieff's only major article to be published (a decade later) in English translation, Kondratieff, 1935.
6. Kondratieff, 1935, p. 115.

7. Ibid.
8. Cited in Garvy, 1943, p. 207.
9. Ibid. p. 208.
10. Ibid.
11. Garvy, 1943, p. 208, points out that Kondratieff recognised the lack of any internal, cyclical necessity for this turning-point, but seems to have assumed it in his explanation for the long waves.
12. Cited by Garvy, 1943, p. 204.
13. Garvy, 1943, pp. 209–16.
14. Rostow, 1960.
15. Rostow, 1978.
16. Rostow, 1979, ch. 28 see especially p. 383.
17. Rostow, 1979, p. 22.
18. Ibid. p. 25.
19. Ibid. p. 34.
20. Schumpeter, 1939.
21. These three issues were raised respectively by Kuznets, 1940; Rose, 1941; and Hansen, 1941. For a detailed survey of contemporary debates surrounding Schumpeter's work see Clemence and Doody, 1950.
22. Schumpeter, 1934, first German edition published in 1912. The conceptual definitions of 'development' and 'innovation' in Schumpeter's work are described succinctly by Heertje, 1977, ch. 6, on whose factual exposition much of this section is based.
23. Schumpeter, 1976, ch. 7 (first published in 1942), is devoted to this process.
24. Mandel, 1983, p. 195.
25. Mensch, 1979 (first published in German in 1975).
26. Aldcroft and Richardson, 1969, p. 35.
27. Kuznets, 1940.
28. Ray, 1980.
29. Freeman, Clark and Soete, 1982, chs 3 and 4.
30. Van Duijn, 1983.
31. Forrester, 1976; Graham and Senge, 1980.
32. Forrester, 1976, p. 203.
33. Cited by Carr and Davies, 1974, pp. 780–1.
34. Trotsky, 1973, p. 226.
35. For an excellent account of Kondratieff's place in the early Soviet debates on economic theory and the prospects for capitalism in the West see Day, 1981, especially pp. 51–5, 87–95.
36. Trotsky, 1973, p. 226.
37. Ibid. pp. 253–4.
38. See Trotsky, 1973, p. 253, where he refers to a survey of foreign trade data in *The Times*.
39. Cited by Day, 1976, p. 71.
40. Mandel, 1975. See also his later book, 1980, where he clarifies the themes of his earlier work and responds to critics.
41. See Marx, 1977b, part III.

42. Mandel, 1975, pp. 109–10.
43. Mandel, 1980, p. 49, original emphasis.
44. See Gordon, 1978, and Mandel's critique of his work, 1980, pp. 51–3.
45. Mandel, 1975, pp. 39, original emphasis.

Chapter 2   Long Waves, Technological Change and the Capitalist Labour Process

1. Rothwell and Zegveld, 1979, pp. 26–35.
2. Friend and Metcalf, 1981, ch. 1.
3. Kaldor, 1954.
4. Marx, 1977a, p. 558, on the motor of capitalist development: 'Accumulate, accumulate! That is Moses and the prophets!'
5. Mattick, 1981, p. 26.
6. Ibid. p. 27.
7. Mandel, 1975, p. 137.
8. Freeman, Clark and Soete, 1982, p. 78.
9. Ibid. pp. 80–1.
10. Wright, 1978, p. 164.
11. See especially Hodgson, 1974; Steedman, 1977.
12. As well as the Sraffian sources see Sweezy, 1970; Meek, 1967; Blaug, 1960.
13. See, for example, Gillman's classic study, 1957, and the critique by Desai, 1974.
14. This conception, which Arun Bose, 1975, p. 95, has called the 'asymptotic' view of abstract values which approach real economic categories, but never coincide with them, has been most strongly represented in the Japanese school of Marxist economists, e.g. see Tsuru, 1952.
15. For the best non-mathematical reviews see Fine and Harris, 1976, 1979; Rowthorn, 1974; Wright, 1979. Collections of articles include Elson (ed.), 1979; Steedman, Sweezy, Wright and others, 1981.
16. E.g. see Elson, 1979, p. 121.
17. Kalecki, 1936.
18. Ibid. pp. 95–6.
19. Mandel, 1980, pp. 56–61.
20. Ibid. p. 49.
21. Mandel's highly impressionistic account of the interrelationship between the so-called subjective and objective factors is well illustrated by an extraordinary graph on p. 21 of his 1980 work purporting to show 'long waves in economic growth' superimposed with 'long waves in European class struggle' from 1871 to 1974. Needless to say Mandel provides no quantitative measure for the vertical axis.
22. Rowthorn, 1976, pp. 63–4.
23. Friedman, 1977.
24. See especially Steedman, 1977.

25. Elson, 1979.
26. See Sraffa, 1960, ch. 12.
27. Leigh and North, 1983.
28. Palloix, 1976.
29. The discussion here draws on the description of Palloix's model by Perrons, 1981.
30. Taylor, 1947.
31. Gramsci, 1971.
32. Marx, 1977a, parts III and IV.
33. Braverman, 1974.
34. Palloix, 1976.
35. For an example of this new form of productive organisation see Coriat, 1980, on the Renault Motor Company's experiments at their Le Mans plant in 1973.
36. Elger, 1979.
37. Friedman, 1977.
38. Aronowitz, 1978.
39. Friedman, 1977.
40. Ibid. p. 56.
41. Ibid. p. 90.
42. Benson and Lloyd, 1983, ch. 2.
43. Ibid. p. 54.

Chapter 3 Long Waves, Capitalist Crisis and the Business Cycle

1. Kalecki, 1943.
2. Salvati, 1983; Phelps Brown, 1975.
3. The degree of autonomy which the state in capitalist society enjoys from the capitalist class has been the subject of ongoing debate in Marxist theory, see particularly the celebrated exchange between Miliband and Poulantzas, 1972.
4. E.g. see Kalecki, 1936.
5. Gordon, 1978, see above, pp. 45–60.
6. Glyn and Harrison, 1980.
7. These exchanges presume the 'transformation' of values into commodity prices, a process which as described above has been the subject of great controversy among Marxist economists. While Marx's analysis provides a useful descriptive framework there are severe limitations on its application as a quantitative theory of exchanges between different elements of the accumulation process.
8. Marx, 1974, chs 20 and 21.
9. For detailed reviews of these alternative Marxist crisis theories see Mandel, 1968, pp. 361–8; Mattick, 1981, ch. 3; Sweezy, 1970, chs 10 and 11; Itoh, 1980, ch. 5.
10. Hilferding, 1980 (first published in 1910); Bukharin, 1972 (German translation first published in 1924).

11. Luxemburg, 1963 (first German edition published in 1912).
12. Glyn and Sutcliffe, 1972.
13. Glyn and Sutcliffe, 1971.
14. Boddy and Crotty, 1975.
15. Ibid. p. 1.
16. Glyn and Harrison, 1980.
17. Itoh, 1980, p. 94.
18. Marx, 1973, p. 748.
19. Marx, 1977b, p. 484.
20. Marx, 1974, p. 414.
21. Wright, 1978, ch. 3.
22. Hilferding, 1980.
23. Lenin, 1973 (first published in 1917).
24. Crouch, 1979, pp. 17–18.
25. O'Connor, 1973.
26. On the role of state expenditure in advanced capitalism see the seminal article by Gough, 1975.
27. Offe, 1973–4, 1975; Habermas, 1976.
28. Itoh, 1980, p. 131.
29. Aglietta, 1979.
30. Ibid. p. 356.
31. Wright, 1978, ch. 3.
32. See Saul, 1969, on the 'Myth of the Great Depression'.
33. Landes, 1969, pp. 232–3.
34. See Van Roon, 1983.
35. Itoh, 1980, p. 141, is generally doubtful of the long-wave thesis and warns in particular that the division of capitalist development into alternate long waves should not be allowed to obscure the unity of the competitive capitalist period and the continuity of the short-term cycles.
36. Aldcroft and Fearon, 1972.
37. Ibid. p. 3.
38. Friend and Metcalf, 1981, p. 34.
39. See also Mitchell, 1950.
40. Itoh, 1980, p. 138.
41. Itoh, 1980, ch. 6.
42. Assuming that there *are* any future economic historians! Emma Rothschild has pointed out that we do not necessarily have to be adherents of Schumpeter or Kondratieff to appreciate the role played by the expansion of US military industry in the post-1945 period, or the importance of the present arms boom in promoting innovation and growth in industries like electronics which many see as the future leaders of the next Kondratieff upturn. See Rothschild, 1980, pp. 181–2.
43. Aldcroft and Richardson, 1969, p. 61.

Chapter 4 Regional Industrial and Employment Change, 1841–1971

1. Lee, 1979.
2. See Mandel, 1975, pp. 130–2.
3. Massey and Meegan, 1982.
4. Van Duijn, 1983. See above, pp. 34–5.
5. Freeman, Clark and Soete, 1982. See above, pp. 33–4.
6. These are not 'activity rates' in the strict sense of the term. The activity rates here are ratios of employees to population rather than to the economically active population.
7. Only a bare outline of the most serious difficulties is provided here. For an exhaustive discussion see Lee, 1979, pp. 6–10.
8. Lee, 1979, p. 9.
9. Ibid. pp. 9–10.
10. Between 1911 and 1931 Scotland's share of the national population fell by 0.9 percentage points compared with only 0.1 in the north of England and in Wales and 0.3 in the north-west.
11. See Williamson, 1965.
12. Secchi, 1977.
13. Ibid. pp. 49–50.

Chapter 5 From Industrial Revolution to Imperialist Workshop: Contrasting Regional Experiences

1. See Gilboy, 1932.
2. Hobsbawm, 1969, p. 45.
3. Ibid. pp. 59–60.
4. Chapman, 1972, p. 12.
5. Hobsbawm, 1969, p. 59.
6. Ashton, 1948, p. 11.
7. Hobsbawm, 1973, p. 52.
8. Hobsbawm, 1969, p.69.
9. Chapman, 1972, pp. 12–13.
10. Ibid. p. 13.
11. See Brown and Burrows's comparison of north-west England with the textiles regions of northern France and the US New England area, 1977, pp. 128–50.
12. Collier, 1964, p. 14.
13. Chapman, 1967, pp. 164–8.
14. See Hobsbawm and Rudé, 1973, maps pp. 167, 170.
15. See Foster, 1974, particularly ch. 4.
16. Rostow, 1960.
17. Deane and Cole, 1967, pp. 42, 185, 188.
18. Habakkuk and Deane, 1963, p. 72.

19. Chapman, 1972, pp. 65–6.
20. Ibid. pp. 67–8.
21. The term 'barbaric' may be an understatement. Hobsbawm, 1969, p. 72, adds the description 'murderous', noting that the average life-expectancy at birth in the Black Country town of Dudley between 1841 and 1850 was just $18\frac{1}{2}$ years.
22. Figures from Lee, 1979.
23. Cottrell, 1980, p. 237.
24. Hamilton, 1942.
25. E.g. see Felix, 1956.
26. Lee, 1980, pp. 167–72.
27. Sigsworth, 1980, p. 189.
28. Slaven, 1980, p. 115.
29. Mitchell, 1964; Kenwood, 1965; Hawke and Reed, 1969.
30. Slaven, 1980, pp. 107–8.
31. Mitchell and Deane, 1971, pp. 131–2.
32. Church, 1975, p. 44. See also Clapham, 1932, pp. 301–2; Hawke, 1970, pp. 396–7.
33. Taylor, 1980, p. 48.
34. Stedman Jones, 1971, p. 26.
35. Ibid. p. 27.
36. Mellor, 1975, p. 110.
37. See, for example, Alexander's study, 1976, of women's work in London between 1820 and 1850.
38. Mellor, 1975, p. 112.
39. Gourvish, 1980, p. 126.
40. Church, 1975, p. 56.
41. Coppock, 1956.
42. Phelps Brown and Handfield-Jones, 1952.
43. Saul, 1969, p. 55.
44. Gayer, Rostow and Schwartz, 1953.
45. Crouzet, 1982, p. 319. The account here draws on Crouzet, 1982, ch. 10.
46. Ibid. p. 322.
47. Church, 1975, pp. 53–4.
48. Saul, 1969, p. 21.
49. Cottrell, 1975, pp. 35–6.
50. Thomas, 1973. See also Williamson, 1962; Kuznets, 1966.
51. Habakkuk, 1962.
52. Harvey, 1978, pp. 116–22.
53. Mathias, 1969, p. 413.
54. Lee, 1971, p. 93.
55. Ibid. p. 96.
56. Mathias, 1969, p. 412.
57. See Landes, 1969, ch. 5.
58. On this 'entrepreneurial stagnation' thesis see Landes, 1969; Aldcroft, 1964.
59. Hobsbawm, 1969, pp. 191–2.

60. See Imlah's data, 1958, pp. 37–8, 70–5, 94–8.
61. Hobsbawm, 1969, p. 192.
62. See Sutcliffe and Smith, 1974, p. 6.
63. Smith, 1964, p. 140.
64. Allen, 1929, pp. 33–4.
65. Crouzet, 1982, pp. 331–2.
66. See, for example, Benwell Community Project, 1978.
67. Carney, Lewis and Hudson, 1977, pp. 52–3.
68. Saul, 1962, p. 87.

Chapter 6 Region, Class and Nation: The Uniqueness of the British Experience

1. Hobsbawm, 1969, pp. 29–30.
2. Anderson, 1979, p. 16.
3. For an account of these twin processes of capitalist expansion see Hill, 1969, pt three.
4. Anderson, 1979, p. 16, emphasis omitted.
5. Nairn, 1977, p. 20.
6. Taylor, 1980, p. 50.
7. On the theoretical issues involved in the relationship between capital and land see Massey and Catalano, 1978, ch. 2.
8. Briggs, 1968, pp. 117–8.
9. Quoted in Briggs, 1968, p. 119.
10. Ibid.
11. Ibid. pp. 119–20.
12. Anderson, 1979, p. 16.
13. See Miliband's thesis on the capitalist state and the 'economic élite', 1973.
14. See Crouzet, 1982, p. 408.
15. Gamble, 1981, p. 51, original emphasis.
16. See above, pp. 148–9.
17. Thomson, 1966, p. 291.
18. Ibid. p. 293.
19. Mingione, 1981, p. 91.
20. von Braunmühl, 1978, p. 171.
21. Aglietta, 1979, pp. 73–9.
22. In so far as a fragmented North American society did exist, the white-settler population were more concerned with avoiding it or liquidating it than integrating and subordinating it to their own.
23. For a discussion of these aspects of the American Civil War see Moore, 1967, ch. 3.
24. For a brief account of the social imperialist movement see Gamble, 1981, pp. 166–74.
25. Lenin, 1973, p. 94.
26. Rhodes's reflections on attending a meeting of the unemployed in

London's East End, quoted in Lenin, 1973, pp. 93–4.
27. See Briggs, 1968, ch. 5.
28. Ibid. p. 187.
29. Ibid. p. 189.
30. Anderson, 1979, p. 18, original emphasis.
31. On this see Moore, 1967, ch. 1.

Chapter 7   Economic Fluctuations and the 'Regional Problem'

1. See Gamble, 1981, pt one, on Britain's 'hundred years' decline'.
2. Mowat, 1968, p. 463–70.
3. McCrone, 1969, p. 16.
4. Aldcroft and Fearon, 1972, p. 3.
5. Thirlwall, 1966.
6. Brechling, 1967, pp. 2–3. He identified these components through a regression analysis of quarterly unemployment percentage rates for the 'old' British statistical regions. This methodology is explained in more detail in Brechling's paper.
7. Brechling, 1967, p. 17. He does not supply specific yearly figures for these residuals, but does provide a table of correlation decision coefficients between the regional figures which, according to Brechling, 'suggests that there are two negatively correlated cyclical components; one in the Northern and the other in the Southern regions of Britain'.
8. Frost and Spence, 1981.
9. Ibid. p. 212.
10. Fothergill and Gudgin, 1982.
11. Ibid. p. 50. Fothergill and Gudgin use the periods 1952–79 and 1952–60, 1960–6, 1966–73, 1973–9, with the initial year as a base year for subsequent calculations. For a concise survey of the shift-share technique, its applications and problems, see Glasson, 1978, pp. 109–15.
12. Fothergill and Gudgin, 1982, p. 63.
13. Ibid. pp. 6–10.

Chapter 8   Industrial Restructuring and the New Spatial Division of Labour

1. See Palloix, 1976; Aglietta, 1979, 1982.
2. Dunford, Geddes and Perrons, 1981.
3. Ibid. p. 388.
4. Aglietta, 1982.
5. Ibid. pp. 18–19.
6. Ibid. pp. 19–26.
7. Stewart, 1972, p. 237.

8. For a detailed account of the 'three traumatic years' from 1964 to 1967 see Brittan, 1971, ch. 8.
9. Fothergill and Gudgin, 1982.
10. Massey and Meegan, 1983.
11. Panić, 1972, p. 13.
12. See Rodger, 1984.
13. See the collection in Blackaby (ed.), 1979.
14. E.g. Massey and Meegan, 1978.
15. E.g. see Blackburn, Green and Liff, 1982, p. 16.
16. Overbeek, 1980, p. 111.
17. Dunning, 1969, pp. 120–1.
18. Glyn and Sutcliffe, 1971, p. 17.
19. Pratten, 1968, p. 39.
20. Glyn and Sutcliffe, 1971, p. 16.
21. Ibid.
22. E.g. Firn, 1975; Susman, 1981; Watts, 1979.
23. McDermott, 1976, p. 326.
24. Dunning, 1969, pp. 120–1.
25. Merseyside Socialist Research Group, 1980, p. 39.
26. See Owen, 1984.
27. Merseyside Socialist Research Group, 1980, pp. 38–9.
28. See above, pp. 196–7.
29. Fothergill and Gudgin, 1982.
30. Massey and Meegan, 1978, p. 81.
31. See Community Development Project, 1977.
32. For an account of the Community Development Projects, their origins, methods and findings see Kraushaar and Loney, 1980.
33. See Community Development Project, 1977, pp. 42–55.
34. Massey, 1979, p. 236. original emphasis.
35. E.g. Chisholm and Oeppen, 1973; Dixon and Thirlwall, 1975; Keeble, 1977.
36. Fothergill and Gudgin, 1982.
37. Smith, 1977.
38. Birmingham City Council, 1982.
39. See Counter Information Services, *Anti-Report no. 14*, p. 19.
40. Gaffikin and Nickson, 1984, p. 71.
41. West Midlands County Council Economic Development Committee, 1984a.
42. Frobel, Heinrichs and Kreys, 1980.
43. Massey and Meegan, 1982, p. 18.
44. Ibid. p. 416.
45. Massey and Meegan, 1983.
46. Massey, 1983.
47. Curiously, Massey does not mention the historical presence of tin-mining in Cornwall and its modern legacy.
48. Massey, 1979, 1984.
49. See Westaway, 1974; Buck, 1979.
50. On the contrasts between these two microelectronics growth areas see Cooke, Morgan and Jackson, 1984.

51. Rosie, 1984.
52. See Breheny, Cheshire and Langridge, 1983; Rapoport, 1984.
53. Electronics Location File, 1984.

Conclusion

1. Itoh, 1980; pp. 138–9, criticises Marxist economists, including Mandel, who have adopted multicausal explanations of capitalist crises.
2. Aronowitz, 1979, p. 32.
3. While recent attention has tended to focus upon the 'microelectronics revolution', technical advances in other fields, such as biotechnology, may yield equal or even greater growth potential. See Blackburn, Green and Liff, 1982.
4. See above, pp. 13–14.
5. Hall, 1981, pp. 537.
6. This debate was revived during the heyday of regional policies in the mid-1960s. See Richardson, and West, 1964; Needleman, 1965.
7. I am thinking here of Norman Tebbit's memorable anecdote concerning his father's bicycle. The December 1983 White Paper on *Regional Industrial Development* stated that 'the Government recognise that it would be unrealistic to expect wage adjustment alone to eliminate regional imbalances in employment opportunities. . . . Natural adjustment can also occur through people moving from areas of persistently high unemployment to areas where employment prospects are better.' See Department of Trade and Industry, 1983, paras 10–11.
8. See Hall, 1982; 1983.
9. See Duncan, 1982; Large, 1983.
10. Brooke, 1983.
11. Whitbread, 1983.
12. See Forester (ed.), 1980, ch. 4; Conference of Socialist Economists' Microelectronics Group, 1980, ch. 7.
13. Counter Information Services *Anti-Report no. 23*, pp. 8–12; *Anti-Report no. 33*, pp. 6–10; Conference of Socialist Economists Microelectronics Group, 1980, ch. 5.
14. Barker and Downing, 1980; Huws, 1982; Schumann, 1984.
15. Cooke, Morgan and Jackson, 1984.
16. Saxenian, 1983.
17. The significance of 'Thatcherism' is a highly contentious issue. Some would argue that the turning-point in the state's orientation to the economy occurred much earlier, e.g. see Blackburn, 1971, and would deny that the present Conservative government represents any fundamental change from post-war social-democratic approaches, e.g. see Tettadoro, 1980.
18. The main principles of the Conservatives' economic strategy are set out in Her Majesty's Treasury, 1979; 1980.

19. I have taken the terms 'slim-down' and 'shake-out' from Tomlinson, 1983, p. 44.

20. I owe the phrase 'new worker' to Mark Gaynor; see West Midlands County Council Economic Development Committee, 1985, p. 8. See also Counter Information Services, *Anti-Report no. 34;* Metcalf, 1982, particularly p. 15.

21. *Financial Times*, 18 July 1979.

22. Cooke, Morgan and Jackson, 1984.

23. See Byrne, 1985, p. 92.

24. Massey and Miles, 1984.

25. Massey, 1983, p. 87.

26. Counter Information Services, *Anti-Report no. 33*, pp. 14–16.

27. E.g. see Birmingham Welfare Rights Group, 1983.

28. Conference of Socialist Economists' London–Edinburgh Weekend Return Group, 1979.

29. See especially Conference of Socialist Economists' London Working Group, 1980.

30. Wainwright and Elliott, 1982. See also Coates (ed.), 1978.

31. It is not possible to capture the enormous richness and diversity of such local initiatives here. See Greater London Council Economic Policy Group, 1982, 1983; West Midlands County Council Economic Development Committee, 1984b; Mawson, Jepson and Marshall, 1984; Marshall, 1985; Blunkett and Green, 1983.

32. This theme is pursued by Blazyca, 1983, who compares and contrasts the Polish economic planning disaster, the experience of national planning under previous Labour governments in the UK and the recent socialist initiatives in Greater London and the West Midlands.

33. Moore and Rhodes, 1982, p. 333.

34. Fothergill and Gudgin, 1982, p. 186, original emphasis.

35. The CEPG have tested their policy prescriptions with econometric forecasts of future employment prospects for the UK regions under a range of alternative national economic policy assumptions, see Gudgin, Moore and Rhodes, 1982. However, other regional forecasts have suggested that the impact of reflationary national policies would be unevenly distributed across the UK regions (see Elias, 1982). Work with which I have been involved on forecasting future employment prospects for the West Midlands Metropolitan County would suggest that, while reflationary policies might arrest the *rate* of decline of manufacturing industry, they would not succeed in *reversing* that decline. The scale of destruction of West Midlands manufacturing over the past five years may be such that the region no longer has the capacity to respond to a relatively sudden upsurge in demand. See West Midlands County Council Economic Development Committee, 1984c.

36. Livingstone, 1983, p. 76.

37. Labour Party Parliamentary Spokesman's Working Group, 1982; Regional Studies Association, 1983.

38. See Briggs, 1968.

Bibliography

Aglietta, M. (1979) *A Theory of Capitalist Regulation: The US Experience* (London: New Left Books).

Aglietta, M. (1982) 'World Capitalism in the Eighties', *New Left Review*, **136**, pp. 5–41.

Aldcroft, D. H. (1964) 'The Entrepreneur and the British Economy, 1870–1914', *Economic History Review*, 2nd series, **17** (1) pp. 113–34.

Aldcroft, D. H. and Fearon, P. (1972) 'Introduction' to Aldcroft, D. H. and Fearon, P. (eds) (1972) *British Economic Fluctuations 1790–1939* (London: Macmillan).

Aldcroft, D. H. and Richardson, H. W. (1969) *The British Economy, 1870–1939* (London: Macmillan).

Alexander, S. (1976) 'Women's Work in Nineteenth Century London: A Study of the Years 1820–50', in Mitchell, J. and Oakley, A. (eds) (1976) *The Rights and Wrongs of Women* (Harmondsworth: Penguin Books).

Allen, G. C. (1929) 'Industrial Organisation in the West Midlands', in *British Industry and Economic Policy* (1979) (London: Macmillan) pp. 20–38.

Anderson, P. (1979) 'Theses on English Class Society', *International* **5** (1) pp. 15–20. Excerpt from "Origins of the Present Crisis", *New Left Review*, **42**, 1964.

Aronowitz, S. (1978) 'Marx, Braverman and the Logic of Capital', *Insurgent Sociologist*, **8** (5) pp. 126–46.

Aronowitz, S. (1979) 'The End of Political Economy', *Social Text*, **2**, pp. 3–52.

Arrighi, G. (1978) 'Towards a Theory of Capitalist Crisis', *New Left Review*, **111**, pp. 3–24.

Asheim, B. (1979) 'Conceptions of Space and Regional Development: On the Fallacies of Current Marxist Approaches to Theories of Regional Development', in Hudson, R. and Lewis, J. (eds) (1979) *The Regional Problem in Europe: Papers presented at the 19th European Congress of the Regional Science Association*, pp. 33–4.

Ashton, T. S. (1948) *The Industrial Revolution, 1760–1850* (London: Oxford University Press).

Barker, J. and Downing, H. (1980) 'Word Processing and the Transformation of the Patriarchal Relations of Control in the Office', *Capital and Class*; **10**, pp. 64–99.

Beckman, R. C. (1983) *The Downwave: Surviving the Second Great Depression*. (London: Pan Books).

Bell, D. and Kristol, I. (eds) (1981) *The Crisis in Economic Theory* (New York: Basic Books).

Benson, I, and Lloyd, J. (1983) *New Technology and Industrial Change: The Impact of the Scientific–Technical Revolution on Labour and Industry* (London: Kogan Page).

Benwell Community Project (1978) *The Making of a Ruling Class: Two Centuries of Capital Development on Tyneside*. Final Report Series no. 6 (Newcastle upon Tyne: Benwell Community Project).

Birmingham City Council (1982) *Economic Bulletin no. 1* (Birmingham City Council).

Birmingham Welfare Rights Group (1983) *Flat Broke: How the Welfare State Collapsed in Birmingham* (Birmingham Welfare Rights Group).

Blackaby, F. (ed.) (1979) *Deindustrialisation* (London: Heinemann).

Blackburn, P., Green, K. and Liff, S. (1982) 'Science and Technology in Restructuring', *Capital and Class* 18, pp. 15–37.

Blackburn, R. (1971) 'The Heath Government: A New Course for British Capitalism', *New Left Review*, 70, pp. 3–26.

Blaug, M. (1960) 'Technical Change and Marxian Economics', in Horowitz, D. (ed.) (1970) *Marx and Modern Economics* (London: MacGibbon & Kee) pp. 227–43.

Blazyca, G. (1983) *Planning is Good For You: The Case for Popular Control* (London: Pluto Press).

Blunkett, D. and Green, G. (1983) 'Building From the Bottom: The Sheffield Experience', *Fabian Tract* 491 (London: Fabian Society).

Boddy, R. and Crotty, J. (1975) 'Class Conflict and Macro-Policy: The Political Business Cycle', *Review of Radical Political Economics*, 7 (1).

Bose, A. (1975) *Marxian and Post-Marxian Political Economy* (Harmondsworth: Penguin Books).

Braunmühl, C. von (1978) 'On the Analysis of the Bourgeois Nation State Within the World Market Context', in Holloway, J. and Picciotto, S. (eds) (1978) *State and Capital: A Marxist Debate* (London: Arnold) pp. 160–77.

Braverman, H. (1974) *Labor and Monopoly Capital: The Degradation of Work in the Twentieth Century* (New York: Monthly Review Press).

Brechling, F. P. R. (1967) 'Trends and Cycles in British Regional Development', *Oxford Economic Papers*, 19, pp. 1–21.

Breheny, M., Cheshire, P. and Langridge, R. (1983) 'The Anatomy of Job Creation? Industrial Change in Britain's M4 Corridor', *Built Environment*, 9 (1) pp. 61–71.

Briggs, A. (1968) *Victorian Cities* (Harmondsworth: Penguin Books).

Brittan, S. (1971) *Steering the Economy: The Role of the Treasury* (Harmondsworth: Penguin Books).

Brooke, R. (1983) 'Why British Industry is Ripe for Major Growth in Buy-outs', *Computer Weekly*, 16 June.

Brown, A. J. and Burrows, E. M. (1977) *Regional Economic Problems: Comparative Experiences of Some Market Economies* (London: Allen & Unwin).

Buck, T. W. (1979) 'Regional Class Differences: An International Study of Capitalism', *International Journal of Urban and Regional Research*, **3** (4) pp. 516–26.

Bukharin, N. I. (1972) 'Imperialism and the Accumulation of Capital', in Tarbuck K. J. (ed.) (1972) *Rosa Luxemburg and Nikolai Bukharin: Imperialism and the Accumulation of Capital* (London: Allen Lane/Penguin Books) pp. 153–270.

Byrne, D. (1985) 'Just Haad On a Minute There: A Rejection of André Gorz's "Farewell to the Working Class"', *Capital and Class*, **24**, pp. 75–98.

Carney, J., Hudson, R., Ive, G. and Lewis, J. (1976) 'Regional Underdevelopment in Late Capitalism: A Study of the North East of England', in Masser, I. (ed.) (1976) *Theory and Practice in Regional Science: London Papers in Regional Science, 6* (London: Pion) pp. 11–29.

Carney, J,. Hudson, R. and Lewis, J. (eds) (1980) *Regions in Crisis: New Perspectives in European Regional Theory* (London: Croom Helm).

Carney, J., Lewis, J. and Hudson, R. (1977) 'Coal Combines and Interregional Uneven Development in the UK', in Massey, D. B. and Batey, P. W. J. (eds) (1977) *Alternative Frameworks For Analysis: London Papers in Regional Science 7* (London: Pion) pp. 52–67.

Carr, E. H. and Davies, R. W. (1974) *Foundations of a Planned Economy:* vol. 1, *1926–29* (Harmondsworth: Penguin Books).

Castells, M. (1976) 'Is There an Urban Sociology?' and 'Theory and Ideology in Urban Sociology', in Pickvance, C. (ed.) (1976) *Urban Sociology: Critical Essays* (London: Tavistock) pp. 33–84.

Central Statistical Office (various) *Abstract of Regional Statistics* (1965–74) *Regional Statistics* (1975–80) *Regional Trends* (1981–4) (London: HMSO).

Chapman, S. D. (1967) *The Early Factory Masters* (Newton Abbot: David & Charles).

Chapman, S. D. (1972) *The Cotton Industry in the Industrial Revolution* (London: Macmillan).

Chisholm, M. and Oeppen, J. (1973) *The Changing Pattern of Employment: Regional Specialisation and Industrial Location in Britain* (London: Croom Helm).

Church, R. A. (1975) *The Great Victorian Boom, 1850–1873* (London: Macmillan).

Clapham, J. H. (1932) *An Economic History of Modern Britain,* vol. II (London: Cambridge University Press).

Cleary, M. N. and Hobbs, G. D. (1983) 'The Fifty-Year Cycle: A Look at the Empirical Evidence', in Freeman, C. (ed.) (1983) *Long Waves in the World Economy* (London: Frances Pinter) pp. 164–82.

Clemence, R. V. and Doody, F. S. (1950) *The Schumpeterian System* (Cambridge, Mass.: Addison-Wesley).

Coates, K. (ed.) (1978) *The Right to Useful Work* (Nottingham: Spokesman Books).

Collier, F. (1964) *The Family Economy of the Working Classes in the Cotton Industry, 1784–1833* (Manchester: Manchester University Press).

Community Development Project (1977) *The Costs of Industrial Change*

(London: Community Development Project Inter-Project Editorial Team).

Conference of Socialist Economists' London–Edinburgh Weekend Return Group (1979) *In and Against the State: Discussion Notes for Socialists* (London: London–Edinburgh Weekend Return Group/ Conference of Socialist Economists).

Conference of Socialist Economists' London Working Group (1980) *The Alternative Economic Strategy: A Labour Movement Response to the Economic Crisis* (London: CSE Books/Labour Co-ordinating Committee).

Conference of Socialist Economists' Microelectronics Group (1980) *Microelectronics: Capitalist Technology and the Working Class* (London: CSE Books).

Cooke, P., Morgan, K. and Jackson, D. (1984) 'New Technology and Regional Development in Austerity Britain: The Case of the Semiconductor Industry', *Regional Studies*, **18** (4) pp. 277–89.

Coppock, D. J. (1956) 'The Climacteric of the 1890s: A Critical Note', *Manchester School*, **24** (1) pp. 1–31.

Coriat, B. (1980) 'The Restructuring of the Assembly Line: A New "Economy of Time and Control"', *Capital and Class*, **11**, pp. 34–43.

Cottrell, P. L. (1975) *British Overseas Investment in the Nineteenth Century* (London: Macmillan).

Cottrell, P. L. (1980) 'Commercial Enterprise', in Church, R. (ed.) *The Dynamics of Victorian Business* (London: Allen & Unwin) pp. 236–49.

Counter Information Services (undated) *Anti-Report no. 14: Who's Next for the Chop? (The Essential Facts on Unemployment)* (London: Counter Information Services).

Counter Information Services (undated) *Anti-Report no. 23: The New Technology* (London: Counter Information Services).

Counter Information Services (undated) *Anti-Report no. 33: Banking on the City* (London: Counter Information Services).

Counter Information Services (undated) *Anti-Report no. 34: Assault on the Unions* (London: Counter Information Services).

Crouch, C. (1979) 'The State, Capital and Liberal Democracy', in Crouch, C. (ed.) (1979) *State and Economy in Contemporary Capitalism* (London: Croom Helm) pp. 13–54.

Crouzet, F. (1982) *The Victorian Economy* (London: Methuen).

Damette, F. and Poncet, E. (1980) 'Global Crisis and Regional Crises', in Carney, J., Hudson, R. and Lewis, J. (eds) (1980) *Regions in Crisis* (London: Croom Helm) pp. 93–116.

Day, R. B. (1976) 'The Theory of the Long Cycle: Kondratiev, Trotsky, Mandel', *New Left Review*, **99**, pp. 67–82.

Day, R. B. (1981) *The 'Crisis' and the 'Crash': Soviet Studies of the West (1917–1939)* (London: New Left Books).

Deane, P. and Cole, W. A. (1967) *British Economic Growth, 1688–1959* (London: Cambridge University Press).

Department of Trade and Industry (1983) *White Paper: Regional Industrial Development*, Cmnd 9111 (London: HMSO).

Desai, M. (1974) *Marxian Economic Theory* (London: Gray-Mills).

Dixon, R. J. and Thirlwall, A. P. (1975) *Regional Growth and Unemployment in the UK* (London: Macmillan).

Duijn, J. J. Van (1983) *The Long Wave in Economic Life* (London: Allen & Unwin).

Duncan, M. (1982) 'The Information Technology Industry in 1981', *Capital and Class*, **17**, pp. 78–113.

Dunford, M. (1977) 'Regional Policy and the Restructuring of Capital', *Sussex Working Papers in Urban and Regional Studies no. 4* (Falmer, Brighton: University of Sussex).

Dunford, M., Geddes, M. and Perrons, D. (1981) 'Regional Policy and the Crisis in the UK: A Long-run Perspective', *International Journal of Urban and Regional Research*, **5** (3) pp. 377–409.

Dunford, M. and Perrons, D. (1983) *The Arena of Capital* (London: Macmillan).

Dunning, J. N. (1969) 'The Role of American Investment in the British Economy', *Political and Economic Planning Broadsheet 35 (507)* (London: PEP).

Electronics Location File (1984) *Outlook for the British Electronics Industry in 1984* (Richmond, Surrey: Urban Publishing Company).

Elger, T. (1979) 'Valorisation and "Deskilling": A Critique of Braverman', *Capital and Class*, **7**, pp. 58–99.

Elias, P. (1982) 'The Regional Impact of National Economic Policies: A Multi-Regional Simulation Approach for the UK', *Regional Studies*, **16** (5) pp. 335–44.

Elson, D. (1979) 'The Value Theory of Labour', in Elson, D. (ed.) (1979) *Value: The Representation of Labour in Capitalism* (London: CSE Books) pp. 115–80.

Elson, D. (ed.) (1979) *Value: The Representation of Labour in Capitalism* (London: CSE Books).

Eversley, D. (1975) 'Planning Without Growth', *Fabian Research Series*, 321 (London: Fabian Society).

Felix, D. (1956) 'Profit Inflation and Industrial Growth: The Historic Record and Contemporary Analogies', *Quarterly Journal of Economics*, **70**, pp. 441–63.

Fine, B. and Harris, L. (1976) 'Controversial Issues in Marxist Economic Theory', in Miliband, R. and Saville, J. (eds) (1976) *The Socialist Register 1976* (London: Merlin).

Fine, B. and Harris, L. (1979) *Rereading 'Capital'* (London: Macmillan).

Firn, J. (1975) 'External Control and Regional Development: The Case of Scotland', *Environmental Planning 7*, pp. 393–414.

Forester, T. (ed.) (1980) *The Microelectronics Revolution: The Complete Guide to the New Technology and its Impact on Society* (Oxford: Blackwell).

Forrester, J. (1976) 'Business Structure, Economic Cycles and National Policy', *Futures*, **8** (3) pp. 195–214.

Foster, J. (1974) *Class Struggle and the Industrial Revolution: Early Industrial Capitalism in Three English Towns* (London: Methuen).

Fothergill, S. and Gudgin, G. (1982) *Unequal Growth: Urban and Regional Employment Change in the UK* (London: Heinemann).

Freeman, C. (ed.) (1981) 'Technical Innovation and Long Waves in World Economic Development', *Futures*, **13** (4), special theme issue.

Freeman, C., Clark, J. and Soete, L. (1982) *Unemployment and Technical Innovation: A Study of Long Waves and Economic Development* (London: Frances Pinter).

Freudenberger, H. and Mensch, G. (1981) 'Regional Differences, Differential Development and Generative Regional Growth', in Bairoch, P. and Lévy-Leboyer, M. (eds) (1981) *Disparities in Economic Development Since the Industrial Revolution* (London: Macmillan) pp. 199–209.

Friedman, A. (1977) *Industry and Labour: Class Struggle at Work and Monopoly Capitalism* (London: Macmillan).

Friend, A. and Metcalf, A. (1981) *Slump City: The Politics of Mass Unemployment* (London: Pluto Press).

Frobel, F., Heinrichs, J. and Kreys, O. (1980) *The New International Division of Labour* (London: Cambridge University Press).

Frost, M. and Spence, N. (1981) 'The Timing of Unemployment Response in British Regional Labour Markets, 1963–76', in Martin, R. L. (ed.) (1981) *Regional Wage Inflation and Unemployment*. (London: Pion) pp. 208–31.

Gaffikin, F. and Nickson, A. (1984) *Jobs Crisis and the Multinationals: The Case of the West Midlands* (Birmingham: Birmingham Trade Union Group for World Development).

Gamble, A. (1981) *Britain in Decline: Economic Policy, Political Strategy and the British State* (London: Macmillan).

Garvy, G. (1943) 'Kondratiev's Theory of Long Cycles', *Review of Economic Statistics*, **25** (4), pp. 203–20.

Gayer, A. D., Rostow, W. W. and Schwartz, A. J. (1953) *The Growth and Fluctuation of the British Economy, 1790–1850* (two volumes) (Oxford: Clarendon Press).

Gilboy, E. W. (1932) 'Demand as a Factor in the Industrial Revolution', in *Facts and Factors in Economic History* (Cambridge, Mass.: Harvard University Press) pp. 620–39.

Gillman, J. (1957) *The Falling Rate of Profit: Marx's Law and its Significance to Twentieth Century Capitalism* (London: Dennis Dobson).

Glasson, J. (1978) *An Introduction to Regional Planning* (London: Hutchinson).

Glasson, J. (1980) 'Major Policy Changes to December 1979 Affecting the Regions', appx to 3rd ed. of *An Introduction to Regional Planning* (London: Hutchinson) pp. 417–9.

Glyn, A. and Harrison, J. (1980) *The British Economic Disaster* (London: Pluto Press).

Glyn, A. and Sutcliffe, B. (1971) 'The Critical Condition of British Capital', *New Left Review*, **66**, pp. 3–33.

Glyn, A. and Sutcliffe, B. (1972) *British Capitalism, Workers and the Profits Squeeze* (Harmondsworth: Penguin Books).

Gordon, D. M. (1978) 'Up and Down the Long Roller Coaster', in Union for Radical Political Economics (1978) *US Capitalism in Crisis* (New York: Union for Radical Political Economics) pp. 22–35.

Gough, I. (1975) 'State Expenditure in Advanced Capitalism', *New Left Review*, **92**, pp. 53–92.

Gourvish, T. R. (1980) 'Railway Enterprise', in Church, R. (ed.) (1980) *The Dynamics of Victorian Business* (London: Allen & Unwin) pp. 126–141.

Graham, A. and Senge, P. (1980) 'A Long-wave Hypothesis of Innovation', *Technological Forecasting and Social Change*, **17**, pp. 283–311.

Gramsci, A. (1971) 'Americanism and Fordism', in *Selections from the Prison Notebooks* (London: Lawrence & Wishart) pp. 277–318.

Greater London Council Economic Policy Group (1982) 'Socialist GLC in Capitalist Britain?' *Capital and Class*, **18**, pp. 117–33.

Greater London Council Economic Policy Group (1983) *Jobs For a Change* (London: Greater London Council).

Gudgin, G., Moore, B. and Rhodes, J. (1982) 'Employment Problems in the Cities and Regions of the UK: Prospects for the 1980s', *Cambridge Economic Policy Review*, **8** (2).

Habakkuk, H. J. (1962) 'Fluctuations in House-building in Britain and the United States in the Nineteenth Century', *Journal of Economic History*, **22** (2) pp. 198–230.

Habakkuk, H. J. and Deane, P. (1963) 'The Take-Off in Britain', in Rostow, W. W. (ed.) (1963) *The Economics of Take-Off into Sustained Growth: Proceedings of a Conference Held by the International Economic Association* (London: Macmillan) pp. 63–82.

Habermas, J. (1976) *Legitimation Crisis* (London: Heinemann).

Hall, P. (1981) 'The Geography of the Fifth Kondratieff Cycle', *New Society*, 26 Mar, pp. 535–7.

Hall, P. (1982) 'Enterprise Zones: A Justification', *International Journal of Urban and Regional Research*, **6** (3) pp. 416–21.

Hall, P. (1983) 'Enterprise Zones and Freeports Revisited', *New Society*, 24 Mar, pp. 460–2.

Hamilton, E. J. (1942) 'Profit Inflation and the Industrial Revolution, 1751–1800', *Quarterly Journal of Economics*, **56** (2) pp. 256–73.

Hanappe, P. and Savy, M. (1981) 'Industrial Port Areas and the Kondratieff Cycle', in Hoyle, B. S. and Pinder, D. A. (eds), *Cityport Industrialisation and Regional Development* (Oxford: Pergamon) pp. 11–21.

Hansen, A. (1941) *Fiscal Policy and Business Cycles* (New York: Norton).

Harvey, D. (1978) 'The Urban Process Under Capitalism: A Framework for Analysis', *International Journal of Urban and Regional Research*, **2** (1) pp. 101–31.

Hawke, G. R. (1970) *Railways and Economic Growth in England and Wales, 1840–1870* (London: Oxford University Press).

Hawke, G. R. and Reed, M. C. (1969) 'Railway Capital in the United Kingdom in the Nineteenth Century', *Economic History Review*, 2nd series, **22** (2) pp. 269–86.

Hechter, M. (1975) *Internal Colonialism: The Celtic Fringe in British National Development, 1536–1966* (London: Routledge & Kegan Paul).

Heertje, A. (1977) *Economics and Technical Change* (London: Weidenfeld & Nicolson).

Her Majesty's Treasury (1979) 'The Budget – A New Beginning', *Economic Progress Report*, **110**, pp. 1–2.

Her Majesty's Treasury (1980) 'The Medium-Term Financial Strategy', *Economic Progress Report*, **120**, pp. 2–7.

Her Majesty's Treasury (1982) 'Recent Trends in Labour Productivity', *Economic Progress Report*, **141**, pp. 1–5.

Hilferding, R. (1980) *Finance Capital* (London: Routledge & Kegan Paul).

Hill, C. (1969) *Reformation to Industrial Revolution* (Harmondsworth: Penguin Books).

Hobsbawm, E. J. (1969) *Industry and Empire* (Harmondsworth: Penguin Books).

Hobsbawm, E. J. (1973) *The Age of Revolution* (London: Sphere).

Hobsbawm, E. J. and Rudé, G. (1973) *Captain Swing* (Harmondsworth: Penguin Books).

Hodgson, G. (1974) 'The Theory of the Falling Rate of Profit', *New Left Review*, **84**, pp. 55–82.

Holland, S. (1975) *The Socialist Challenge* (London: Quartet).

Huws, U. (1982) *Your Job in the Eighties: A Woman's Guide to the New Technology* (London: Pluto Press).

Imlah, A. H. (1958) *Economic Elements in the Pax Britannica* (Cambridge, Mass.: Harvard University Press).

Institute of Measurement and Control (1981) *Long-term Economic Cycles: Their Causes and Consequences*. Papers presented at symposium, London, 3 Dec 1981.

Itoh, M. (1980) *Value and Crisis: Essays on Marxian Economics in Japan* (London: Pluto Press).

Kaldor, N. (1954) 'The Relation of Economic Growth and Cyclical Fluctuations', *Economic Journal*, **64**, pp. 53–71.

Kalecki, M. (1936) 'A Theory of the Business Cycle', *Review of Economic Studies*, **4**, pp. 77–97.

Kalecki, M. (1943) 'Political Aspects of Full Employment', *The Political Quarterly*, **14 (4)**, pp. 322–31.

Keeble, D. (1977) 'Spatial Policy in Britain: Regional or Urban?', *Area*, **9**, pp. 3–8.

Kenwood, A. G. (1965) 'Railway Investment in Britain, 1825–75', *Economica*, new series, **32** (127) pp. 313–21.

Kondratieff, N. (1935) 'The Long Waves in Economic Life', *Review of Economic Statistics*, **17** (6) pp. 101–15. (Reprinted in *Lloyds Bank Review*, **129**, 1978.)

Kraushaar, R. and Loney, M. (1980) 'Requiem for Planned Innovation: The Case of the Community Development Project', in Brown, M. and Baldwin, S. (eds) (1980) *The Yearbook of Social Policy in Britain 1978* (London: Routledge & Kegan Paul) pp. 225–47.

Kuznets, S. (1940) 'Schumpeter's Business Cycles', *American Economic Review*, **30** (2) pp. 257–71.

Kuznets, S. (1966) 'Long Swings in Population Growth and Related Economic Variables', in *Economic Growth and Structure: Selected Essays* (London: Heinemann) pp. 328–78.

Labour Party Parliamentary Spokesman's Working Group (1982) *Alternative Regional Strategy: A Framework for Discussion* (London: Labour Party).

Landes, D. S. (1969) *The Unbound Prometheus: Technological Change and Industrial Development in Western Europe from 1750 to the Present* (London: Cambridge University Press).

Large, P. (1983) 'Financial Extra [slump in the US semiconductor industry]', *The Guardian* 31 Jan.

Lebas, E. (1977) 'Regional Policy Research: Some Theoretical and Methodological Problems', in Harloe, M. (ed.) (1978) *Captive Cities* (London: Wiley) pp. 79–88.

Lee, C. H. (1971) *Regional Economic Growth in the United Kingdom Since the 1880s* (London: McGraw-Hill).

Lee, C. H. (1979) *British Regional Employment Statistics, 1841–1971* (London: Cambridge University Press).

Lee, C. H. (1980) 'The Cotton Textile Industry', in Church, R. (ed.) (1980) *The Dynamics of Victorian Business* (London: Allen & Unwin) pp. 161–80.

Leigh, R. and North, D. (1983) 'The Clothing Sector in the West Midlands', *West Midlands County Council Economic Development Unit Sector Report no. 3*.

Lenin, V. I. (1973) *Imperialism, the Highest Stage of Capitalism* (Peking: Foreign Languages Press).

Lipietz, A. (1980) 'The Structuration of Space, the Problem of Land and Spatial Policy', in Carney, J., Hudson, R. and Lewis, J. (eds) (1980) *Regions in Crisis* (London: Croom Helm) pp. 60–75.

Livingstone, K. (1983) 'Monetarism in London', *New Left Review* **137**, pp. 68–77.

Lorenz, C. (1982) 'How Design May Fit the Theory of Economic "Long Waves"', *Financial Times*, 18 Aug.

Luxemburg, R. (1963) *The Accumulation of Capital* (London: Routledge & Kegan Paul).

McCrone, G. (1969) *Regional Policy in Britain* (London: Allen & Unwin).

McDermott, P. J. (1976) 'Ownership, Organisation and Regional Dependence in the Scottish Electronics Industry', *Regional Studies*, **10** (3) pp. 319–35.

Mandel, E. (1968) *Marxist Economic Theory* (London: Merlin).

Mandel, E. (1975) *Late Capitalism* (London: New Left Books).

Mandel, E. (1980) *Long Waves of Capitalist Development: The Marxist Interpretation* (London: Cambridge University Press).

Mandel, E. (1983) 'Explaining Long Waves of Capitalist Development', in Freeman, C. (ed.) (1983) *Long Waves in the World Economy* London: Frances Pinter) pp. 195–201.

Marglin, S. (1974) 'What Do Bosses Do? The Origin and Functions of Hierarchy in Capitalist Production', in Gorz, A. (ed.) (1976) *The*

Division of Labour: The Labour Process and Class Struggle in Modern Capitalism (Brighton, Sussex: Harvester) pp. 13–54.

Marshall, M. (1985) 'Technological Change and Local Economic Strategy in the West Midlands', *Regional Studies* **19 (6)**, pp. 570–78.

Martinelli, A. (1974) 'The Concept of Dualism in the Analysis of Underdevelopment', *International Journal of Sociology*, **4** (2–3) pp. 7–30.

Marx, K. (1973) *Grundisse* (Harmondsworth: Penguin Books).

Marx, K. (1977a) *Capital*, vol. i (London: Lawrence & Wishart).

Marx, K. (1974) *Capital*, vol. ii (London: Lawrence & Wishart).

Marx, K. (1977b) *Capital*, vol. iii (London: Lawrence & Wishart).

Massey, D. (1978) 'Regionalism: Some Current Issues', *Capital and Class*, **6**, pp. 106–25.

Massey, D. (1979) 'In What Sense a Regional Problem?', *Regional Studies*, **13** (2) pp. 233–43.

Massey, D. (1983) 'Industrial Restructuring as Class Restructuring: Production Decentralization and Local Uniqueness', *Regional Studies*, **17** (2) pp. 73–89.

Massey, D. (1984) *Spatial Divisions of Labour: Social Structures and the Geography of Production* (London: Macmillan).

Massey, D. and Catalano, A. (1978) *Capital and Land: Land Ownership by Capital in Great Britain* (London: Arnold).

Massey, D. and Meegan, R. (1978) 'Industrial Restructuring versus the Cities', *Urban Studies*, 15; and in Evans, A. and Eversley, D. (eds) (1980) *The Inner City: Employment and Industry* (London: Heinemann) pp. 78–107.

Massey, D. and Meegan, R. (1982) *The Anatomy of Job Loss: The How, Why and Where of Employment Decline* (London: Methuen).

Massey, D. and Meegan, R. (1983) 'The New Geography of Jobs', *New Society*, 17 Mar, pp. 416–18.

Massey, D. and Miles, N. (1984) 'Mapping Out the Unions', *Marxism Today*, May, pp. 19–22.

Mathias, P. (1969) *The First Industrial Nation*: An Economic History of Britain, 1700–1914 (London: Methuen).

Mattick, P. (1981) *Economic Crisis and Crisis Theory* (London: Merlin).

Mawson, J., Jepson, D. and Marshall, M. (1984) 'Economic Regeneration in the West Midlands: The Role of the County Council', *Local Government Policy Making* (Nov) pp. 61–72.

Meek, R. (1967) 'Karl Marx's Economic Method', in *Economics and Ideology and Other Essays* (London: Chapman & Hall) pp. 93–106.

Mellor, R. (1975) 'The British Experience: Combined and Uneven Development', in Harloe, M. (ed.) (1975) Proceeding of the Conference on Urban Change and Conflict. *Centre for Environmental Studies Conference Papers 14* (London: Centre for Environmental Studies) pp. 100–35.

Mensch, G. (1979) *Stalemate in Technology: Innovations Overcome the Depression* (New York: Ballinger).

Merseyside Socialist Research Group (1980) *Merseyside in Crisis* (Birkenhead: Merseyside Socialist Research Group).

Metcalf, D. (1982) 'Special Employment Measures: An Analysis of Wage Subsidies, Youth Schemes and Worksharing', *Midland Bank Review* (autumn/winter) pp. 9–21.

Miliband, R. (1973) *The State in Capitalist Society* (London: Quartet).

Miliband, R. and Poulantzas, N. (1972) 'The Problem of the Capitalist State', in Blackburn, R. (ed.) (1972) *Ideology in Social Science: Readings in Critical Social Theory* (London: Fontana) pp. 238–62.

Mingione, E. (1981) *Social Conflict and the City* (Oxford: Blackwell).

Mitchell, B. R. (1964) 'The Coming of the Railway and United Kingdom Economic Growth', *Journal of Economic History*, **24** (3) pp. 315–36.

Mitchell, B. R. and Deane, P. (1971) *Abstract of British Historical Statistics* (London: Cambridge University Press).

Mitchell, B. R. and Jones, H. G. (1971) *Second Abstract of British Historical Statistics* (London: Cambridge University Press).

Mitchell, W. C. (1950) *Business Cycles and their Causes* (Berkeley: University of California Press).

Moore, B. Jnr. (1967) *Social Origins of Dictatorship and Democracy* (London: Allen Lane/Penguin Books).

Moore, B. and Rhodes, J. (1982) 'A Second Great Depression in the UK Regions: Can Anything Be Done?', *Regional Studies*, **16** (5) pp. 323–33.

Morgan, K. (1980) 'The Reformulation of the Regional Question, Regional Policy and the British State', *Sussex Working Papers in Urban and Regional Studies*, p. 18 (Falmer, Brighton: University of Sussex).

Mowat, C. L. (1968) *Britain Between the Wars, 1919–1940* (London: Methuen).

Nairn, T. (1977) *The Break-Up of Britain: Crisis and Neo-Nationalism* (London: New Left Books).

Needleman, L. (1965) 'What Are We To Do About the Regional Problem?', *Lloyds Bank Review*, **75**, pp. 45–58.

O'Connor, J. (1973) *The Fiscal Crisis of the State* (New York: St James's Press).

Offe, C. (1973–4) 'The Abolition of Market Control and the Problem of Legitimacy', *Kapitalistate*, May 1973, pp. 109–16; Dec–Jan 1973–4, pp. 73–5.

Offe, C. (1975) 'The Theory of the Capitalist State and the Problem of Policy Formation', in Lindberg, L. *et al.* (eds) *Stress and Contradiction in Modern Capitalism* (Lexington, Mass.: D. C. Heath) pp. 125–44.

Organisation for Economic Co-operation and Development (1979) *Structural Determinants of Employment and Unemployment*, vol. 2 (Paris: OECD).

Overbeek, H. (1980) 'Finance Capital and the Crisis in Britain', *Capital and Class*, **11**, pp. 99–120.

Owen, I. (1984) 'Nissan Decision Draws Backbench Criticism', *Financial Times*, 2 Feb.

Palloix, C. (1976) 'The Labour Process: From Fordism to Neo-Fordism' in *The Labour Process and Class Strategies*, Conference of Socialist Economists' Pamphlet no. 1 (London: Stage 1) pp. 46–67.

Panić, M. (1972) 'Capital Utilisation in the Manufacturing Industry', *National Westminster Bank Quarterly Review* (Feb) pp. 7–16.

Perrons, D. (1981) 'The Role of Ireland in the New International Division of Labour: A Proposed Framework for Regional Analysis', *Regional Studies*, **15** (2) pp. 81–100.

Phelps Brown, E. H. and Handfield-Jones, S. J. (1952) 'The Climacteric of the 1890s: A Study in the Expanding Economy', *Oxford Economic Papers*, **4** (3) pp. 266–307.

Phelps Brown, E. H. (1975) 'A Non-Monetarist View of the Pay Explosion', *Three Banks Review* p. 105.

Pickvance, C. G. (1981) 'Policies as Chameleons: An Interpretation of Regional Policy and Office Policy in Britain', in Dear, M. and Scott, A. (eds) (1981) *Urbanization and Urban Planning in Capitalist Societies* (London: Methuen) pp. 231–65.

Politics and Profit (1982) 'The Things They Say about Profit and Politics', *Politics and Profit*, newspaper of the Conference of Socialist Economists, Dec.

Pratten, C. F. (1968) 'The Merger Boom in Manufacturing Industry', *Lloyds Bank Review*, pp. 39–55.

Rapoport, C. (1984) 'Britain's Silicon Valley Revisited: Life in the Fast Lane', *Financial Times*, 28 Apr.

Ray, G. F. (1980) 'Innovation in the Long Cycle', *Lloyds Bank Review*, **135**, pp. 14–28.

Regional Studies Association (1983) *Report of an Inquiry into Regional Problems in the United Kingdom* (Norwich: GEO Books).

Richardson, H. W. and West, E. G. (1964) 'Must We Always Take Work to the Workers?', *Lloyds Bank Review*, **71**, pp. 35–48.

Rodger, I. (1984) 'Hard Truths on Britain's Industrial Decline', *Financial Times*, 23 Jan.

Roon, G. Van (1983) 'Historians and Long Waves', in Freeman, C. (ed.) (1983) *Long Waves in the World Economy* (London: Frances Pinter) pp. 237–44.

Rose, A. (1941) 'Wars, Innovations and Long Cycles: A Brief Comment', *American Economic Review*, p. 31.

Rosie, G. (1984) 'High Tech on the High Road', *Sunday Times*, 11 Mar.

Rostow, W. W. (1960) *The Stages of Economic Growth: A Non-Communist Manifesto* (London: Cambridge University Press).

Rostow, W. W. (1978) *The World Economy: History and Prospect* (London: Macmillan).

Rostow, W. W. (1979) *Getting From Here to There: A Policy for the Post-Keynesian Age* (London: Macmillan).

Rothschild, E. (1980) 'The American Arms Boom', in Thompson, E. P. and Smith, D. (eds) *Protest and Survive* (Harmondsworth: Penguin Books) pp. 170–85.

Rothwell, R. (1982) 'The Role of Technology in Industrial Change: Implications for Regional Policy', *Regional Studies*, **16** (5) pp. 361–9.

Rothwell, R. and Zegveld, W. (1979) *Technical Change and Employment* (London: Frances Pinter).

Rowthorn, R. (1974) 'Neo-Classicism, Neo-Ricardianism and Marxism', *New Left Review*, **86**, pp. 63–87.

Rowthorn, R. (1976) 'Mandel's "Late Capitalism"', *New Left Review* **98**, pp. 59–83.

Salvati, M. (1983) 'Political Business Cycles and Long Waves in Industrial Relations: Notes on Kalecki and Phelps Brown', in Freeman, C. (ed.) (1983) *Long Waves in the World Economy* (London: Frances Pinter) pp. 202–24.

Saul, S. B. (1962) 'The Motor Industry in Britain to 1914', *Business History*, **5** (1) pp. 22–44.

Saul, S. B. (1969) *The Myth of the Great Depression* (London: Macmillan).

Saxenian, A.-L. (1983) 'The Urban Contradictions of Silicon Valley: Regional Development and the Restructuring of the Semiconductor Industry', *International Journal of Urban and Regional Research*, **7** (2) pp. 237–62.

Schumann, G. (1984) 'The Macro- and Microeconomic Social Impact of Advanced Computer Technology', *Futures*, **16** (3) pp. 260–85.

Schumpeter, J. A. (1934) *The Theory of Economic Development* (London: Cambridge University Press).

Schumpeter, J. A. (1939) *Business Cycles: A Theoretical, Historical and Statistical Analysis of the Capitalist Process* (London: McGraw-Hill).

Schumpeter, J. A. (1976) *Capitalism, Socialism and Democracy* (London: Allen & Unwin).

Searjeant, G. (1983) 'World Recovery: A Question of Belief', *The Times*, 28 Apr.

Secchi, B. (1977) 'Central and Peripheral Regions in a Process of Economic Development: The Italian Case', in Massey, D. B. and Batey, P. W. J. (eds) (1977) *Alternative Frameworks for Analysis*. London Papers in Regional Science, 7 (London: Pion) pp. 36–51.

Shearlock, P. (1981) 'From Stalin's Salt Mines to Belgrave Square', *Sunday Times*, 20 Sep.

Sigsworth, E. M. (1980) 'The Woollen Textile Industry', in Church, R. (ed.) (1980) *The Dynamics of Victorian Business* (London: Allen & Unwin) pp. 181–98.

Slaven, A. (1980) 'The Shipbuilding Industry', in Church, R. (ed.) (1980) *The Dynamics of Victorian Business* (London: Allen & Unwin) pp. 107–25.

Smith, B. M. D. (1964) 'Industry and Trade, 1880–1960', *Victorian County History of Warwickshire*, **7**, pp. 140–208.

Smith, B. M. D. (1977) 'Industry in Metropolitan Area Plans: Proposals and Experience in the West Midlands County Area', *Joint Centre for Regional, Urban and Local Government Studies* (University of Birmingham).

Sraffa, P. (1960) *Production of Commodities By Means of Commodities: Prelude to a Critique of Economic Theory* (London: Cambridge University Press).

Stedman Jones, G. (1971) *Outcast London* (Oxford: Clarendon Press).

Steedman, I. (1977) *Marx After Sraffa* (London: New Left Books).

Steedman, I., Sweezy, P., Wright, E. O., *et al.* (1981) *The Value Controversy* (London: New Left Books).

Stewart, M. (1972) *Keynes and After* (Harmondsworth: Penguin, Books).

Susman, P. (1981) 'Regional Restructuring and Transnational Corporations', *Antipode*, **13** (2) pp. 15–24.

Sutcliffe, A. and Smith, R. (1974) *History of Birmingham*, vol. III: *Birmingham 1939–1970* (London: Oxford University Press).

Sweezy, P. (1970) *The Theory of Capitalist Development* (New York: Monthly Review Press).

Taylor, A. J. (1980) 'The Coal Industry', in Church, R. (ed.) (1980) *The Dynamics of Victorian Business* (London: Allen & Unwin) pp. 46–62.

Taylor, F. W. (1947) *Scientific Management* (New York: Harper & Bros).

Tettadoro, D. (1980) 'Analysing the Tories', *International*, **5** (2) pp. 2–5.

Thirlwall, A. P. (1966) 'Regional Unemployment as a Cyclical Phenomenon', in Blunden, J., Brook, C., Edge, G. and Hay, A. (eds) (1973) *Regional Analysis and Development* (London: The Open University Press) pp. 42–9.

Tinbergen, J. (1983) 'Kondratiev Cycles and So-called Long Waves: The Early Research', in Freeman, C. (ed.) (1983) *Long Waves in the World Economy*. (London: Frances Pinter), pp. 13–18.

Thomas, B. (1973) *Migration and Economic Growth: A Study of Great Britain and the Atlantic Economy* (London: Cambridge University Press).

Thomson, D. (1966) *Europe Since Napoleon* (Harmondsworth: Penguin Books).

Tomlinson, J. (1983) 'Does Mass Unemployment Matter?', *National Westminster Bank Quarterly Review* (Feb) pp. 35–45.

Trotsky, L. D. (1973) 'Report on the World Economic Crisis and the New Tasks of the Communist International', in *The First Five Years of the Communist International*, vol. 1 (London: New Park) pp. 226–78.

Tsuru, S. (1952) 'Business Cycle and Capitalism: Schumpeter vs. Marx', in Howard, M. and King, J. (eds) (1976) *The Economics of Marx: Selected Readings of Exposition and Criticism* (Harmondsworth: Penguin Books) pp. 179–84.

Wainwright, H. and Elliott, D. (1982) *The Lucas Plan: A New Trade Unionism in the Making?* (London: Allison & Busby).

Warren, J. P. (1982) *The 50-Year Boom–Bust Cycle: The Case for Kondratieff's Long Wave Theory* (Godalming, Surrey: Warren, Cameron & Co.).

Watts, H. D. (1979) 'Large Firms, Multinationals and Regional Development: Some New Evidence from the United Kingdom', *Environment and Planning*, **11**, pp. 7–81.

West Midlands County Council Economic Development Committee (1984a) 'Combatting Industrial Decline', *Economic Review no. 1* (Birmingham: WMCC).

West Midlands County Council Economic Development Committee (1984b) *Action in the Local Economy* (Birmingham: WMCC).

West Midlands County Council Economic Development Committee (1984c)

'Future Employment Prospects for the West Midlands County', *Research Paper no. 2* (Birmingham: WMCC).

West Midlands County Council Economic Development Committee (1985) 'Jobs and Technology', *Economic Review no. 3* (Birmingham: WMCC).

Westaway, J. (1974) 'The Spatial Hierarchy of Business Organisations and its Implications for the British Urban System', *Regional Studies*, **8**, pp. 145–55.

Whitbread, C. (1983) 'The Car of the Future in Western Europe: The Application of High Technology for the Cars of Tomorrow', *Economist Intelligence Unit Special Report no. 115*.

Williamson, J. G. (1962) 'The Long Swing: Comparisons and Interactions Between British and American Balance of Payments, 1820–1913', *Journal of Economic History*, **22** (1) pp. 21–46.

Williamson, J. G. (1965) 'Regional Inequality and the Process of National Development: A Description of the Patterns', in Needleman, L. (ed.) (1968) *Regional Analysis: Selected Readings* (Harmondsworth: Penguin Books) pp. 99–158.

Wright, E. O. (1978) *Class, Crisis and the State* (London: New Left Books).

Wright, E. O. (1979) 'The Value Controversy and Social Research', *New Left Review* **116**, pp. 53–82.

Author Index

269

Subject Index